First World War
and Army of Occupation
War Diary
France, Belgium and Germany

30 DIVISION
Divisional Troops
200 Field Company Royal Engineers
3 November 1915 - 17 May 1919

WO95/2322/1

The Naval & Military Press Ltd
www.nmarchive.com
Published in association with The National Archives

Published by

The Naval & Military Press Ltd

Unit 10 Ridgewood Industrial Park,
Uckfield, East Sussex,
TN22 5QE England
Tel: +44 (0) 1825 749494

www.naval-military-press.com
www.nmarchive.com

Contents

Document type	Place/Title	Date From	Date To
Heading	WO95/2322 30 Div Engineers 200th Fld Coy R.E. Nov' 15-May' 19		
Heading	30th Division Divl Engineers 200th Fld Coy R.E. Nov. 1915-May 1919		
War Diary		03/11/1915	08/11/1915
War Diary	Le Harve	09/11/1915	09/11/1915
War Diary	Pont-Remy	10/11/1915	10/11/1915
War Diary	Monflieres	10/11/1915	17/11/1915
War Diary	Bouchon	17/11/1915	17/11/1915
War Diary	Vignacourt	18/11/1915	28/11/1915
War Diary	Epecamps.	28/11/1915	04/12/1915
War Diary	Lanches	04/12/1915	10/12/1915
War Diary	Candas	11/12/1915	11/12/1915
War Diary	Bienvillers-Au-Bois	12/12/1915	12/12/1915
War Diary	Souastre	12/12/1915	12/12/1915
War Diary	Bienvillers-Au-Bois.	16/12/1915	17/12/1915
War Diary	Souastre	19/12/1915	19/12/1915
War Diary	Bienvillers-Au-Bois	19/12/1915	19/12/1915
War Diary	Bienvillers-Au-Bois & Souastre	26/12/1915	26/12/1915
War Diary	Halloy	27/12/1915	27/12/1915
War Diary	Lanches	27/12/1915	04/01/1916
Miscellaneous	The Following Messages Has Been Received From His Majesty The King. Appendix A.	03/11/1915	03/11/1915
Miscellaneous	Derby House, Stratford Place, W. Appendix B.	04/11/1915	04/11/1915
Miscellaneous	Disembarkation. A.L. 1632	04/11/1915	04/11/1915
Miscellaneous	Move Of Division. Appendix C.	05/11/1915	05/11/1915
Heading	A.G. 1033		
Miscellaneous	200th Field Coy R.E. Appendix D.	08/11/1915	08/11/1915
Diagram etc			
Diagram etc	200 Fd Co. R.E.		
Miscellaneous			
Miscellaneous	G.9	10/11/1915	10/11/1915
Operation(al) Order(s)	Reference 30th Division Operation Order No. (1) Para. 4. Transport And Supply Arrangements During The Move Of The Division.	16/11/1915	16/11/1915
Miscellaneous		16/11/1915	16/11/1915
Operation(al) Order(s)	89th Brigade Operation Order No. 1. March Orders For 17th November. Appendix E.	17/11/1915	17/11/1915
Operation(al) Order(s)	89th Brigade Operation Order No. 2	18/11/1915	18/11/1915
Operation(al) Order(s)	89th Brigade Operation Order No. 3. Appendix F.	28/11/1915	28/11/1915
Miscellaneous	March Table For 28th November 1915. Issued With 89th Brigade Operation Order No. 3	28/11/1915	28/11/1915
Miscellaneous	Billeting Orders November 28th. 1915	28/11/1915	28/11/1915
Map	Amiens Appendix G.		
Operation(al) Order(s)	Transport And Supply Arrangement Issued With Operation Order No. 6. Dated 29th December 1915	29/12/1915	29/12/1915
Heading	30th Divisional Engineers 200th Field Company R.E. January 1916		
War Diary	Lanches	04/01/1916	04/01/1916
War Diary	Wargnies	05/01/1916	05/01/1916

War Diary	Pont-Noyelles	06/01/1916	06/01/1916
War Diary	Bray-Sur-Somme	06/01/1916	31/01/1916
Operation(al) Order(s)	89th Brigade Operation Order No. 5. Appendix J.	01/01/1916	01/01/1916
Miscellaneous	Table B. 3. No. 3. Column. Commander Lt. Col. B.C. Fairfax. 17th Liverpools.		
Heading	30th Divisional Engineers 200th Field Company R.E. February 1916		
War Diary	Bray-Sur-Somme	02/02/1916	04/02/1916
War Diary	Cappy	04/02/1916	04/02/1916
War Diary	Bray-Sur-Somme	04/02/1916	05/02/1916
War Diary	Chipilly	05/02/1916	05/02/1916
War Diary	Bray-Sur-Somme	05/02/1916	05/02/1916
War Diary	Chipilly	06/02/1916	06/02/1916
War Diary	Bray-Sur-Somme	06/02/1916	29/02/1916
Diagram etc	Sketch. Appendix K.		
Miscellaneous	O.C., 200th. Field Company, R.E. Appendix M	13/02/1916	13/02/1916
Miscellaneous	G.177 13th. Feb. 1916	13/02/1916	13/02/1916
Diagram etc	Outpost-Position At Cappy Corner Appendix L.		
Heading	30th Divisional Engineers 200th Field Company R.E. March 1916		
War Diary	Bray-Sur-Somme.	01/03/1916	17/03/1916
War Diary	Sailly-Le-Sec.	17/03/1916	18/03/1916
War Diary	Frechencourt	18/03/1916	30/03/1916
War Diary	Behencourt	30/03/1916	30/03/1916
War Diary	Frechencourt	31/03/1916	31/03/1916
Miscellaneous	O.C., 200th. Field Company, R.E. Appendix N.	07/03/1916	07/03/1916
Miscellaneous	O.C., 200th. Field Company, R.E.	14/03/1916	14/03/1916
Miscellaneous	Extract from March Table No. 3		
Operation(al) Order(s)	Instructions in Connection With Operation Order No. 11	16/03/1916	16/03/1916
Heading	30th Divisional Engineers 200th Field Company R.E. :: April 1916		
War Diary	Frechencourt	01/04/1916	01/04/1916
War Diary	Somme	01/04/1916	04/04/1916
War Diary	La Neuville-Les-Bray.	04/04/1916	10/04/1916
War Diary	Bray-Sur Somme	10/04/1916	30/04/1916
Miscellaneous	O.C. 200th Field Coy. R.E. Appendix N.	01/04/1916	01/04/1916
Miscellaneous	C Form (Duplicate). Messages And Signals.		
Miscellaneous	A Form. Messages And Signals.		
Miscellaneous	Chief Engineer, 13th Corps.	01/04/1916	01/04/1916
Miscellaneous	Relief Of 202nd Field Company, R.E. By 200th Field Company, R.E. Table Of Moves.	31/03/1916	31/03/1916
Map	France. Appendix O.		
Heading	30th Divisional Engineers 200th Field Company R.E. F: May 1916		
War Diary	Bray And Maricourt		
War Diary	Bray And Maricourt	12/05/1916	18/05/1916
Heading	30th Divisional Engineers 200th Field Company R.E. June 1916		
War Diary	Bray And Maricourt	01/06/1916	10/06/1916
War Diary	Bray And Maricourt	01/06/1916	17/06/1916
War Diary	Bray And Maricourt	11/06/1916	30/06/1916
War Diary	Bray & Maricourt	21/06/1916	28/06/1916
War Diary	Bray & Maricourt	25/06/1916	25/06/1916
War Diary	Bray & Maricourt	07/06/1916	16/06/1916
War Diary	Bray & Maricourt	04/06/1916	27/06/1916
War Diary	Bray & Maricourt	13/06/1916	13/06/1916

War Diary	Bray & Maricourt	06/06/1916	18/06/1916
Heading	30th Divisional Engineers 200th Field Company R.E. July 1916		
Miscellaneous	Headquarters, 30th Division.	06/08/1916	06/08/1916
War Diary	Maricourt	01/07/1916	05/07/1916
War Diary	Bray	05/07/1916	31/07/1916
War Diary	Bray	01/07/1916	12/07/1916
War Diary	Bray	02/07/1916	29/07/1916
War Diary	Bray	08/07/1916	29/07/1916
Heading	30th Divisional Engineers 200th Field Company R.E. August 1916		
War Diary	Bray.	01/08/1916	31/08/1916
War Diary	Bray	30/07/1916	30/07/1916
War Diary	Hocquincourt	03/08/1916	03/08/1916
War Diary	Merville	09/08/1916	10/08/1916
War Diary	Gorre	14/08/1916	24/08/1916
War Diary	Bray	30/07/1916	30/07/1916
War Diary	Merville	03/08/1916	03/08/1916
War Diary	Gorre	13/08/1916	20/08/1916
War Diary	Gorre	11/07/1916	21/08/1916
War Diary	Gorre	19/08/1916	23/08/1916
War Diary	Gorre	21/08/1916	21/08/1916
Heading	30th Divisional Engineers 200th Field Company R.E. September 1916		
War Diary	Gorre	01/09/1916	12/09/1916
War Diary	Bruay	13/09/1916	13/09/1916
War Diary	Ecoivres	14/09/1916	16/09/1916
War Diary	ACQ	17/09/1916	17/09/1916
War Diary	Cambligneul	19/09/1916	21/09/1916
War Diary	Cezaincourt	21/09/1916	27/09/1916
War Diary	Vignacourt	27/09/1916	27/09/1916
War Diary	Allonville	28/09/1916	28/09/1916
War Diary	Camp	29/09/1916	29/09/1916
War Diary	Montauban	30/09/1916	30/09/1916
War Diary	Gorre	29/08/1916	11/09/1916
War Diary	Vignacourt	25/09/1916	25/09/1916
War Diary	Cambligneul	17/09/1916	17/09/1916
War Diary	Vignacourt	24/09/1916	24/09/1916
War Diary	Gorre	11/09/1916	11/09/1916
War Diary	Cambligneul	19/09/1916	19/09/1916
War Diary	Vignacourt	26/09/1916	26/09/1916
War Diary	Vignacourt	12/09/1916	12/09/1916
Heading	30th Divisional Engineers 200th Field Company R.E. October 1916		
War Diary	Montauban (S.26.d.8.8.)	01/10/1916	11/10/1916
War Diary	Montauban (S.26.d.8.8.)	11/10/1916	17/10/1916
War Diary	Montauban S.21.a.8.4	18/10/1916	22/10/1916
War Diary	Mametz Wood (S.19.d.9.7)	23/10/1916	24/10/1916
War Diary	Buire	25/10/1916	26/10/1916
War Diary	Doullens	27/10/1916	27/10/1916
War Diary	Pommier	28/10/1916	28/10/1916
War Diary	Grenas	29/10/1916	29/10/1916
War Diary	Bienvillers	29/10/1916	31/10/1916
War Diary	Bavincourt	31/10/1916	31/10/1916
War Diary	Pommier	31/10/1916	31/10/1916

Miscellaneous	Report On Operations On 12-13 October 1916. 200th Field Co. R.E.	12/10/1916	12/10/1916
Miscellaneous	Operation	18/10/1916	18/10/1916
Miscellaneous	O.C. 200th Field Co. R.E. 9.10.16	09/10/1916	09/10/1916
Miscellaneous	O.C. 200th Field Co. R.E. 10.Oct. 1916	10/10/1916	10/10/1916
Miscellaneous	Disposition of R.E. and Pioneers.	10/10/1916	10/10/1916
Miscellaneous	O.C. 200th Field Co. R.E.	11/10/1916	11/10/1916
Miscellaneous	O.C. 200th Field Co. R.E.	12/10/1916	12/10/1916
Miscellaneous	Extract from "System of Liaison and Communication. Appendix "B".		
Miscellaneous	Extract from "Amendments and Addenda to O.O. No. 40". Appendix "C".		
Miscellaneous	Disposition of R.E. and Pioneers.		
Miscellaneous	Rations & Water Supply. Appendix F.		
Miscellaneous	Medical Arrangements. Appendix H.		
Miscellaneous	O.C. 200th Field Co. R.E.	11/10/1916	11/10/1916
Operation(al) Order(s)	30th Division Operation Order No. 40	11/10/1916	11/10/1916
Miscellaneous	O.C. 200th Field Co. R.E.	12/10/1916	12/10/1916
Operation(al) Order(s)	21st Infantry Brigade Order No. 4	11/10/1916	11/10/1916
Heading	30th Divisional Engineers 200th Field Company R.E. November 1916		
War Diary	Bienvillers	01/11/1916	01/11/1916
War Diary	Pommier	01/11/1916	01/11/1916
War Diary	Bavincourt	01/11/1916	18/11/1916
War Diary	Berles	19/11/1916	19/11/1916
War Diary	Bavincourt	19/11/1916	19/11/1916
War Diary	La Cauchie	19/11/1916	19/11/1916
War Diary	Berles	20/11/1916	30/11/1916
Miscellaneous	Works Report From 6 p.m. 2.11.16 1916 to 6 p.m. 3.11.16 1916. 200 Field Co. R.E.	02/11/1916	02/11/1916
Miscellaneous	To O.C. 200th Field Coy R.E. Report On Work-Section No. 4	04/11/1916	04/11/1916
Miscellaneous			
Miscellaneous	Works Report From 6 p.m. 3.11.16 To 6 p.m. 4.11.16. 200th Fd. Co. R.E.	03/11/1916	03/11/1916
Miscellaneous	R.E. 46th Division. Daily Work Report.	04/11/1916	04/11/1916
Miscellaneous	Works Report From 6 P.M. 4-11-16 To PM 5-11-16 200th Field Coy R.E.	04/11/1916	04/11/1916
Miscellaneous	Works Report From 6 pm. 4/11/1916 To 6 pm. 5/11/1916. 200th Field Co. R.E.	05/11/1916	05/11/1916
Miscellaneous	Works Report From 6 pm. 1916 To 6 pm. 6.9.16 1916. 200th Field Coy. R.E.	06/11/1916	06/11/1916
Miscellaneous	Works Report From 6 P.M. 5/11/1916 To 6 PM. 6/11/1916 200th Field Coy. R.E.	05/11/1916	05/11/1916
Miscellaneous	Works Report From 6 P.M. 6/11/1916 To 6 PM. 7/11/1916 200th Field Coy. R.E.	06/11/1916	06/11/1916
Miscellaneous	Works Report From 6 P.M. 7/11/1916 To 6 PM. 8/11/1916 200th Field Coy. R.E.	07/11/1916	07/11/1916
Miscellaneous	Works Report From 6 pm. 7/11 1916 to 6 pm. 8/11 1916. Field Co. R.E.	07/11/1916	07/11/1916
Miscellaneous	Works Report From 6 P.M. 8 Nov. 1916 To 6 P.M. 9th Nov. 1916. 200th Field Coy. R.E.	08/11/1916	08/11/1916
Miscellaneous	Works Report From 6 P.M. 8/11/1916 To 6 P.M. 9/11/1916. 200th Field Coy. R.E.	08/11/1916	08/11/1916
Miscellaneous	Works Report From 6 P.M. 8/11/1916 To 6 P.M. 9/11/1916. Field Coy. R.E.	08/11/1916	08/11/1916

Miscellaneous	Works Report From 6 p.m. 9th Nov. 1916 To 6 p.m. 10th Nov. 1916. 200th Field Coy. R.E.	09/11/1916	09/11/1916
Miscellaneous	Works Report From 6 pm. 9/11/1916 to 6 pm. 10/11/1916. 200 Field Co. R.E.	09/11/1916	09/11/1916
Miscellaneous	Works Report From 6 pm. 10th Nov 1916 To 6 pm. 11th Nov 1916. 200th Field Co. R.E.	10/11/1916	10/11/1916
Miscellaneous	Works Report From 6 pm. 10/11/1916 To 6 pm. 11/11/1916. 200th Field Co. R.E.	10/11/1916	10/11/1916
Miscellaneous	Works Report From 6 pm. 11th Nov 1916 To 6 pm. 12th Nov 1916. 200th Field Co. R.E.	11/11/1916	11/11/1916
Miscellaneous	Works Report From 6 pm. 11/11/1916 to 6 pm. 12/11/1916. 200th Field Co. R.E.	11/11/1916	11/11/1916
Miscellaneous	Works Report From 6 pm. 12-11-1916 to 6 pm. 13-11-1916. 200th Field Co. R.E.	12/11/1916	12/11/1916
Miscellaneous	Works Report from 6 pm. 13th Nov 1916 to 6 pm. 14th Nov 1916. 200th Field Co. R.E.	13/11/1916	13/11/1916
Miscellaneous	Works Report from 6 pm. 13/11/1916 to 6 pm. 14/11/1916. 200th Field Co. R.E.	13/11/1916	13/11/1916
Miscellaneous	Works Report from 6 pm. 14th Nov 1916 to 6 pm. 15th Nov 1916 200th Field Co. R.E.	14/11/1916	14/11/1916
Miscellaneous	Works Report From 6 pm. 15/11/1916 to 6 pm. 14/11/1916. 200th Field Co. R.E.	15/11/1916	15/11/1916
Miscellaneous	Works Report from 6 pm. 15/11/1916 to 6 pm. 16/11/1916. 200th Field Coy. R.E.	15/11/1916	15/11/1916
Miscellaneous	Works Report from 6 pm. 15/11/1916 to 6 pm. 16/11/1916. 200th Field Co. R.E.	15/11/1916	15/11/1916
Miscellaneous	Works Report From 6 pm. 16th Nov 1916 to 6 pm. 17th Nov 1916 200th Field Coy. R.E.	16/11/1916	16/11/1916
Miscellaneous	Works Report from 6 pm. 1916 to 6 pm. 1916. Field Coy. R.E.		
Miscellaneous	Works Report from 6 pm. 17/11/1916 to 6 pm. 18/11/1916 200th Field Coy R.E.	17/11/1916	17/11/1916
Miscellaneous	Works Report from 6 pm. 18th Nov 1916 to 6 pm. 19th Nov 1916 200th Field Coy R.E.	18/11/1916	18/11/1916
Miscellaneous	Works Report from 6 pm. 18/11/1916 to 6 pm. 19/11/1916. 200th Field Co. R.E.	18/11/1916	18/11/1916
Miscellaneous	Works Report from 6 pm. 19/11/1916 to 6 pm. 20/11/1916. 200th Field Coy R.E.	19/11/1916	19/11/1916
Miscellaneous	Works Report from 6 pm. 19/11/16 to 6 pm. 20/11/16. 200th Field Co. R.E.	19/11/1916	19/11/1916
Miscellaneous	Works Report from 6 pm. 20th 11/1916 to 6 pm. 21st 11/1916. 200th Field Coy R.E.	20/11/1916	20/11/1916
Miscellaneous	Works Report from 6 pm. 20/11/1916 to 6 pm. 21/11/1916. 200th Field Coy R.E.	20/11/1916	20/11/1916
Miscellaneous	Works Report from 6 pm. 21st 11/1916 to 6 pm. 22nd 11/1916. 200th Field Coy R.E.	21/11/1916	21/11/1916
Miscellaneous	Works Report from 6 pm. 21/11/1916 to 6 pm. 22/11/1916. 200th Field Coy R.E.	21/11/1916	21/11/1916
Miscellaneous	Works Report from 6 pm. 22nd 11/1916 to 6 pm. 23rd 11/1916. 200th Field Coy R.E.	22/11/1916	22/11/1916
Miscellaneous	Works Report from 6 pm. 22/11/1916 to 6 pm. 23/11/1916. 200th Field Coy R.E.	22/11/1916	22/11/1916
Diagram etc			
Miscellaneous	Works Report from 6 pm. 23rd 11/1916 to 6 pm. 24th 11/1916. 200th Field Coy R.E.	23/11/1916	23/11/1916

Miscellaneous	Work Report from 6 pm. 23/11/1916 to 6 pm. 24/11/1916. 200th Field Coy R.E.	23/11/1916	23/11/1916
Miscellaneous	Report Of Works From 6 pm. 24/11/1916 to 6 pm. 25/11/1916. 200th Field Coy R.E.	24/11/1916	24/11/1916
Miscellaneous	Works Report from 6 pm. 24/11/1916 to 6 pm. 25/11/1916 200th Field Coy R.E.	24/11/1916	24/11/1916
Miscellaneous	Works Report from 6 pm. 25/11/1916 to 6 pm. 26/11/1916. 200th Field Coy R.E.	25/11/1916	25/11/1916
Miscellaneous	Works Report from 6 pm. 25/11/1916 to 6 pm. 26/11/1916. 200th Field Co. R.E.	25/11/1916	25/11/1916
Miscellaneous	Works Report from 6 pm. 26/11/1916 to 6 pm. 27/11/1916. 200th Field Coy R.E.	26/11/1916	26/11/1916
Diagram etc			
Miscellaneous	Works Report from 6 pm. 27/11/1916 to 6 pm. 28/11/1916. 200th Field Co. R.E.	27/11/1916	27/11/1916
Miscellaneous	Works Report from 6 pm. 28/11/1916 to 6 pm. 29/11/1916. 200th Field Co. R.E.	28/11/1916	28/11/1916
Miscellaneous	Works Report from 6 pm. 28/11/1916 to 6 pm. 29/11/1916. 200th Field Co. R.E.	27/11/1916	27/11/1916
Miscellaneous	Works Report from 6 pm. 29/11/1916 to 6 pm. 30/11/1916. 200th Field Co. R.E.	29/11/1916	29/11/1916
Heading	30th Divisional Engineers 200th Field Company R.E. December 1916		
War Diary	Berles And Bavincourt	01/12/1916	31/12/1916
War Diary	Berles And Laherliere	03/12/1916	26/12/1916
War Diary	Berles And Laherliere	03/12/1916	17/12/1916
War Diary	Berles And Laherliere	10/12/1916	24/12/1916
War Diary	Berles And Laherliere	19/12/1916	19/12/1916
War Diary	Berles And Laherliere	02/12/1916	20/12/1916
War Diary	Berles And Laherliere	05/12/1916	05/12/1916
Heading	War Diary Of The 200th Field Company Royal Engineers For The Month Of January 1917 (Volume XIII).		
War Diary	Berles And Bavincourt And Humbercamps	01/01/1917	08/01/1917
War Diary	Halloy	09/01/1917	09/01/1917
War Diary	Ivergny	09/01/1917	10/01/1917
War Diary	Rebreuviette	10/01/1917	15/01/1917
War Diary	Beaudricourt	16/01/1917	21/01/1917
War Diary	Lucheux	22/01/1917	22/01/1917
War Diary	Grouches	22/01/1917	22/01/1917
War Diary	Sus St Leger	23/01/1917	23/01/1917
War Diary	Le Cauroy	24/01/1917	25/01/1917
War Diary	Ivergny	26/01/1917	28/01/1917
War Diary	Simencourt	28/01/1917	28/01/1917
War Diary	Achiecourt	28/01/1917	31/01/1917
War Diary	Berles And Laherliere	02/01/1917	19/01/1917
War Diary	Berles And Laherliere	31/12/1916	15/01/1917
War Diary	Berles And Laherliere	06/01/1917	24/01/1917
War Diary	Berles And Laherliere	03/01/1917	20/01/1917
War Diary	Ivergny	22/01/1917	22/01/1917
Miscellaneous	Ivergny	11/12/1916	11/12/1916
Heading	War Diary Of The 200th Field Company Royal Engineers For The Month Of February 1917 (Volume XIV)		
Miscellaneous	Direct Hit on Dugout by Heavy Mineuwerfer-Bomb. Appendix A.	22/02/1917	22/02/1917

War Diary	Achicourt	01/02/1917	01/02/1917
War Diary	Simencourt	01/02/1917	08/02/1917
War Diary	Agny	09/02/1917	13/02/1917
War Diary	Dainville	14/02/1917	23/02/1917
War Diary	Agny	23/02/1917	23/02/1917
War Diary	Simencourt.	23/02/1917	23/02/1917
War Diary	Monchiet	23/02/1917	28/02/1917
War Diary	Achicourt	01/02/1917	01/02/1917
War Diary	Simencourt	01/02/1917	01/02/1917
War Diary	Agny	01/02/1917	01/02/1917
War Diary	Dainville	01/02/1917	17/02/1917
War Diary	Monchiet.	17/02/1917	27/02/1917
War Diary	Monchiet.	07/02/1917	07/02/1917
War Diary	Monchiet.	05/02/1917	23/02/1917
War Diary	Monchiet.	07/02/1917	11/02/1917
War Diary	Monchiet.	27/01/1917	23/02/1917
Heading	War Diary Of The 200th Field Company, Royal Engineers. For The Month Of March 1917 (Volume XV)		
War Diary	Dainville	01/03/1917	01/03/1917
War Diary	Agny	01/03/1917	01/03/1917
War Diary	Monchiet	01/03/1917	19/03/1917
War Diary	Agny	20/03/1917	20/03/1917
War Diary	Monchiet	20/03/1917	22/03/1917
War Diary	Blaireville	23/03/1917	31/03/1917
War Diary	Dainville	02/03/1917	02/03/1917
War Diary	Agny	02/03/1917	02/03/1917
War Diary	Monchiet	02/03/1917	02/03/1917
War Diary	Blaireville	02/03/1917	17/03/1917
War Diary	Blaireville	14/03/1917	22/03/1917
War Diary	Blaireville	01/03/1917	20/03/1917
War Diary	Blaireville	06/03/1917	06/03/1917
War Diary	Blaireville	02/03/1917	17/03/1917
War Diary	Blaireville	05/03/1917	25/03/1917
War Diary	Dainville	04/03/1917	04/03/1917
War Diary	Agny	04/03/1917	04/03/1917
War Diary	Monchiet	04/03/1917	04/03/1917
War Diary	Blaireville	04/03/1917	28/03/1917
War Diary	Beaurains	24/04/1917	27/04/1917
War Diary	Gouy En Artois	28/04/1917	28/04/1917
War Diary	Sibiville	28/04/1917	30/04/1917
War Diary	Blaireville	31/03/1917	31/03/1917
War Diary	Beaurains	31/03/1917	31/03/1917
War Diary	Sibiville	31/03/1917	23/04/1917
War Diary	Sibiville	02/04/1917	28/04/1917
War Diary	Sibiville	02/04/1917	22/04/1917
War Diary	Sibiville	23/11/1916	26/04/1917
Heading	War Diary Of The 200th Field Company, Royal Engineers. For The Month Of May 1917 (Volume: XVII).		
War Diary	Sibiville	01/05/1917	02/05/1917
War Diary	Boffles	03/05/1917	19/05/1917
War Diary	Sericourt	20/05/1917	20/05/1917
War Diary	Belval	21/05/1917	21/05/1917
War Diary	Ecquedecques	22/05/1917	23/05/1917
War Diary	Tanny	24/05/1917	24/05/1917

War Diary	Caestre	25/05/1917	26/05/1917
War Diary	Brandhoek	27/05/1917	28/05/1917
War Diary	Ypres	29/05/1917	31/05/1917
War Diary	Boffles	06/05/1917	19/05/1917
War Diary	Ecquedecques	23/05/1917	23/05/1917
War Diary	Brandhoek	28/05/1917	28/05/1917
War Diary	Brandhoek	18/05/1917	19/05/1917
War Diary	Brandhoek	18/05/1917	30/05/1917
War Diary	Brandhoek	23/04/1917	25/05/1917
Heading	War Diary Of The 200th Field Company Royal Engineers. For The Month Of June 1917 Volume XVIII.		
War Diary	Ypres Brandhoek	01/06/1917	13/06/1917
War Diary	Dickebush Huts Camp.	14/06/1917	22/06/1917
War Diary	Zillebeke Bund	22/06/1917	30/06/1917
War Diary	Dickebush Huts Camp.	30/06/1917	30/06/1917
War Diary	Ypres Brandhoek	03/06/1917	03/06/1917
War Diary	Dickebush Huts Camp.	05/06/1917	05/06/1917
War Diary	Zillebeke Bund	06/06/1917	18/06/1917
War Diary	Zillebeke Bund	07/06/1917	27/06/1917
War Diary	Zillebeke Bund	09/06/1917	28/06/1917
War Diary		06/06/1917	26/06/1917
War Diary		24/06/1917	24/06/1917
War Diary		18/06/1917	25/06/1917
War Diary		01/06/1917	24/06/1917
War Diary		02/06/1917	26/06/1917
War Diary		18/06/1917	27/06/1917
Heading	War Diary Of 200th Field Company, Royal Engineers For The Month Of July 1917. (Volume XIX).		
War Diary	Zillebeke Bund.	01/07/1917	01/07/1917
War Diary	Dickebush Huts Camp.	01/07/1917	31/07/1917
War Diary	Zillebeke	30/06/1917	30/06/1917
War Diary	Dickebusch	30/06/1917	03/07/1917
War Diary	Dickebusch	02/07/1917	26/07/1917
War Diary	Dickebusch	06/07/1917	19/07/1917
War Diary	Dickebusch	02/07/1917	02/07/1917
War Diary	Dickebusch	27/06/1917	27/06/1917
War Diary	Dickebusch	21/06/1917	12/07/1917
War Diary	Dickebusch	03/07/1917	18/07/1917
War Diary	Dickebusch	11/07/1917	11/07/1917
War Diary	Zillebeke	01/07/1917	04/07/1917
War Diary	Zillebeke	01/07/1917	31/07/1917
War Diary	Zillebeke	03/07/1917	11/07/1917
War Diary	Zillebeke	07/07/1917	24/07/1917
Heading	War Diary Of The 200th Field Company Royal Engineers. For The Month Of August 1917. (Volume XX).		
War Diary	H.29.a.7.6 and Dickebusch Huts Camp.	01/08/1917	04/08/1917
War Diary	Eecke	05/08/1917	07/08/1917
War Diary	Outtersteene	08/08/1917	09/08/1917
War Diary	Cx. De. Poperingue	10/08/1917	15/08/1917
War Diary	Kemmel	16/08/1917	22/08/1917
War Diary	Lindenhoek.	23/08/1917	31/08/1917
War Diary		02/08/1917	28/08/1917
War Diary		11/08/1917	31/08/1917
War Diary		03/08/1917	18/08/1917

War Diary		30/07/1917	28/08/1917
War Diary		21/08/1917	21/08/1917
War Diary		29/07/1917	29/09/1917
War Diary		03/09/1917	24/09/1917
War Diary		22/09/1917	27/09/1917
War Diary		01/09/1917	11/09/1917
War Diary		06/09/1917	14/09/1917
War Diary		02/09/1917	16/09/1917
War Diary		11/09/1917	23/09/1917
Heading	War Diary Of The 200th Field Company Royal Engineers. For The Month Of December 1917. (Volume XXI).		
War Diary	Lindenhoek	01/09/1917	30/09/1917
Heading	War Diary Of The 200th Field Company Royal Engineers. For The Month Of October 1917 (Volume XXII).		
War Diary	N.28.b.2.6	01/10/1917	01/10/1917
War Diary	Taffin Farm	02/10/1917	19/10/1917
War Diary	Kemmel Camp	21/10/1917	21/10/1917
War Diary	N.21.b.1.4	22/10/1917	31/10/1917
War Diary		04/10/1917	05/10/1917
War Diary		02/10/1917	31/10/1917
War Diary		22/10/1917	28/10/1917
War Diary		05/10/1917	10/10/1917
War Diary		08/10/1917	08/10/1917
War Diary		05/10/1917	25/10/1917
War Diary		24/10/1917	30/10/1917
War Diary		21/10/1917	21/10/1917
War Diary		06/10/1917	15/10/1917
War Diary		11/10/1917	11/10/1917
War Diary		05/10/1917	12/10/1917
Heading	War Diary Of The 200th Field Company Royal Engineers For The Month Of November 1917. (Volume. XXIII).		
War Diary	Kemmel Camp.	01/11/1917	01/11/1917
War Diary	N.21.b.1.4	02/11/1917	10/11/1917
War Diary	Ypres.	11/11/1917	13/11/1917
War Diary	Kaaie & Vlamertinghe	14/11/1917	23/11/1917
War Diary	Canada St Dugouts & Vierstraat	24/11/1917	30/11/1917
War Diary		08/11/1917	28/11/1917
War Diary		04/11/1917	25/11/1917
War Diary		13/11/1917	28/11/1917
War Diary		17/11/1917	17/11/1917
War Diary		08/11/1917	30/11/1917
War Diary		04/11/1917	19/11/1917
War Diary		16/11/1917	16/11/1917
Heading	War Diary Of The 200th Field Company Royal Engineers For The Month Of December 1917. (Volume XXIV).		
War Diary	Canada St Dugouts & Vierstraat	01/12/1917	31/12/1917
War Diary		02/12/1917	26/12/1917
War Diary		03/12/1917	03/12/1917
War Diary		01/12/1917	14/12/1917
War Diary		10/12/1917	11/12/1917
War Diary		10/12/1917	23/12/1917
War Diary		13/12/1917	23/12/1917

War Diary		03/12/1917	28/12/1917
War Diary		18/12/1917	18/12/1917
War Diary		06/12/1917	21/12/1917
War Diary		19/12/1917	19/12/1917
Heading	War Diary Of The 200th Field Company Royal Engineers. For The Month Of January 1918. (Volume XXV).		
War Diary	Ypres	01/01/1918	31/01/1918
Heading	War Diary 200th Field Company Royal Engineers. For The Month Of February 1918. (Volume XXVI).		
War Diary	Attilly	01/02/1918	24/02/1918
War Diary	Douchy	25/02/1918	28/02/1918
War Diary	Attilly	11/02/1918	11/02/1918
War Diary	Douchy	11/02/1918	11/02/1918
War Diary	Douchy	09/02/1918	23/02/1918
War Diary	Douchy	17/02/1918	17/02/1918
Heading	War Diary Of The 200th Field Company Royal Engineers. For The Month Of April 1918 (Volume XXVIII).		
Heading	30th Div. War Diary 200th Field Company, R.E. March 1918. Attached:- Appendix "A".		
Heading	War Diary 200th Field Company, Royal Engineers. For The Month Of March 1918 (Volume XXVII).		
War Diary	Douchy	01/03/1918	21/03/1918
War Diary	Aubigny	22/03/1918	23/03/1918
War Diary	Esmery Hallon	23/03/1918	24/03/1918
War Diary	Solente	25/03/1918	25/03/1918
War Diary	Plessier	26/03/1918	26/03/1918
War Diary	Bouchoir	27/03/1918	27/03/1918
War Diary	Moreuil	28/03/1918	28/03/1918
War Diary	Rouvrel	29/03/1918	31/03/1918
Heading	Appendix "A".		
Miscellaneous	C.R.E., 30th Division. Appendix "A".	03/04/1918	03/04/1918
Miscellaneous	200th Field Company R.E. Order	10/03/1918	10/03/1918
Heading	War Diary 200th Field Company, Royal Engineers. For The Month Of April 1917 (Volume XVI).		
War Diary	Blaireville	01/04/1917	12/04/1917
War Diary	Bailleulmont	13/04/1917	13/04/1917
War Diary	Famechon	14/04/1917	20/04/1917
War Diary	Achicourt	20/04/1917	20/04/1917
War Diary	Beaurains	20/04/1917	24/04/1917
War Diary	Vaudricourt	01/04/1917	04/04/1917
War Diary	Elverdinghe	05/04/1917	15/04/1917
War Diary	Elverdinghe	12/04/1917	17/04/1917
War Diary	Brandhoek	18/04/1917	30/04/1917
Heading	War Diary Of The 200th Field Company, R.E. For The Month Of May 1918 (Volume XXIX).		
War Diary	Near Houtkerque	01/05/1918	01/05/1918
War Diary	E.7.a.6.8	02/05/1918	25/05/1918
War Diary	Nr. Proven	26/05/1918	26/05/1918
War Diary	E.18.b.9.5	26/05/1918	31/05/1918
Heading	War Diary Of The 200th Field Company, Royal Engineers For The Month Of June 1918. (Volume XXX).		
War Diary	Proven	01/06/1918	02/06/1918
War Diary	Eecke	03/06/1918	21/06/1918

Miscellaneous			
Heading	War Diary Of The 200th Field Company, Royal Engineers. For The Month Of July 1918. (Volume XXXI).		
War Diary	Eecke 27/Q.28.c.0.5	01/07/1918	10/07/1918
War Diary	Cassel (Mt Recollet)	11/07/1918	19/07/1918
War Diary	Cassel	20/07/1918	28/07/1918
Heading	War Diary Of The 200th Field Company, Royal Engineers For The Month Of August 1918 (Volume XXXII)		
War Diary	Cassel	01/08/1918	30/08/1918
Miscellaneous	C.R.E. 30th British Division Appendix "A".	22/08/1918	22/08/1918
Heading	War Diary Of The 200th Field Company, Royal Engineers For The Month Of September 1918 (Volume XXXIII).		
War Diary	M.21.a.2.2	01/09/1918	05/09/1918
War Diary	N.3.1.d.1.7	06/09/1918	30/09/1918
Heading	War Diary Of The 200th Field Company, Royal Engineers For The Month Of October 1918 (Volume XXIV).		
War Diary	N.3.1.d.1.7	01/10/1918	15/10/1918
War Diary	P.12.b.	15/10/1918	17/10/1918
War Diary	Q.27.b.5.0	18/10/1918	19/10/1918
War Diary	Rolleghem.	20/10/1918	20/10/1918
War Diary	Dottignies	21/10/1918	31/10/1918
Heading	War Diary Of The 200th Field Company, Royal Engineers. For The Month Of November 1918 (Volume XXV)		
War Diary	29/U.2.b.95.40	01/11/1918	05/11/1918
War Diary	Knokke	06/11/1918	09/11/1918
War Diary	Escanaffles	10/11/1918	10/11/1918
War Diary	Beauregard	11/11/1918	16/11/1918
War Diary	Heestert	17/11/1918	17/11/1918
War Diary	Luingne	18/11/1918	28/11/1918
War Diary	Linselles	29/11/1918	29/11/1918
War Diary	Croix Au Bois	30/11/1918	30/11/1918
Heading	War Diary Of The 200th Field Company, Royal Engineers For The Month Of December 1918. (Volume XXVI).		
War Diary	Bac St Maur	01/12/1918	01/12/1918
War Diary	St. Venant	02/12/1918	02/12/1918
War Diary	Aire	03/12/1918	31/12/1918
Heading	War Diary Of The 200th Field Company, R.E. For The Month Of January 1919 (Volume XXVII).		
War Diary		01/01/1919	24/01/1919
War Diary	Bergues	25/01/1919	31/01/1919
Heading	War Diary Of The 200th Field Company, Royal Engineers For The Month Of February 1919. (Volume XXVIII).		
War Diary	Bergues	01/02/1919	28/02/1919
Heading	War Diary Of The 200th Field Company, Royal Engineers. For The Month Of March 1919. (Volume XXXIX).		
War Diary	Bergues	01/03/1919	31/03/1919
Heading	War Diary Of The 200th Field Company, Royal Engineers For The Month Of April 1919 (Volume XL.)		

War Diary	Bergues	01/04/1919	30/04/1919
Heading	War Diary Of 200th Field Coy. R.E. For May 1919		
War Diary	Bergues	01/05/1919	17/05/1919
Miscellaneous	Account Of Operations On 3rd-4th June 1917. Appendix A.	03/06/1917	03/06/1917
Miscellaneous	Orders.	03/06/1917	03/06/1917

1

WO 95/2322

30 Div Engineers

200th Fld Coy RE,

Nov'15 – May'19

30TH DIVISION
DIVL ENGINEERS

200TH FLD COY R.E.

NOV 1915-MAY 1919

One

Instructions regarding War Diaries and Intelligence Summaries are contained in F. S. Regs., Part II. and the Staff Manual respectively. Title pages will be prepared in manuscript.

WAR DIARY
or
~~INTELLIGENCE SUMMARY.~~ 200th Field Company, R.E.
(Erase heading not required.)

Army Form C. 2118.

Place	Date	Hour	Summary of Events and Information	Remarks and references to Appendices
			The first week in November was spent in completing our preparations and collecting the necessary stores for the move overseas.	
Nov 15 / May 19	Wed. 3-11-15	11.45 pm	The Division was paraded for inspection by Rt. Hon. The Earl of Derby K.G. G.C.V.O. C.B. The message from the King to the Officers N.C.O's and men was read by the G.O.C. Major-General W. Fry C.V.O. C.B. (Copy attached)	Appendix A.
			A letter of appreciation and farewell from Lord Derby was sent to the G.O.C. (Copy attached)	Appendix B.
	Sunday 7-11-15	11.20 pm	The Company less 15 Details under command of 2nd Lieut. J. A. D. Richmond R.E. left Larkhill, Salisbury Plain, on Sunday November 7th 1915, and marched to Amesbury Station where they entrained at 11.20 p.m. for Southampton, arriving at Southampton Docks	
	Monday 8-11-15	2.0 am	at 2.0 a.m. Monday, 8th November 1915. (Copy of Orders and Timetable attached)	Appendix C.
Le Havre	Tuesday 9-11-15	2.30 am	The Company embarked on board the transports "Australind" and "Mona's Queen", sailing from Southampton 4.0 p.m. & arriving at le Havre at 2.30 a.m. Tuesday, November 9th 1915	

2353 Wt. W2544/1454 700,000 5/15 D. D. & L. A.D.S.S./Forms/C. 2118.

(2) Two

Instructions regarding War Diaries and Intelligence Summaries are contained in F. S. Regs., Part II. and the Staff Manual respectively. Title pages will be prepared in manuscript.

WAR DIARY
or
~~INTELLIGENCE SUMMARY~~. 200th Field Company R.E.

(*Erase heading not required.*)

Army Form C. 2118.

Place	Date	Hour	Summary of Events and Information	Remarks and references to Appendices
			Disembarking at 7.0 a.m.	
			The Company then proceeded to Rest Camp No 5 marching from there to Le Gare des Merchandises, Point No 3 where they entrained at midnight.	
			(Copy of Standing Orders attached)	Appendix D
Pont-Remy	10-11-15	3 p.m.	On arrival at PONT-REMY at 3 p.m. the Company detrained and proceeded to MONFLIERES arriving in this billeting	
Monflieres	10-11-15	6 p.m.	area at 6 p.m. November 10th 1915.	
-do-	12-11-15		On the night of November 12th the weather turned cold & frosty and there was a heavy fall of snow.	
			After resting in billets for two days the men were exercised in Company Drill and Manoeuvres, a night alarm	
-do-	15-11-15	9.0 p.m.	and march taking place Monday, November 15th 1915.	
-do-	17-11-15		On November 17th the Company had orders to move to	
Bouchon	17-11-15	1.30 p.m.	BOUCHON, en route to VIGNACOURT where they arrived at	
Vignacourt	18-11-15	2.30 p.m.	2.30 p.m. November 18th 1915. (Copy of Orders & March Table attached)	Appendix E
			Here the Company were put through a course of Bomb throwing, a casualty occurred during this practice, one Sapper being slightly hit in the shoulder	

2353 Wt. W2544/1454 700,000 5/15 D. D. & L. A.D.S.S./Forms/C. 2118.

Three

Instructions regarding War Diaries and Intelligence Summaries are contained in F. S. Regs., Part II, and the Staff Manual respectively. Title pages will be prepared in manuscript.

WAR DIARY
or
~~INTELLIGENCE SUMMARY.~~ 200th Field Company, R.E.

(Erase heading not required.)

Army Form C. 2118.

Place	Date	Hour	Summary of Events and Information	Remarks and references to Appendices
			by a splinter when standing 15 yards in rear of the Bomb Trench.	
			A lecture and demonstration was given by a member of the Technical Staff to Officers and men of the 89th Brigade billeted in that area upon the use and care of gas helmets, the men passing through a room charged with asphyxiating gas.	
Vignacourt	28-11-15	9.30am	The Company had orders to move to ÉPÉCAMPS on Sunday 28th November. (Copy of March Orders attached)	Appendix F.
Épécamps	25-11-15	12.20pm	They arrived in this area at 12.20 pm. the same day. ÉPÉCAMPS is a small village of 27 inhabitants, in a poor and very delapidated condition. A scheme for the general improvement of billets was begun by the 89th Brigade to which this Company was attached and	
Épécamps	4-12-15	12.30pm	the Company was ordered to proceed to LANCHES on	
LANCHES	4-12-15	2.20pm	Saturday, 4th December 1915, for the purpose of carrying out this scheme.	
			A reconnaissance was made of the 89th Brigade area	

2353 Wt. W2544/1454 700,000 5/15 D. D. & L. A.D.S.S./Forms/C. 2118.

Four

Instructions regarding War Diaries and Intelligence Summaries are contained in F. S. Regs., Part II. and the Staff Manual respectively. Title pages will be prepared in manuscript.

WAR DIARY
or
~~INTELLIGENCE SUMMARY.~~ 200th Field Company R.E.

(Erase heading not required.)

Army Form C. 2118.

Place	Date	Hour	Summary of Events and Information	Remarks and references to Appendices
			and the R.A. area with a view to ascertain the possibilities of local resources for this purpose. Assistance was given to all O.C.s in procuring suitable material and advice. (Copy of Map attached)	Appendix G.
LANCHES			One Sergeant and One Sapper were evacuated to the Base Clearing Station.	
-do-	10-12-15	11 am	On Friday 10th December 1915 the Company moved to Candas,	
CANDAS	11-12-15		on the 11th December to HALLOY, on the 12th December arriving at BIENVILLERS-au-BOIS	
Bienvillers au-Bois	12-12-15		in the 37th Division Area to which Division they were attached for trench training (Copy of March Table attached)	Appendix H
Souastre	12-12-15		The Headquarters Section, all the transport horses and mules remained at SOUASTRE just behind the Army Corps, 3rd line of defence, remaining Sections being attached to the 153rd Field Company R.E. Next few days were spent in repairing and improving billets damaged by shell fire.	

Five

Instructions regarding War Diaries and Intelligence Summaries are contained in F. S. Regs., Part II. and the Staff Manual respectively. Title pages will be prepared in manuscript.

WAR DIARY
or
~~INTELLIGENCE SUMMARY~~. 200th Field Coy. R.E.

(Erase heading not required.)

Army Form C. 2118.

Place	Date	Hour	Summary of Events and Information	Remarks and references to Appendices
Bienvillers-au-Bois			Sections were allotted to various Sectors in the line to carry on the necessary construction and repairs.	
-do-	16-12-15		One Sapper slightly wounded.	
-do-	17-12-15		Enemy active. Artillery fire on FONCQUEVILLERS severe, several shells also falling in the billets of the men in BIENVILLERS-au-BOIS.	
Souastre	19-12-15		A German aeroplane flew over SOUASTRE, dropped a bomb but without causing any material damage.	
Bienvillers-au-Bois			A report is current that we have the Prussian Guard opposite to us in this sector. Our trenches in the front line are in very bad condition, being full of mud and water in many places and almost impassable. Pumping revetting and re-construction is carried on with systematic order, and our men fully understand the work that is required of them in keeping front line trenches in good condition. Most of the specially employed Tradesmen assist in the various works carried out at the Divisional Workshops at SOUASTRE.	

2353 Wt. W2544/1454 700,000 5/15 D. D. & L. A.D.S.S./Forms/C. 2118.

Six

Instructions regarding War Diaries and Intelligence Summaries are contained in F. S. Regs., Part II. and the Staff Manual respectively. Title pages will be prepared in manuscript.

WAR DIARY
or
~~INTELLIGENCE SUMMARY.~~
(Erase heading not required.)

Army Form C. 2118.

200th Field Coy R.E.

Place	Date	Hour	Summary of Events and Information	Remarks and references to Appendices
			The Section Sappers supervised and materially assisted in trench improvements, gun emplacements, mine shelters, steel tubular shelters, barbed wiring, hut erection.	
			The transport was used for the collection and conveyance of material to the various points of distribution	
Bienvillers au-Bois + Souastre.	26.12.15	11.30am	The Company moved from BIENVILLERS-au-BOIS, and SOUASTRE and arrived at HALLOY at 2.0 pm.	
HALLOY	27.12.15	8.30am	Leave HALLOY at 8.30 am via DOULLENS, CANDAS, FIENVILLERS, & BERNEUIL arriving at LANCHES at 5.45 pm	
LANCHES			The next week is spent in improving existing billets and enlarging and constructing others arranging horse and transport standings, improving water supply making a reconnaissance and report of all the villages in the near neighbourhood with a view to increase the billeting accomodation in this area.	
-do-	4.1.16		Orders were given to move to the front line to relieve	

Appendix a

THE FOLLOWING MESSAGE HAS BEEN RECEIVED FROM

HIS MAJESTY THE KING.

3rd November, 1915.

Officers, Non-Commissioned Officers, and Men of the 30th Division, on the eve of your departure for Active Service, I send you my heartfelt good wishes.

It is a bitter disappointment to me, that, owing to an unfortunate accident, I am unable to see the Division on Parade before it leaves England, but I can assure you that my thoughts are with you all.

Your period of training has been long and arduous, but the time has now come for you to prove on the Field of Battle the results of your instruction.

From the good accounts that I have received of the Division, I am confident that the high traditions of the British Army are safe in your hands, and that with your comrades now in the Field, you will maintain the unceasing efforts necessary to bring this War to a victorious ending.

Goodbye and God-speed.

GEORGE, R.I.

To be read out on parade. [initials]

Appendix 6.

Derby House,

Stratford Place, W.

4 November 1915.

My dear General,

I want to thank you most sincerely for having given me an opportunity today of saying good-bye to a Division with which from its very inception I have had so much to do. I confess to having had very mixed feelings during that Inspection: Feelings of pride in the splendid men that Lancashire has sent to fight for the King, but on the other hand the anxiety for those who are going out and still more deep sympathy for the anxieties of those who, like myself, have relations in the Division.

I feel perfectly certain, thanks to your able instruction, that proud as we are in Lancashire of the men of the Division at this moment, we shall be even prouder in a very short time when they will have been put to the test and not found wanting.

I wish I could have said good-bye to every Officer and indeed every man individually. May I do so through you and may I at the same time beg that every one of them will remember that there is nothing too much to ask me to do for them and that I shall be only too happy, if they write to me to put my words into deeds and place myself at their service.

Good luck to you all.

Yours very sincerely,

DERBY.

Major - General W. Fry, C.V.O., C.B.

SUBJECT: DISEMBARKATION.

A.L.1632.

The following points on Disembarkation at Havre have arisen in connection with other Divisions which have proceeded overseas, and are circulated for your information:

WAGON POLES. These nominally are inter-changeable, in reality they are not so. Each Pole should be labelled so that it can with certainty be affixed to its own wagon.

SWINGLE BARS should be made fast to wagons, much delay has been caused by these not being forthcoming immediately the wagon is landed.

PINS should be secured.

The Landing Authorities state that at times it is impossible not to mix the Transport of various details of the Division and even of other Divisions. They suggest that each Unit should have a distinctive mark on its wagons and horses etc. The last Division which came through here had its animals marked with luminous paint in different positions to indicate different Regiments and in consequence the Disembarkation proceeded without a hitch.

All animals should carry a label with the Driver's name in addition to their distinctive mark.

Picketting Ropes, Lanterns & Camp Kettles should not be packed away, as has often been done, but should be available for immediate use.

Every man should land with his kit on and with his quota of Ammunition, this rule apparently has not been universally observed.

The unconsumed portion of the days ration and forage must respectively be carried by the men and accompany the animals.

Maps if issued to the Division before starting should be served out and not carried in bulk. They are a very difficult weight to handle when in bulk.

Indents by Quarter Masters should be ready to hand in on landing. It is the practice to make good deficiencies from the Stores at this Base. Units use their own fatigue parties and their own Transport for the purpose of drawing Stores.

Interpreters are in some cases attached to Units here and in some cases up Country. The fact of an Interpreter not being attached here does not mean that the Unit has been overlooked.

LARKHILL.
4/11/1915.

L.Hume-Spry. Lieut. Colonel.
A.A. & Q.M.G., 30th Division.

SUBJECT: MOVE OF DIVISION.

Appendix. C.

A.L.1632.

Attached are Time Tables for the move of Division.

Full instructions as to entrainment, embarkation, the voyage, disembarkation, entrainment at the Base, and detrainment in the area of concentration have already been issued in book form. It is of the utmost importance that these instructions are fully and carefully complied with in every respect.

DRESS. All men will parade wearing their greatcoats. All water bottles will be filled.

ENTRAINING. In entraining at Amesbury the following points will be observed:

Horses and Vehicles and Baggage will be at the Station 1½ hours and Men 30 minutes before the departure time of the train. A Mounted Officer will be sent ahead to ascertain from the R.T.O. the platform from which the troops will entrain.

A loading party of 50 men, under an Officer, will be detailed for each train and this party must arrive at the Station in advance of the Horses and Vehicles. The R.T.O. will issue all instructions to this party, part of which will be utilised for loading the vehicles and the remainder for the Baggage.

Care must be taken to see that all Vehicle Poles can be readily removed.

No Rifles are to be left on Transport Vehicles - each man will take his rifle into the carriage with him.

HORSES. Horse wagons will usually be found at head of the trucks for transport wagons. All riders and spare horses must be sent ahead to the leading horse wagons and entrained without delay. The men so released will give a hand with the Team Horses which will be led forward as soon as unhooked well clear of all Transport Wagons.

Bits will be removed and girths slightly loosened, nose bags will be secured to truck rails in rear of the horses.

BAGGAGE. Requisitions for transport for baggage will be forwarded to the O.C., A.S.C., No.2 A Camp, Canada Lines, Larkhill, immediately on receipt of these instructions. In no case will the Baggage sent by Units exceed in amount and weight the scale authorised to be carried in the Baggage Section of Train as laid down in the Field Service Manuals, plus such articles carried in the Supply Section as are articles of Regimental Equipment.

RATIONS. Attention is drawn to para.5 of the "Instructions for Entrainment and Embarkation", and to para.5 of "Instructions for the Voyage" &c. already issued.

R. S. Clarke
Captain.
D.A.A. & Q.M.G., 30th Division.

LARKHILL.
5/11/1915.

30 27

Officer Commanding .... 200th Field Coy R.E. .... *appendix 504 d*

1. Please note that the .... Field Coy. .... under your command will entrain as detailed in Para. 4 below.

2. Units must be very careful that every man in their unit is told the station and "point of Entrainment" before marching off from camp. Most of the numerous cases of men left behind have occurred through neglect of this precaution.

3. The entrance to Points Nos. 1, 2, and 4 is at No. 70 Cours de la République and to Point 3 at the Boulevard d'Harfleur.

4. Place of entrainment **Gare des Merchandises.**
~~**Gare Maritime.**~~ Point No. 3

Time Midnight Date 9-10/XI/15

~~Ration~~ Ration Party (strength 1 officer 15 men) to report to Officer i/c Detail Issue Store at **Gare des Merchandises.**

~~**Gare Maritime.**~~ ~~Point 6.~~

Time 23-30 pm. Date 9/XI/15

N.B.—The time given is the hour at which units are to arrive **AT THE POINT** specified (*i.e.*, place of entrainment).

5. As soon as orders for entrainment are received the units will at once notify the strength of the unit to the Officer i/c Detail Issue Store at place of entrainment.

6. Your attention is directed to the "**Special Orders for Units Passing through Havre Base,**" especially para. 6 and to "**Standing Orders for Entrainment.**"

Any further information about Entrainment can be obtained from the D.A.D.R.T., GARE DES VOYAGEURS.

The Orderly Room Serjeants, if any, should report to this office, at .... ready in all respects for immediate entrainment on being posted to the D.A.G., 3rd Echelon, for duty.

[illegible]

Issued at 21 45 .... CAPTAIN,

Date 8/XI/15. D.A.Q.M.G., Havre Base.

Stationery Services Press, P 420, 1000. 9/15.

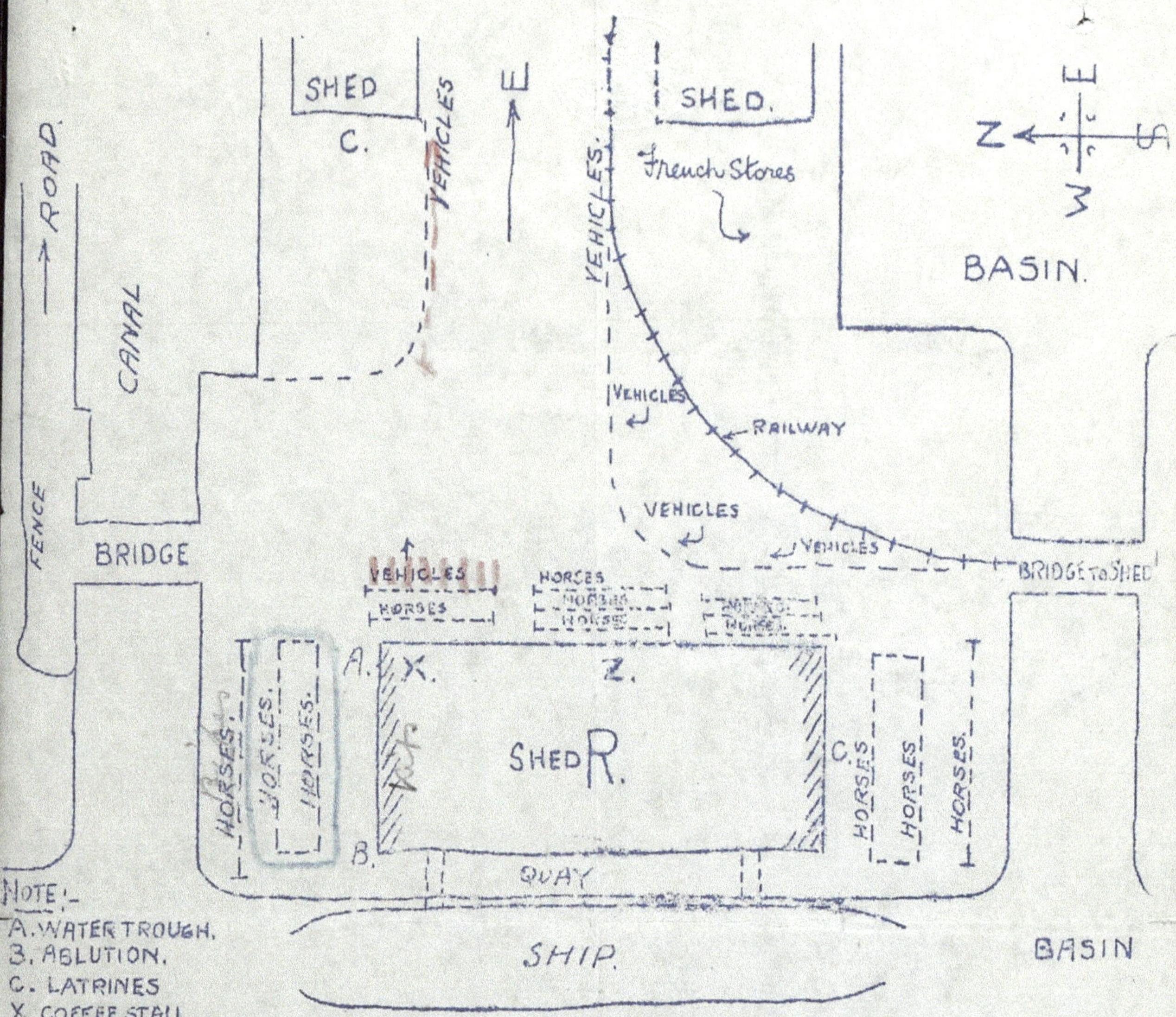

NOTE:-
A. WATER TROUGH.
B. ABLUTION.
C. LATRINES
X. COFFEE STALL
Z. RATIONS & FORAGE

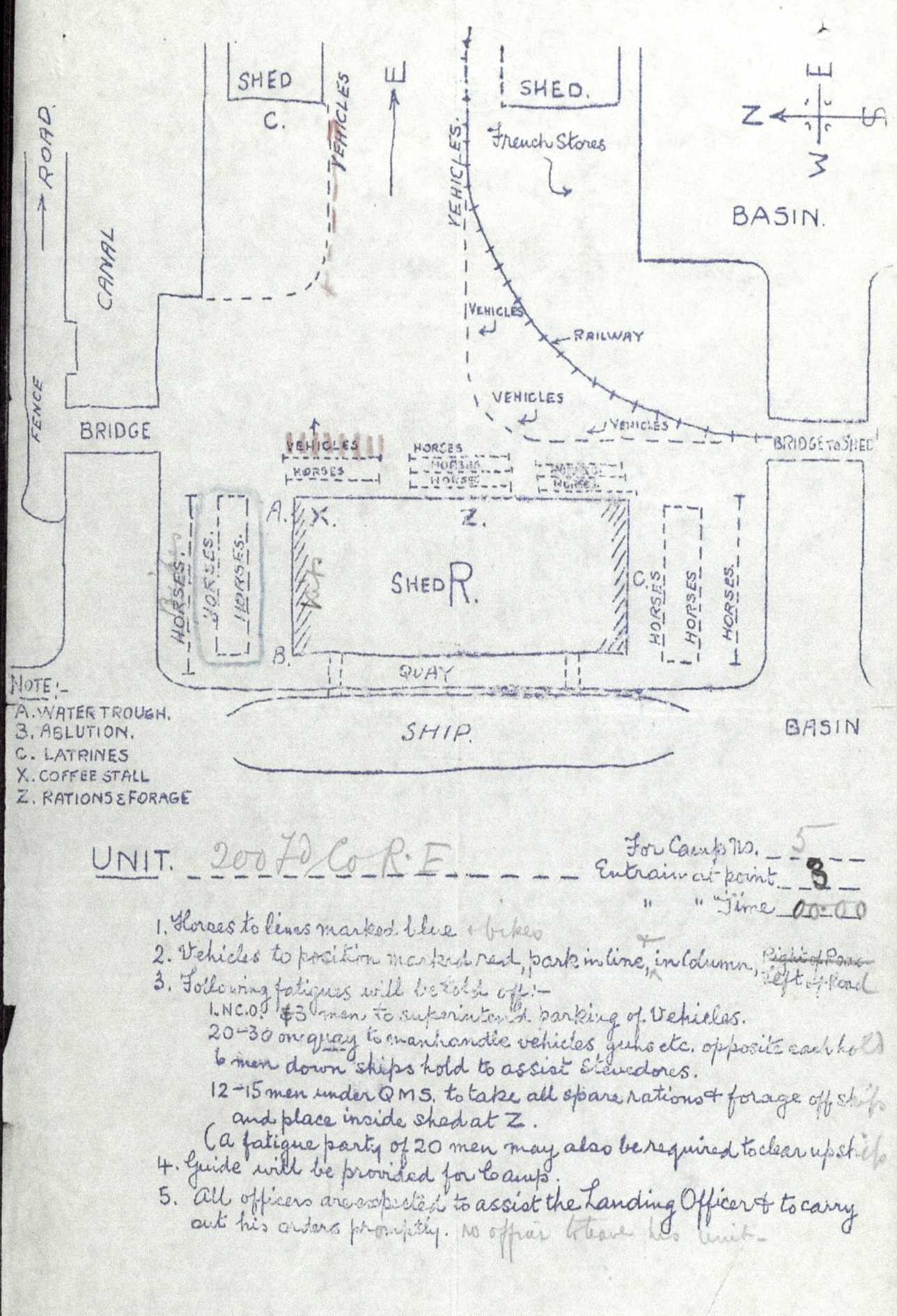

UNIT. 200 Fd Co R.E.

For Camp No. 5
Entrain at point 3
" " Time ~~00-00~~

1. Horses to lines marked blue + bikes
2. Vehicles to position marked red, park in line, + in column, ~~Right of Road~~ Left of Road
3. Following fatigues will be told off:-
   1 N.C.O. & 3 men to superintend parking of Vehicles.
   20-30 on quay to manhandle vehicles, guns etc. opposite each hold
   6 men down ships hold to assist Stevedores.
   12-15 men under Q.M.S. to take all spare rations & forage off ship and place inside shed at Z.
   (a fatigue party of 20 men may also be required to clear up ship
4. Guide will be provided for Camp.
5. All officers are expected to assist the Landing Officer & to carry out his orders promptly. No officer to leave his unit.

SECRET.

Train No.	UNIT.	O.	O.R.	H.	Vehicles 4-Wh.	Vehicles 2-Wh.	From	To	Starting Times. Day NOV.	Starting Times. Time.	Arrival Times. Day NOV.	Arrival Times. Time
X.176.	H.Q.Div.R.E. & Cyclist Co.	8	193	3	1	1 (204 bikes.)	Amesbury	Southampton Docks.	7th	1 pm.	7th	2-45 p.m.
X.195	½ 200th Fd.Co.R.E.	3.	113.	39	5	4	"	--- do ----	"	11.30 pm	8th	1-15 a.m.
X.196	½ -- do ----	3	113	40	5	5	"	"	8th	12.45 am	"	2-30 a.m.
X.198	½ 201st "	3	113	39	5	4	"	"	"	2-45 am	"	4-30 a.m.
X.200	½ " "	3	113	40	5	5	"	"	"	3.45 am	"	5-30 a.m.
X.216.	½ 202nd "	3	113	39	5	4	"	"	9th	9-45 am	9th	11-30 a.m.
X.217	½ 202nd "	3	113	40	5	5	"	"	"	10.40 am.	9th	12.25 p.m.

66

HEADQUARTERS B.1 10 NOV. 1915 ... INFANTRY BRIGADE

G. 9.

....

....

(1). The following road space tables are issued for the guidance of all concerned.

It is assumed that the rate of march is 100 yards per minute and for all practical purposes the distances shown in the second column against units may be taken as correct.

	Exact length in yards.	Approximate length in yards.
Divisional H.Q.	210	200
H.Q. No.1 Section Divl. Signal Coy.	390	400
Infantry Brigade H.Q.	105	100
No. 2,3 or 4 Section Signal Coy.	70	50
Squadron Cavalry	335	300
F.A. Brigade H.Q.	90	100
F.A. Brigade.	2210	2000
F.A. Brigade less Ammunition Column.	1595	1500
Divisional Ammunition Column	2165	2000
Motor Machine Gun Battery	400	400
Cyclist Company (mounted)	610	600
Cyclist Company (wheeling)	300	300
Field Company.	475	500
Field Company (less bridging equipment)	400	400
Battalion of Infantry	780	600
Pioneer Battalion.	895	1000
Divisional Train.	2260	2000
Divisional Train H.Q. Company.	1000	1000
Divisional Train H.Q. Coy. Baggage Section.	340	300
Divisional Train H.Q. Coy. Supply section.	510	500
Divisional Train, other coys. Baggage section.	190	200
Divisional Train, other coys. Supply section.	100	100
Field Ambulance	430	500
Workshop for Motor Ambulances.	150	150
Mobile veterinary section.	60	50
Infantry Brigade	3295	3000

(2). On the march the following spaces will be left in rear of units as shewn below.

In rear of a section of a field company or signal company..............................6 yards
In rear of a squadron, battery or infantry company....................................10 yards
In rear of an artillery brigade or infantry battalion....................................20 yards
In rear of an infantry brigade..................30 yards.

These spaces have been included in the lengths of the columns shewn in paragraph 1.

J.H. Hardy(?)

Major

General Staff

30th. Division.

10:11:15.

REFERENCE 30TH DIVISION OPERATION ORDER NO. (1) PARA. 4.

TRANSPORT AND SUPPLY ARRANGEMENTS DURING THE MOVE
OF THE DIVISION.

---

1 BAGGAGE WAGONS will remain with Units until the move is completed.

BLANKET WAGONS will be issued today at the following scale:-

2 per Infantry Battalion.
1 per Infantry Brigade Headquarters.

These wagons will be returned to the Headquarter Company, Divisional Train at FLESSELLES immediately after the move is completed.

SUPPLY WAGONS will join their units this evening loaded with rations for consumption on the 18th instant; these wagons will march on the 17th with their units until the Units arrive at their billets allotted to them that night, they will issue the rations as soon as possible after the units have reached their billets; stay the night with the unit and will be led by an Officer on the 18th instant to the re-filling point for the Brigade Area. Refilling points as under:-

2 DIVISIONAL TROOPS at the Junction of the FLESSELLES - VIGNACOURT-CANAPES ROADS. (1/4 mile N.W. of OLINCOURT CH^au)
89TH BRIGADE point 70 on the VAUX-FLESSELLES cross roads. (3/4 mile N of VAUX
90TH BRIGADE at the cross road from COISY to BERTANGLES and (in VAUX
PONTAMEVILLE to VILLERS BOCAGE.
91ST BRIGADE. at the entrance to PIERREGOT on the RAINNEVILLE road.

3. No. 202 Company R.E. will be in the Divisional Troops area.

No. 98th Field Ambulance and 200 Field Company will be in the 89th Area.

No. 96th Field Ambulance and the 201st Field Company will be in the 90th Area.

No. 97th Field Ambulance in the 91st Area.

4 O.C. Units will be responsible that men falling out do not ride on the Supply wagons, and that the Supply wagons reach the re-filling point for the Brigade Area concerned not later than 3.0 p.m. on the 18th. inst.

5 The following units will be issued with 2 days rations today for consumption on the 17th and 18th instants. The Supply wagons of these Units will return to the Headquarter Company of the Train after issuing rations tonight:-

Divisional Headquarters;	Headquarters, R.E.
Sanitary Section;	Signal Company.
A.K. Cable Section;	Mobile Veterinary Section.

6 All Units will arrange to draw soft-soap for their horses feet from D.A.D.O.S. at 5.0 p.m. today.

This soft-soap is used to prevent balling.

16th November, 1915.

J.H. Humphreys (signature)
Lieut. Colonel,
A.A. & Q.M.G. 30th Division.

Formation Brigade Headquarters will be established at MOUFLERS at 12 noon on the 17th. instant at which time the present Brigade Headquarters will be closed.

On arrival each Unit Commander will report to Brigade Headquarters that his Unit has arrived in its billets.

Edward Seymour,

Captain,
BRIGADE MAJOR.

November 16th. 1915.

Breakfast 6.0
Parade: 7.30.
Pt. 98. 10.0

Copy No 4.

Appendix C.

89TH BRIGADE OPERATION ORDER NO. 1.

S E C R E T. MARCH ORDERS FOR 17TH NOVEMBER.

The 17th Battalion K.L.R. will move on November 17th to VAUCHELLES-les-Domart and SURCAMPS, via AILLY and BRUCAMPS. Head of the column will pass point 98 on Route Nationale at 9.30 a.m.

The 18th Battalion K.L.R. will move on November 17th to MOUFLERS and BOUCHON, via AILLY and thence by Route Nationale to MOUFLERS. Head of the column will pass point 98 on Route Nationale at 9.45 a.m.

The 19th Battalion K.L.R. will remain at BUIGNY.

The 20th Battalion K.L.R. will move on November 17th to L'ETOILE, via COCQUEREL and LONG and will start at 9.0 a.m.

Headquarters will move on November 17th to MOUFLERS, via AILLY and thence Route Nationale. They will start at 9.0 a.m. and will march in rear of the 17th Battalion K.L.R.

98th Field Ambulance will remain at YAUCOURT.

200th Field Company R.E. will move to MOUFLERS or BOUCHON, via AILLY and will follow the 18th Battn. K.L.R Head of the column will pass point 98 on Route Nationale at 10.0 a.m.

Issued to Signals at
Copy No 1 Hd Qrs 30 Divn
No 2. 17th Bn KLR
No 3 18th "
No 4 19 "
No 5 20th "
No 6 98 Fd Amb
No 7 200 Field Coy RE
No 8 Signal Coy #2 Section
No 9 War Diary
No 10. No 2 Coy Divl Train

Edward Seymour. Captain.
Brigade Major.

SECRET. 89th Brigade Operation Order No 2

March Orders for the 18th November 1915-

****

Brigade Head Quarters will move from MOUFLERS to

FREMONT via FLIXECOURT. - BELLOY - ST, VAST.
Starting at 9 a,m,
****

17th Battn K.L,R. will move to VIGNACOURT via

ST OUEN.
Starting from SURCAMPS at 9 a,m,
****

18th Battnb K,L.R. will move to ST. VAST via

FLIXECOURT and BELLOY.
Starting from MOUFLERS at 8-50 a,m.
****

19th Battn K.L.R. will move to VIGNACOURT via AILLY -

FLIXECOURT.
Starting from BUIGNY at 8-- a.m.
****

20th Battn K.L.R. will move to VAUX via FLIXECOURT -

BELLOY - ST. VAST.
Starting from L'ETOILE at 8,30 a.m.
****

200th Field Coy R.E., will move to VIGNACOURT -

from MOUFLERS or BOUCHON at 910 a,m.
****

98th Field Ambulance will move to VIGNACOURT via

AILLY and FLIXECOURT.
Starting from YAUCOURT at 9- a.m.

Edward Seymour, Captain,

Brigade Major 89th Brigade,

16th November 1915-

Appendix F.

S E C R E T. Copy No. 6....

89th BRIGADE OPERATION ORDER NO. 3.

26th November 1915.

(Reference 1/80,000 Amiens Sheet 12.)

1. The 89th Brigade will move into the BERNAVILLE - PROUVILLE - BEAUMETZ - RIBEAUCOURT - LANCHES - DOMESMONT - EPECAMPS area on the 28th instant in accordance with the attached March Table.

2. Supply arrangements ~~are attached.~~ issued to you by CRE

3. Divisional Headquarters will open at FIENVILLERS at 11.0 a.m. at which hour it will close at FLESSELLES.

4. Brigade Headquarters will open at Chateau at RIBEAUCOURT at 12.0 noon, at which hour it will close at VAUX-en-Amienois.

5. Units will report to Brigade Headquarters immediately on arrival in billets in new area.

6. Reports to Brigade Headquarters in rear of the 20th Battalion on the march.

Seymour Captain.

Brigade Major.

Issued to Signals at 7 A.M. 27/11/15

No. 1 Copy H.Q. 30th Division.
No. 2 Copy 17th Batt. K.L.R.
No. 3 Copy 18th -do-
No. 4 Copy 19th -do-
No. 5 Copy 20th -do-
No. 6 Copy 200th Field Coy.R.E
No. 7 Copy 98th Field Ambulance.
No. 8 Copy No.3 Coy. 30th Divisional Train A.S.C
No. 9 Copy Supply Officer. 89th Infantry Brigade.
No.10 Copy O.C., No.2 Section Signal Company.
No.11 Copy File.
No.12 Copy War Diary.

S E C R E T.

MARCH TABLE for 28th November 1915.
Issued with 89th Brigade Operation Order No. 3.

UNIT	FROM	TO	STARTING POINT	TIME	ROUTE	REMARKS
19th Batt.K.L.R.	VIGNACOURT	PROUVILLE	Road junction 200 yds. S.W. of B of BERTEAUCOURT.	11. 0 a.m.	ST LEGER - DOMART-EN-PONTHIEU.	Branches off at DOMART-EN-PONTHIEU through RIBEAUCOURT to PROUVILLE.
17th Batt.K.L.R	"	(BEAUMETZ) (PROUVILLE)	"	11. 7 a.m.	"	Branches off at DOMART-EN-PONTHIEU through RIBEAUCOURT to BEAUMETZ.
200th Field Coy. Royal Engineers.	"	EPECAMPS	"	11.14 a.m.	"	Branches off at DOMART-EN-PONTHIEU through ST HILAIRE to EPECAMPS.
18th Batt.K.L.R.	FREMONT	BERNAVILLE	"	11.19 a.m.	"	Branches off at DOMART-EN-PONTHIEU through ST HILAIRE and EPECAMPS to BERNAVILLE.
20th Batt.K.L.R.	VAUX	(BERNAVILLE) (DOMESMONT) (LANCHES)	"	11.26 a.m.	"	Branches off at DOMART-EN-PONTHIEU to LANCHES. DOMESMONT. and BERNAVILLE.
Brigade Head-Quarters.	"	RIBEAUCOURT	"	11.33 a.m.	"	To RIBEAUCOURT.
No. 2 Company A.S.C	"	BERNAVILLE	"	11.34 a.m.	"	Branches off at DOMART-EN-PONTHIEU to BERNAVILLE.
98th Field Ambulance.	VIGNACOURT	HOUDENCOURT	"	11.36 a.m.	"	Branches off at DOMART-EN-PONTHIEU through FRANQUEVILLE to HOUDENCOURT.

N.B. This order of march will not be altered without direct orders from Brigade Headquarters.

BILLETING ORDERS

NOVEMBER 28TH.1915.

---

1. BILLETS.

Brigade Headquarters at	RIBEAUCOURT
17th.L'pools.	BEAUMETZ and PROUVILLE,
18th. "	BERNAVILLE,
19th. "	PROUVILLE,
20th. "	BERNAVILLE, DOMESMONT and LANCHES.
200th.Field Co.R.E.	EPECAMPS,
98th.Field Ambulance	HOUD ENCOURT,
No.2 Co.Dvsnl. Train	BERNAVILLE.

---

2. ADVANCE PARTIES. All Units will send forward the billeting parties as on previous occasions as early as possible on Sunday morning, or may send forward an Officer and the Interpreter on Saturday night, the remainder of the Billeting party to report to the Officer i/c Billeting Party on Sunday morning at such place as he shall direct. As there will very likely be troops in the Area on Saturday night it will probably be difficult to find accommodation for more than the Officer and Interpreter.

3. A. Distribution. As there is not sufficient accommodation in BEAUMETZ for a full Battalion the Officer i/c Billeting party 17th.Btln. will arrange to take over from the Officer i/c 19th.Btln. Billeting party room in PROUVILLE for not more than 1 Company. PROUVILLE will hold one Battalion of Infantry plus 1 Company. The Mayor at PROUVILLE is on active service and the list of billets is in charge of the Schoolmistress.

B. Distribution at BERNAVILLE. Accommodation will approximately be as follows,

18th.L'pools.	All east of cross roads to the West of Church.
20th. "	All west of cross roads to the West of Church
No.2 Coy.Dvsnl.Train.	In the empty house on the road junction south of B in BERNAVILLE on the main road FIENVILLERS-BEAUMETZ.

C. Distribution suggested for 20th.L'pools. is as follows

BERNAVILLE	- 2 Companies & H.Qrs.(?)
DOMESMONT	- 1 "
LANCHES	- 1 "

E.Seymour Captain
Brigade Major

Opperwex ?

AMIENS

Type 1889

Prix : 0 fr 30

5

TRANSPORT AND SUPPLY ARRANGEMENT ISSUED WITH OPERATION ORDER NO. 6. dated 29th December 1915.

(a) TRANSPORT ARRANGEMENTS.

All Infantry Battalions will be issued with two motor lorries or 5 G.S. Wagons for the conveyance of blankets and additional authorised stores.

2. Infantry Brigade Head Quarters and Field Company R.E. will be issued with 1 additional G.S. Wagon for the conveyance of blankets etc.

The above additional transport and baggage wagons as per War Establishment will be issued to Units by 3 p.m. on the day previous to the commencement of the march and will accompany Units as far as the 1st Line Transport billets in the 5th Divisional Area. The contents will be unloaded as soon as possible and the lorries returned to their Units.

The Baggage Wagons and additional G.S.Wagons will be withdrawn on the day following day of arrival under instructions which will be issued to Units by the O.C. 30th Divisional Train. Similarly after arrival at final destination Supply Wagons will return to the Divisional Train as soon as possible after supplies have been issued.

(b). SUPPLY ARRANGEMENTS.

Each Unit will draw 2 day's supplies on the day previous to commencement of their march; 1 day's supplies will be carried in the cookers, the other in Supply Wagons.

2. 2 Day's supplies will be issued at PONT NOYELLES to all troops billeted on the evening of 2nd day's march in the PONT NOYELLES - LA HOUSSOYE area. The Supply Officer will post a man outside the main door of the Church at PONT NOYELLES to direct Units to the refilling point.

P. T. O.

4. On the evening of the 4th day's march Units will draw rations from the 5th Divisional Refilling point, under instructions which will be issued by the Senior Supply Officer, 30th Division, as soon as Units arrive at the end of the 3rd day's march.

4. All Train Transport and personnel will be rationed by the Unit to which they are attached. They will require rations from and including the first day's march of the Unit.

5. All troops billeting at DAOURS on the second day's march will be issued with rations at DAOURS, two day's rations being issued the day before leaving the present area.

The Refilling Point at DAOURS will be notified later to all troops concerned.

(Signed). L. Hume-Spry. Lt. Col.

30/12/1915. A.A. & Q.M.G., 30th Division.

With reference to para. 2. please arrange that train vehicles are returned to the O.C., Divisional Train, at E T I N E H E M, the day following arrival in New Area with one day's supply for men and horses.

30th Divisional Engineers

200th FIELD COMPANY R. E.

JANUARY 1916.

Seven

Instructions regarding War Diaries and Intelligence Summaries are contained in F. S. Regs., Part II. and the Staff Manual respectively. Title pages will be prepared in manuscript.

WAR DIARY
or
~~INTELLIGENCE SUMMARY~~.
(Erase heading not required.)

Army Form C. 2118.

200th Field Coy R.E.

Place	Date	Hour	Summary of Events and Information	Remarks and references to Appendices
			The 5th Division	
Lanches	4-1-16	9.0am	We left LANCHES at 9.0am. via BERNEUIL, CANAPLES and arrive at WARGNIES at 2.0 pm.	
Wargnies	5-1-16	9.45am	Leave WARGNIES at 9.45am. marching via SAINT GRATEIN, QUERRIEU, arriving at PONT-NOYELLE at 3.0pm. Two Officers Lieut. L A Hill and 2nd Lieut. G J Gibbins were detailed to attend a lecture at VIGNACOURT on the recent fighting at LOOS.	
Pont-Noyelle	6-1-16	9.0am	Leave PONT-NOYELLE at 9-0 am. via CORBIE, arriving at BRAY-SUR-SOMME at 4.30pm. (Copies of Orders and March Table attached)	Appendices I. and J.
Bray-sur-Somme			Here we occupied the billeting area and take over the various works that were in the hands of the 1/2nd Durham Field Company R.E. The Sector allotted to us Fire Trench 62 on the CARNOY-MAMETZ road to Fire French 76 S.E. FRICOURT. Works requiring our immediate and special attention improvement and reconstruction of light narrow guage railway which conveys all stores and material to the Sub-Sector on the	

2353 Wt. W2544/1454 700,000 5/15 D. D. & L. A.D.S.S./Forms/C. 2118.

Eight

Instructions regarding War Diaries and Intelligence Summaries are contained in F. S. Regs., Part II. and the Staff Manual respectively. Title pages will be prepared in manuscript.

WAR DIARY
or
~~INTELLIGENCE SUMMARY~~. 200th Field Coy R.E.

(*Erase heading not required.*)

Army Form C. 2118.

Place	Date	Hour	Summary of Events and Information	Remarks and references to Appendices
Bray-sur-Somme.			extreme of our lines. The erection and construction of steel tubular, mined and other shelters. Siteing and constructing machine gun emplacements and carrying out other works necessary to keep the Section in a high state of efficiency. The next week is fairly wet with two or three fine mornings. Sectors fairly quiet so work is progressing fast. The next few days Artillery duels take place, some shells dropped into BRAY-SUR-Somme.	
-do-	17-1-16		Quiet day and wet weather also the same on the 18-1-16.	
-do-	19-1-16		Weather fine, in the evening heavy machine gun duel in front lines, one casualty Sapper slightly wounded.	
-do-	21-1-16		In the early morning two or three heavy shells came over BRAY-SUR-Somme.	
-do-	22-1-16		Weather wet, BRAY-CORBIE road heavily shelled throughout the day S.W. of BRAY-SUR-Somme. For the next few days, Artillery active.	
-do-	26-1-16		Accurate and complete survey of the whole Sector begun.	

Aire

Instructions regarding War Diaries and Intelligence Summaries are contained in F. S. Regs., Part II. and the Staff Manual respectively. Title pages will be prepared in manuscript.

WAR DIARY
or
~~INTELLIGENCE~~ SUMMARY.
(Erase heading not required.)

Army Form C. 2118.

200th Field Coy. R.E.

Place	Date	Hour	Summary of Events and Information	Remarks and references to Appendices
Bray-sur-Somme	26-1-16		Company workshop developed, introduction of Steam plant and Saws.	
-do-	27-1-16		Destruction of several blind shells, casualty two 2nd Lieut. E. E. Billington, seriously wounded and 2nd Lieut. G. G. Gibbins slightly wounded. Artillery very active all night. Wind, light. Atmosphere, heavy.	
-do-	28-1-16	9-0am	Weather, heavy + misty. Wind light N.E. Artillery duel all day. SUZANNE heavily shelled, at 10.30 p.m. Orders to	
"		10.30pm	"Stand to" pending Gas attack. One casualty, Sergeant wounded with Shrapnel.	
-do-	29-1-16		Wind, light N.E. morning heavy and foggy.	
"		6.45am	At 6.45 am Gas attack alarm, but cloud did not reach BRAY-SUR-Somme. Refugees from SUZANNE come into BRAY-SUR-Somme and are sent on to CORBIE. Artillery very active.	
-do-	30-1-16		Weather, damp + misty. Artillery active during the morning. Refugees continue to come from SUZANNE into BRAY-SUR-Somme.	
		4pm	At 4-0 pm. received a Gas alarm from the 90th Brigade at	

2353 Wt. W2544/1454 700,000 5/15 D. D. & L. A.D.S.S./Forms/C. 2118.

Ten

Instructions regarding War Diaries and Intelligence Summaries are contained in F. S. Regs., Part II. and the Staff Manual respectively. Title pages will be prepared in manuscript.

WAR DIARY
or
~~INTELLIGENCE SUMMARY~~. 200th Field Coy. RE.
(Erase heading not required.)

Army Form C. 2118.

Place	Date	Hour	Summary of Events and Information	Remarks and references to Appendices
Bray-sur-Somme.	30-1-16	4 pm	Suzanne, and this was cancelled at 4.50 pm.	
– do –	31-1-16		Weather dull and misty. Company had orders to be prepared to hand over our Sector of the Line and all other works. Great progress has been made whilst the Company has had charge of this Sector in re-constructing and erecting shelters of various kinds, improvement to railway, developing the Company workshop.	
		11.45am	A quantity of heavy German shells fell in the valley N.E. of Bray-sur-Somme.	
		9.0pm	Artillery active	

Christopher [illegible] Major.
R.E.
O.C. 200TH FIELD CO., (COUNTY PALATINE) R.E.

2353 Wt. W2544/1454 700,000 5/15 D. D. & L. A.D.S.S./Forms/C. 2118.

Copy. No. 6

1st January 1916.

Appendix J.

SECRET.

89th Brigade Operation Order No. 5.

Reference Maps	Sheet 11.	LENS.	1/100.000.
	Sheet 17.	AMIENS.	1/100.000.
	Combined Sheet	ALBERT.	1/40.000.

1. The 30th Division will march commencing Sunday 2nd January to relieve the 5th Division (less one B rigde) of the 10th Corps.

2. The Division is to be attached to the 10th Corps and the troops enter the 10th Corps Area in their second day's march.

(PONT NOYELL ES LA HOUSSOYE).

The relief will be carried out under the orders of the G. C. C., 5th Division in whose area the troops will arrive on their third day's march.

(V AUX - SAILLY LAURETTE - ETINEHEM).

3. i. Moves will be in accordance with the attached march table.

ii. Route TALMA S. SEPTENVILLE. PIERREGOT. MOLLIENS.-AU-B OIS. ST. GRATIEN. CORBIE., then by the lower (River) road. The troops of the 5th Division will use the upper road to CORBIE via point 108.

iii. Moves on the fourth day and afterwards will take place after dark, and will be under orders of the 5th Division, who may also issue special orders as regards moves on the third day into their area.

iv. Column Commanders will report arrival of their troops at their destinations and the position of their Head Quarters.

(a) Daily to 30th Division. for this purpose a motor cyclist from the Signal Company will accompany the C olumn Commander on the first day's march. Second day's report will be sent through 10th Corps, third day's through 5th Division.

(b) In the PONT NOYELLES - LA HOUSSOYE. area to 10th Corps at QUERRIEUX.

(c) In the VAUX SUR SOMME - ETINEHEM area to 5th D ivision at ETINEHEM.

v. Baggage section of the train will accompany troops on the march.

4. Billetting accomodation is approximately as follows:-

1st day.	TALMAS.	1 Battalion.
	NAOURS.	1 Battalion. - more could be obtained.
	WARGNIES.	1/2 Battalion.
2nd day.	LA HOUSSOYE	1 Battalion.
	PONT NOYELLES.	1500.- more could be obtained.
3rd day	CHIPILLY.) ETINEHAM.)	1 Battalion.
	SAILLY LAURETTE.	2 B attalions.
	VAUX SUR SOMME.	1 Battalion.

This area will be in occupation by 5th Division and 30th Division troops throughout the relief, and billetting in it will be arranged by 5th Division.

5. Every man on entering the trenches will carry with him 120 rounds of ammunition. Arrangements are being made by 5th Division to allow of 1 Officer and 1 N.C.O. per Coy. and one N.C.O. per platoon besides representatives of Brigade and Battalion Head Quarters visiting the trenches before relief, as well as taking over by daylight trench stores, trench ammunition and grenades.

6. Copy of instructions as regards communication during the move attached.

7. Copy of arrangements as regards transport and supply attached.

8. Divisional Head Quarters will remain at LE MAILLARD until 4 p.m. 8th January when they will close and re-open at DAOURS.

Communications with Divisional Head Quarters after this time will be via 10th Corps Signal Office.

9. Column Commanders will issue their own orders to the Units concerned.

E Seymour

Captain.
Brigade Major.
89th Infantry Brigade.

Issued to Signals at 1 pm on 2/1/16

Copy No 1. 30th Division.
Copy No. 2. 17th Battn K.L.R.
Copy No. 3 19th Battn K.L.R.
Copy No. 4. 20th Battn K.L.R.
Copy No. 5. 2nd Battn Bedford Regiment.
Copy No. 6. 200th Field Coy R.E.
Copy No. 7. 2 Coy 30th Divisional Train.
Copy No. 8. 89th Brigade Supply Officer.
Copy No.10. War Diary.
Copy No.11. War Diary.
Copy No 9 98th Field Ambulance

TABLE B. 3.

No. 3 Column. Commander Lt. Col. B. C. Fairfax. 17th Liverpools.

1	2	3	4	5	6	7
Troops	4th Jan.	5th Jan.	6th Jan	7th Jan.	8th Jan.	Remarks.
200th Field Coy. R. E.	WARGNIES	PONT NOYELLES	BRAY			Via Upper Road (pts. 102, 108, 105)
17th Liverpools.	NAOURS	PONT NOYELLES	SAILLY LAURETTE	SUZANNE	Trenches Sector A.4.	
2nd Royal Scots Fusiliers.	TALMAS	LA HOUSSOYE	ETINEHEM and CHIPILLY	SUZANNE	Trenches Sector A.2.	

30th Divisional Engineers

----- -----

200th FIELD COMPANY R. E. ::: FEBRUARY 1916

"Eleven."

Instructions regarding War Diaries and Intelligence Summaries are contained in F. S. Regs., Part II. and the Staff Manual respectively. Title pages will be prepared in manuscript.

WAR DIARY
or
~~INTELLIGENCE SUMMARY~~. 200th Field Company, R.E.

(*Erase heading not required.*)

Army Form C. 2118.

Place	Date	Hour	Summary of Events and Information	Remarks and references to Appendices
Bray-sur-Somme	2-2-16	3.45pm	Weather cold & dull. At 3.45pm enemy dropped a quantity of shells in the valley N.E. of BRAY. One heavy shell dropping into the middle of the square in BRAY, the Place de la Liberté, demolishing all the windows of the Maire and damaging windows and facade of the Church. Artillery were active at night.	
-do-	3-2-16		Hand over Sector of the line C1 & C2 and are relieved in this Sector, by the 1/3rd Durham Field Company R.E. (T.)	
		4.50pm	Civilian population moving out of BRAY. At 4.50pm the enemy again shell BRAY. Two officer reinforcements 2nd Lt. R. W. R. Rankin R.E. and 2nd Lieut. J. A. Bickel R.E. arrive and report, and are taken on to the strength of this Company. Artillery active during the night.	
-do-	4.2.16	3.5pm	Weather rough and wet. At 3.5pm BRAY was heavilly shelled for quarter of an hour. Considerable damage was done to Officers Mess and men's billets.	

2353 Wt. W2544/1454 700,000 5/15 D. D. & L. A.D.S.S./Forms/C. 2118.

Twelve

Instructions regarding War Diaries and Intelligence Summaries are contained in F. S. Regs., Part II. and the Staff Manual respectively. Title pages will be prepared in manuscript.

WAR DIARY
or
~~INTELLIGENCE SUMMARY.~~ 200th Field Company R.E.
(Erase heading not required.)

Army Form C. 2118.

Place	Date	Hour	Summary of Events and Information	Remarks and references to Appendices
Bray-Sur-Somme	4-2-16		Two casualties No 81516 Sapper Wright W. and No. 99787 Sapper Hughes J. killed and a further casualty No 83332 Sapper Hughes P. wounded.	
-do- Cappy			Take over work on fortified position at CAPPY CORNER on the BRAY-CAPPY road. This defence takes the form of three fortified buildings with machine gun emplacements and loop-holed walls on ground level. The cellars and loop holes being made shell proof with communication trenches in rear leading to support line, flanked by fire-trenches with three machine gun emplacements to sweep the approaches from CAPPY. Barbed wire entanglement and other obstacles placed in front on E. side of river the whole forming a strong point-d'appui. (Attached copies of plan & sketch as appendices)	Appendices K. & L.
Bray-Sur-Somme	4-2-16		Also take over construction of barbed wire entanglements on the S.E. of BRAY from River Somme to the marshes S. of the BRAY-FROISSY Road at a point	

Thirteen

Instructions regarding War Diaries and Intelligence Summaries are contained in F. S. Regs., Part II. and the Staff Manual respectively. Title pages will be prepared in manuscript.

WAR DIARY

or

~~INTELLIGENCE SUMMARY.~~ 200th Field Company R.E.

(*Erase heading not required.*)

Army Form C. 2118.

Place	Date	Hour	Summary of Events and Information	Remarks and references to Appendices
BRAY-SUR SOMME	4-2-16		½ a mile S. of la Neuville. Bray	
-do-	5-2-16		No 81516 Sapper Wright W. buried at CHIPILLY Cemetery	
Chipilly	"	2pm.	at 2 p.m.	
BRAY-SUR SOMME			Enemy's aeroplanes very active. Extensive air reconnaissance between 2 pm and 5.30 p.m. took place by Allied aircraft.	
Chipilly	6-2-16	2pm.	No 99787 Sapper Hughes J. buried at CHIPILLY Cemetery at 2pm. Artillery active. Enemy heavilly shelled	
BRAY-SUR SOMME		2.55pm	BRAY at 2.55 pm for about 15 minutes, but little or no material damage was done.	
-do-	7-2-16		Weather fine, a little rain at intervals. Wind W. One Officer casualty 2nd Lieut. T. A. Bickel R.E. being accidently shot in the foot whilst loading his revolver.	
-do-	8-2-16		Weather dull. Artillery active, About 9 pm. Snow during the night.	
-do-	9-2-16		Weather cold and fine. Considerable air reconnaissance by Allied air-craft taking place in the afternoon.	

Fourteen

Instructions regarding War Diaries and Intelligence Summaries are contained in F. S. Regs., Part II. and the Staff Manual respectively. Title pages will be prepared in manuscript.

WAR DIARY
or
~~INTELLIGENCE SUMMARY.~~ 200th Field Company R.E.

(*Erase heading not required.*)

Army Form C. 2118.

Place	Date	Hour	Summary of Events and Information	Remarks and references to Appendices
Bray-sur Somme	9-2-16	5 pm	Artillery active from 5 pm. to 8 pm.	
-do-	10-2-16	12.45am	Enemy shelled BRAY at 12-45 am. no material damage being done.	
-do-	11-2-16		Morning wet and cold. During the day French Artillery on our right very active.	
-do-	12-2-16		Dull and wet. Artillery active.	
-do-	13-2-16		Wet. 1 O.R. reinforcement arrived and reported & was taken on the strength of this Company.	
-do-	14-2-16		Wet. Enemy shelled BRAY-CORBIE road W. of BRAY, several shells dropping in BRAY.	
		3 pm	At 3 pm. they shelled the town, one shell hitting the Church Tower.	
-do-	15-2-16	4 pm	Fine & windy. Enemy shelled the town at 4 pm. several shells also dropped into the town during the night.	
-do-	16-2-16	9.15am	Weather wet & windy. Enemy's Artillery active BRAY being shelled at 9-15 am. and also in the afternoon. One Officer reinforcement. 2nd Lieut. F.A.D. Richmond R.E.	

2353 Wt. W2544/1454 700,000 5/15 D. D. & L. A.D.S.S./Forms/C. 2118.

Fifteen

Instructions regarding War Diaries and Intelligence Summaries are contained in F. S. Regs., Part II. and the Staff Manual respectively. Title pages will be prepared in manuscript.

WAR DIARY
or
~~INTELLIGENCE SUMMARY.~~ 200th Field Coy. R.E.

(Erase heading not required.)

Army Form C. 2118.

Place	Date	Hour	Summary of Events and Information	Remarks and references to Appendices
Bray-sur-Somme	16-2-16		arrived and reported and is taken on to the strength of this Company. This officer was Reserve Officer and remained in England as O. i/c Details left at the base on the Company leaving for duty overseas.	
-do-	17-2-16		Weather fine. Had orders to prepare to take over the Sector of the line A1 + A2. including the defences of MARICOURT. An officer of the 1/1st Highland Field Company R.E. arrived and reported to take over this Sector, the Company receiving orders to move into another area for rest.	
-do-	18-2-16		Weather very wet. A reconnaissance is made of Sector A1 + A2.	
-do-	19-2-16	11 p.m.	Weather dull and wet. Orders for the Company to move are cancelled. At 11 p.m. Artillery active.	
-do-	20-2-16		Weather fine. French + English Artillery co-operate during day and night with great activity.	

2353 Wt. W2544/1454 700,000 5/15 D. D. & L. A.D.S.S./Forms/C. 2118.

Sixteen

Instructions regarding War Diaries and Intelligence Summaries are contained in F. S. Regs., Part II. and the Staff Manual respectively. Title pages will be prepared in manuscript.

WAR DIARY
or
~~INTELLIGENCE SUMMARY~~. 200th Field Coy. R.E.
(Erase heading not required.)

Army Form C. 2118.

Place	Date	Hour	Summary of Events and Information	Remarks and references to Appendices
Bray-sur-Somme	21-2-16		Weather fine, cold. One casualty O.R. No 81653 C.Q.M.S. J.A. Wood, broken arm through a fall from his horse. Artillery active all day.	
-do-	22-2-16	7.30pm	Weather fine, snow during the night. In the late afternoon Artillery very active the troops in the town had orders to "stand to". Artillery activity ceased at 7.30 pm.	
-do-	23-2-16		Weather fine, very cold, Wind E. later turned to snow.	
-do-	24-2-16		Weather cold, hard frost.	
-do-	25-2-16		Weather very cold. Snowing all morning. Leave for all Officers and troops cancelled. Heavy fall of snow during the night.	
-do-	26-2-16	8.10pm	Weather fine & dull. At 8.10 pm. BRAY was heavily shelled by enemy. Bombardment ceased at 9.5 pm. Sudden thaw set in.	
-do-	27-2-16		Weather dull.	
-do-	28-2-16		Weather dull.	
-do-	29-2-16	5.40pm	Weather fine, turned to rain later. Artillery active. At 5.40pm	

Seventeen

Instructions regarding War Diaries and Intelligence Summaries are contained in F. S. Regs., Part II. and the Staff Manual respectively. Title pages will be prepared in manuscript.

WAR DIARY
or
~~INTELLIGENCE SUMMARY~~. 200th Field Coy R.E.
(Erase heading not required.)

Army Form C. 2118.

Place	Date	Hour	Summary of Events and Information	Remarks and references to Appendices
BRAY-SUR-SOMME	29/2/16	5.40pm	The enemy shelled BRAY-SUR-SOMME.	

[illegible] Major R.E.
O.C. 200TH FIELD CO., (COUNTY PALATINE) R.E.
3/iii/16

2353 Wt. W2544/1454 700,000 5/15 D. D. & L. A.D.S.S./Forms/C. 2118.

Appendix K.

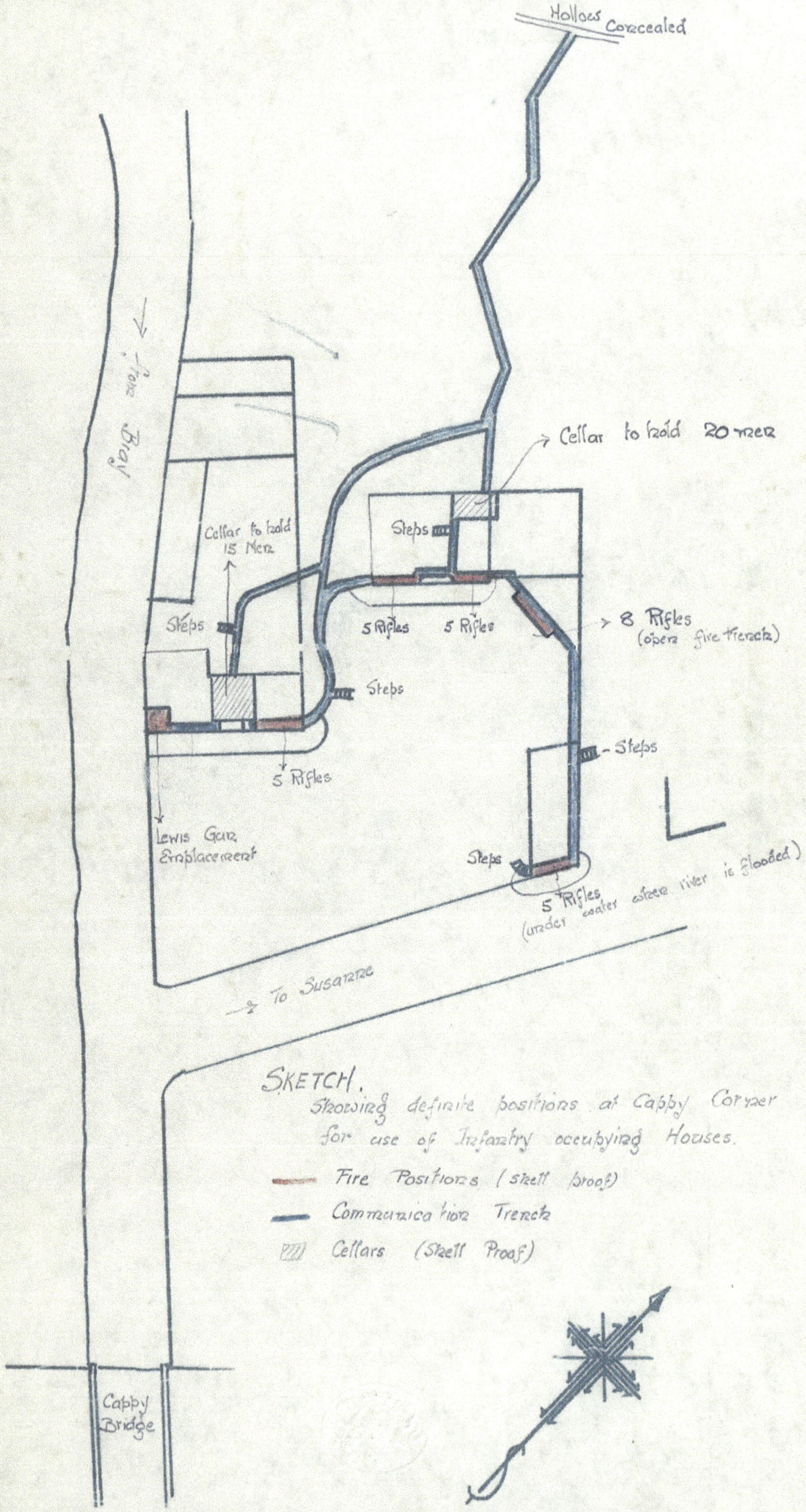
Hollow Concealed
From Bray
Cellar to hold 20 men
Cellar to hold 15 Men
Steps
Steps
5 Rifles
5 Rifles
8 Rifles
(open fire trench)
Steps
Steps
Steps
5 Rifles
Lewis Gun Emplacement
Steps
5 Rifles
(under water when river is flooded)
To Susanne
SKETCH.
Showing definite positions at Cappy Corner for use of Infantry occupying Houses.
Fire Positions (shell proof)
Communication Trench
Cellars (Shell Proof)
Cappy Bridge

Secret Appendix M

O.C.,200th. Field Company, R.E.,

Copy of 30th. Division No.G.177 of 13/2/1916, forwarded for information and guidance.

When the Redistribution comes into force 2 Sections will be in the front line at disposal of G.O.C. Brigade and 2 Sections at C.R.E's disposal.

For the present the Sections at C.R.E's disposal will be employed on following works:-

CAPPY Bridge Defences.

BILLON AVENUE.

LAUNDRY at CERISY.

BOIS des TAILLES Well.

R.J. Stall Capt
for. Lt-Col.R.E.,

13/2/1916. C.R.E., 30th. Division.

C O P Y.

S E C R E T.

C.R.E.,

G.177 13th. Feb.1916.

Reference 1/10,000 MARICOURT Sheet, 62c N.W. 1.

1. The Redistribution of this Divisional Front will come into force at midday 16th. inst.

2. Lieut.Colonel Cobham will be in command of 'A' Sector, pending the arrival of Br.Gen. The Hon. F. C. Stanley, D.S.O.,

3. The limits of the two Sectors will be as follows:-

Z Sector: Bri.Gen. Steavenson. H.Q. SUZANNE.
Z.1. from the River SOMME at ECLUSIER to MOULIN de FARGNY (exclusive).
Z.2. from MOULIN de FARGNY (inclusive) to Trench 17 (inclusive).
3 Battalions.
Includes 'R' Works.

A Sector: Brig.Gen. The Hon. F. C. Stanley,D.S.O. H.Q. BRAY.
A.1. from Trench 18 (inclusive) to Trench 27 (inclusive).
A.2. from Trench 28 (inclusive) to Trench 36 (exclusive).
4 Battalions.
Includes 'S' and 'U' Works.

4. (i). The Brigade Reserve to 'Z' Sector will be at SUZANNE.
As regards 'A' Sector, 2 Battalions will be in the front line, 1 Battalion at MARICOURT; the remaining Battalion is earmarked for the Divisional Reserve. It will continue for the present to be located at SUZANNE, but it is proposed later to move it to BRAY.
BILLON WOOD AVENUE is now being renovated as a communication trench leading to 'A' Sector. It may later become advisable to prolong this trench back towards BRAY.

5. Battle Headquarters for 'A' Sector are in course of construction about A.25.d.5/5; telephone lines now being buried.
For the moment the Brigade Grenade Store will be at SUZANNE with an advanced Store at MARICOURT. Later the main Store will be located, probably, at BRAY.

(sd). W. F. WEBER, Lt-Col.

30th. Divn. General Staff.

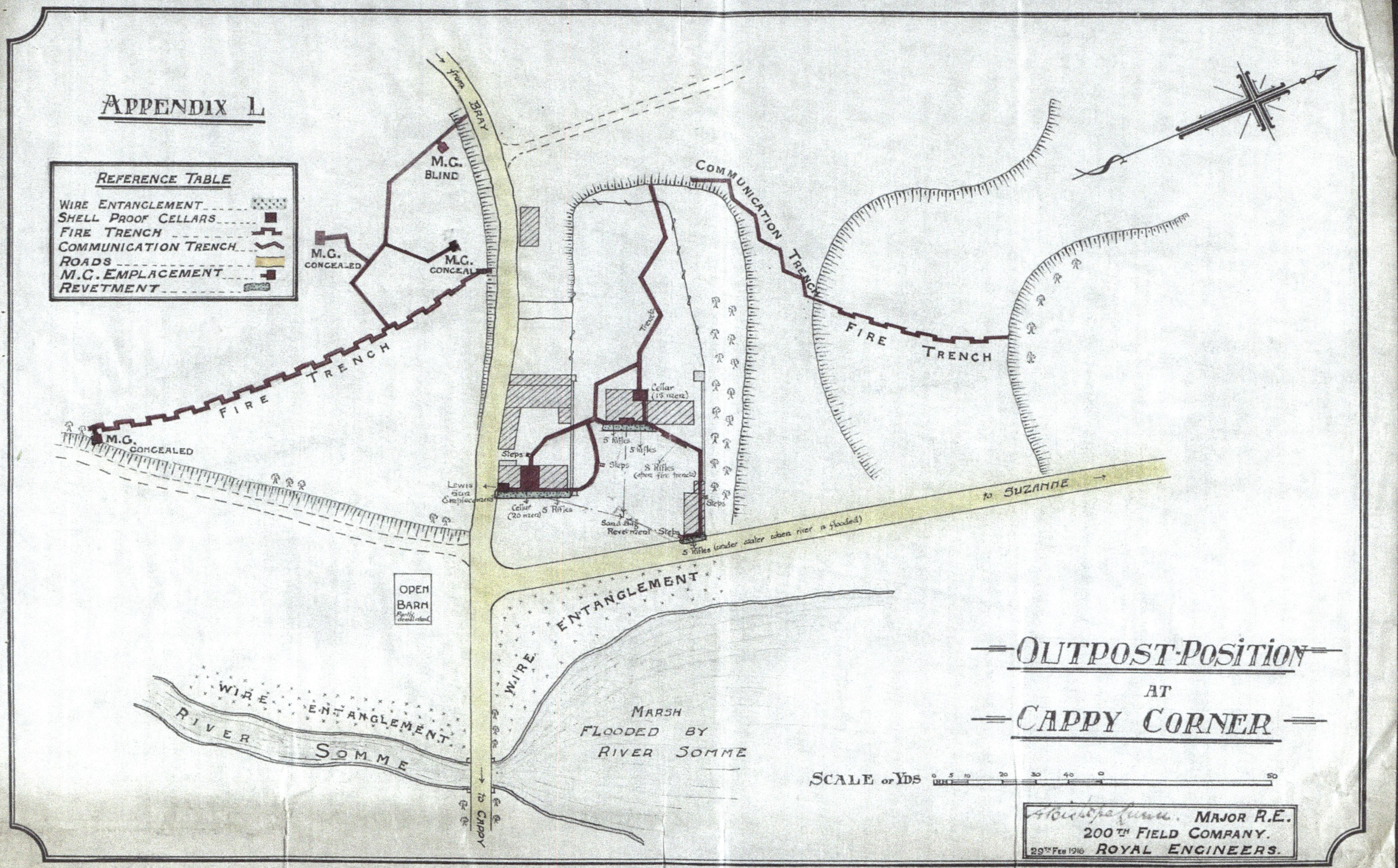
APPENDIX L
REFERENCE TABLE
WIRE ENTANGLEMENT
SHELL PROOF CELLARS
FIRE TRENCH
COMMUNICATION TRENCH
ROADS
M.C. EMPLACEMENT
REVETMENT
from BRAY
M.G. BLIND
M.G. CONCEALED
M.G. CONCEALED
FIRE TRENCH
M.G. CONCEALED
COMMUNICATION TRENCH
FIRE TRENCH
Trench
Cellar (15 men)
5 Rifles
5 Rifles
Steps
8 Rifles (above fire trench)
Steps
Lewis Gun Emplacement
Cellar (20 men)
5 Rifles
Sand Bag Revetment
Steps
Steps
5 Rifles (under water when river is flooded)
to SUZANNE
OPEN BARN
WIRE ENTANGLEMENT
WIRE ENTANGLEMENT
MARSH FLOODED BY RIVER SOMME
RIVER SOMME
to CAPPY
OUTPOST-POSITION AT CAPPY CORNER
SCALE OF YDS
MAJOR R.E.
200TH FIELD COMPANY.
29TH FEB 1916 ROYAL ENGINEERS.

30th Divisional Engineers

200th FIELD COMPANY R. E. :: MARCH 1916.

Eighteen

Instructions regarding War Diaries and Intelligence Summaries are contained in F. S. Regs., Part II. and the Staff Manual respectively. Title pages will be prepared in manuscript.

WAR DIARY
~~or~~
~~INTELLIGENCE SUMMARY.~~ 200th Field Coy R.E.
(Erase heading not required.)

Army Form C. 2118.

Place	Date	Hour	Summary of Events and Information	Remarks and references to Appendices
Bray-sur-Somme	1-3-16		Weather fine, but dull. Very quiet day. 7 O.R. reinforcements reported their arrival. One Section of this unit was detailed to carry out work in fortifying a house directly N.W. of bridge in LA NEUVILLE-les-BRAY on the BRAY-FROISSY Road. These premises were taken over and occupied by the 89th Infantry Brigade as Brigade Headquarters. The work consisted of excavation of 4 cellars strengthening roofs revetting and making them shell proof. Construction of a dug-out shelter, underground protected communication between these, rendering the whole a complete and safe unit against shell bombardment. Another Section carrying out Divisional R.E. work, deep well boring at CÉRISY, Baths and the construction and erection of Divisional Laundry.	

Nineteen

Instructions regarding War Diaries and Intelligence Summaries are contained in F. S. Regs., Part II. and the Staff Manual respectively. Title pages will be prepared in manuscript.

WAR DIARY
or
~~INTELLIGENCE SUMMARY~~. 200th Field Company R.E.
(Erase heading not required.)

Army Form C. 2118.

Place	Date	Hour	Summary of Events and Information	Remarks and references to Appendices
Bray-sur-Somme			The remainder of the Company carried out the ordinary routine work in improving and making good trenches in that Sector occupied by the 89th Infantry Brigade. The construction of shell-proof shelters in MARICOURT, improvement of water supply, and the erection of 3 large dug-out shelters in BILLON VALLEY has been undertaken. (Copy of orders attached)	Appendix M.
-do-	2-3-16		Weather fine, but dull.	
-do-	3-3-16		Morning fine, but dull, night, wind N.E. very gusty with snow.	
-do-	4-3-16		Dull, damp and cold. Snowing all day. gusty wind. The enemy put several shells into BRAY during the afternoon.	
-do-	5-3-16		Day fine. A certain amount of air reconnaissance undertaken by Allied aeroplanes, which were subjected considerable shell fire from hostile anti-aircraft guns.	

Twenty

Instructions regarding War Diaries and Intelligence Summaries are contained in F. S. Regs., Part II. and the Staff Manual respectively. Title Pages will be prepared in manuscript.

WAR DIARY
or
~~INTELLIGENCE SUMMARY~~ 200th Field Company R.E.

(Erase heading not required.)

Army Form C. 2118.

Place	Date	Hour	Summary of Events and Information	Remarks and references to Appendices
BRAY-sur-Somme.	5-3-16		No 83269 Lance Corporal Fielding A. recommended to notice for consideration, for good services rendered. This N.C.O. showed considerable courage and devotion to duty, under shell fire on the night of February 26th 1916 whilst in charge of transport, passing through SUZANNE which was being heavily shelled by the enemy. His transport came under direct shell fire causing the animals to bolt, he gave orders to his drivers to proceed along the SUZANNE - CAPPY Road, whilst he himself returned to SUZANNE for the purpose of ascertaining the direction in which the transport had gone. He was instrumental in stopping two pairs of horses which were bolting in his direction and returning them to their unit. Not finding his transport he returned, and proceeding along the BRAY-CAPPY road.	

2449 Wt. W14957/M90 750,000 1/16 J.B.C. & A. Forms/C.2118/12.

Twenty one.

Instructions regarding War Diaries and Intelligence Summaries are contained in F. S. Regs., Part II. and the Staff Manual respectively. Title Pages will be prepared in manuscript.

WAR DIARY
or
~~INTELLIGENCE~~ SUMMARY
(Erase heading not required.)

Army Form C. 2118.

200th Field Coy. R.E.

Place	Date	Hour	Summary of Events and Information	Remarks and references to Appendices
Bray-sur Somme	5-3-16		again came under their direct shell fire. His clothes being perforated, at length finding his transport at CAPPY, he returned to his units Headquarters at BRAY.	
-do-	6-3-16		Day fine.	
-do-	7-3-16		Day fine, cold, a little snow at night.	
-do-	8-3-16		Cold and frosty. Air reconnaissance during the day.	
-do-	9-3-16		Day fine, cold, a fall of snow at night.	
-do-	10-3-16		Day cold, dull, some snow.	
-do-	11-3-16		Morning dull, cold. Artillery fairly active during the afternoon and night.	
-do-	12-3-16		No 48822 Sergt. Carter A. was tried by F.G.C.M. for drunkenness and reduced to the ranks. No. 16316 Sergt. Weaver A. transferred to 69th Field	

2449 Wt. W14957/M90 750,000 1/16 J.B.C. & A. Forms/C.2118/12.

Twenty two

Instructions regarding War Diaries and Intelligence Summaries are contained in F. S. Regs., Part II. and the Staff Manual respectively. Title Pages will be prepared in manuscript.

WAR DIARY
or
~~INTELLIGENCE~~ SUMMARY
(Erase heading not required.)

200th Field Company R.E.

Army Form C. 2118.

Place	Date	Hour	Summary of Events and Information	Remarks and references to Appendices
Bray-sur-Somme	12-3-16		Company R.E. 12th Division, 1st Army.	
			The following men were promoted to the ranks as under:-	
			No. 81341 Sergt. Smith W.H. to be A/C.Q.M.S.	
			No. 81647 Corpl. Peacock J. to be A/Sergeant.	
			No 83351 Corpl Turner C. to be A/Sergeant.	
			No. 81814 II Cpl. Helm J. to be A/Corporal.	
			No. 81336 L/Cpl. Parry J.H. to be A/2nd Corporal.	
			No. 83211 Sapr. Burgess H. to be Lance Corporal	
-do-	13-3-16		Day fine and warm. Artillery active aircraft active. Enemy shelled road S.W. of BRAY at	
		5.30pm	5-30 p.m. Artillery active during the night.	
-do-	14-3-16		Day fine, warm. Air reconnaissance by Allied aircraft during morning. Hostile shells dropped in valley S.E. of Bray at 1.0 p.m. Enemy aircraft	
		9.0pm	flew over Bray at 9 p.m. dropping two bombs in	

Twenty three

Instructions regarding War Diaries and Intelligence Summaries are contained in F. S. Regs., Part II. and the Staff Manual respectively. Title Pages will be prepared in manuscript.

WAR DIARY
or
~~INTELLIGENCE~~ SUMMARY
(Erase heading not required.)

200th Field Coy. R.E.

Army Form C. 2118.

Place	Date	Hour	Summary of Events and Information	Remarks and references to Appendices
Bray. sur Somme	14-3-16	9 pm	valley N.E. of BRAY. Artillery active during night. Receive orders to prepare for move from this Sector to back area for rest on the 17th inst.	
-do-	15-3-16		Day fine, dull, cloudy.	
-do-	16-3-16		Day fine, dull. The Sector is handed over to the 79th Field Company, R.E.	
-do-	17-3-16		This unit marched from BRAY at 7.30 am. arriving	
Sailly. le-Sec	"	10.30 am	at SAILLY-LE-SEC at 10.30 a.m., remaining in billets for the rest of the day and night.	
-do-	18-3-16		marched from SAILLY-LE-SEC via CORBIE arriving in billets at FRÉCHENCOURT at 1.20 p.m. Two	
Fréchencourt	"	1-20 pm	Sections being detached for work on hutments and general work under C.E. at the 4th Army Headquarters at QUERRIEU (Attached copy of march table &c).	Appendix N.
"	19-3-16		Relieve the 92nd Field Company R.E. One Section and Headquarters with Transport carry on Company	

2449 Wt. W14957/M90 750,000 1/16 J.B.C. & A. Forms/C.2118/12.

Twenty four

Instructions regarding War Diaries and Intelligence Summaries are contained in F. S. Regs., Part II. and the Staff Manual respectively. Title Pages will be prepared in manuscript.

WAR DIARY
or
~~INTELLIGENCE SUMMARY~~ 200th Field Company R.E.

(Erase heading not required.)

Army Form C. 2118.

Place	Date	Hour	Summary of Events and Information	Remarks and references to Appendices
Fréchencourt	19-3-16		Training Pontooning etc.	
-do-	20-3-16		Day fine, warm.	
-do-	21-3-16		Day dull, rather cold. Water scheme commenced for storage of water obtained from springs S. from FRÉCHENCOURT. Pipe line commenced.	
-do-	22-3-16		Day wet. Major A. Bishope Lunn R.E. went on leave. Command of the Company is taken over by Captain G. H. Irvin R.E.	
-do-	23-3-16		Day dull, very cold.	
-do-	24-3-16		Day cold, snow.	
-do-	25-3-16		Day cold.	
-do-	26-3-16		Day wet. Necessary repairs were undertaken on the water system at LA HOUSSOYE.	
-do-	27-3-16		Day wet, windy. Take over saw mill and plant as a running concern at FRÉCHENCOURT.	

2449 Wt. W14957/M90 750,000 1/16 J.B.C. & A. Forms/C.2118/12.

Twenty five.

Instructions regarding War Diaries and Intelligence Summaries are contained in F. S. Regs., Part II. and the Staff Manual respectively. Title Pages will be prepared in manuscript.

WAR DIARY
or
INTELLIGENCE SUMMARY 200th Field Company, R.E.

(Erase heading not required.)

Army Form C. 2118.

Place	Date	Hour	Summary of Events and Information	Remarks and references to Appendices
Fréchencourt	28.3.16		Day cold, snow.	
- do -	29.3.16		Day cold, snow.	
- do -	30.3.16		Day fine. At 1 p.m. Lord Kitchener inspected troops at BÉHENCOURT.	
Béhencourt	"		Lieut. L A Hill R.E. went on leave.	
Fréchencourt	31.3.16		Day fine. Received advance orders to be prepared to take over work and relieve the 202nd Field Company, R.E. at BRAY-SUR-SOMME.	

[illegible] Major. R.E.

O.C. 200TH FIELD CO., (COUNTY PALATINE) R.E.

200th FIELD COMPANY (COUNTY PALATINE) R.E. No. .... Date ....

2449 Wt. W14957/M90 750,000 1/16 J.B.C. & A. Forms/C.2118/12.

Appendix A

COMMANDING ROYAL ENGINEERS
No. 160
7 - MAR 1916
30th DIVL. (COUNTY PALATINE) ENGINEERS

SECRET.

O.C., 200th. Field Company, R.E.

For information.

The Relief of 89th Brigade takes place on night 15th/16th March. The remainder of the relief of 30th Division takes place immediately after.

R.J. Hall
Captain.R.E.

7/3/1916. Adjt. 30th Divisional Engineers.

COMMANDING ROYAL ENGINEERS
No. 638
14 MAR 1916
30th DIVL. (COUNTY PALATINE) ENGINEERS

S E C R E T.

O.C. 200th Field Company, R.E.

The attached extract from Addendum to Operation Order No.11 is forwarded for your information.

Outgoing units on meeting incoming units on roads will halt and allow the latter to pass.

R.G. [signature]

Captain.R.E.

Adjt. 30th Divisional (County Palatine) Engineers.

14/3/1916.

S E C R E T.

Extract from MARCH TABLE No.3.

Date.	Unit.	From.	To.	Remarks.
17th March.	200th Field Coy.R.E. (less 1 Section)	BRAY	SAILLY LE SEC	Relieved by the 79th Field Coy.R.E.
18th March.	200th Field Coy. R.E. (less 1 Section)	SAILLY LE SEC	FRECHENCOURT	To relieve the 92nd Field Coy. R.E.

Secret

INSTRUCTIONS IN CONNECTION WITH OPERATION ORDER No.11.

O.C.,

200th. Field Company, R.E.

In continuation of the extract from March Table No. 3 already sent you. Times at which your Company will move on 17th instant will be as follows:

(1) All transport to be clear of BRIQUETRIE Square K.16.d on BRAY - CORBIE road by 8 am.

(2) Remainder of Company to pass BRIQUETRIE Square K.16.d on BRAY - CORBIE road at 9-20 am.

N.B: (a). In moving from BRAY and until reaching the BRIQUETRIE the Company will move in sections at 150 yards distance.

(b). The detachment of 6 men of 200th Field Coy. now attached to Hd.Qrs. R.E. will rejoin at SAILLY LE SEC on 17th instant.

R.G. Stone

Captain.R.E.

Adjt. 30th Divisional (County Palatine) Engineers.

16/3/1916.

~~200th~~ 30th Divisional Engineers

<u>200th FIELD COMPANY R.E. ::: APRIL 1916.</u>

Twenty eight

Instructions regarding War Diaries and Intelligence Summaries are contained in F. S. Regs., Part II. and the Staff Manual respectively. Title Pages will be prepared in manuscript.

WAR DIARY
or
INTELLIGENCE SUMMARY
(Erase heading not required.)

Army Form C. 2118.

XXX

200th Field Company R.E.

Vol 4 6

Place	Date	Hour	Summary of Events and Information	Remarks and references to Appendices
FRECHENCOURT SOMME	1-4-16		Weather fine. Carried on training	
"	2.4.16		Weather fine, warm. Major A. Bishope Lunn R.E. returned from leave and took up again command of the Company	
"	3.4.16		Weather fine, hot. Received advanced orders to prepare to move to BRAY-SUR-SOMME to relieve the 202nd Field Company R.E. on work on the RANGÉE d' ARBRES	
"	4.4.16	8.55a	Weather fine, warm. Left FRECHENCOURT at 8.55 am. owing to weather conditions and abnormal traffic on the main road it was decided to march through LA NEUVILLE, CORBIE SAILLY-LE-SEC halting at the latter place at mid day, leaving there at 4.30 p.m. marching through BRAY-SUR-SOMME and	
LA NEUVILLE-LES-BRAY	"	7 pm	arriving at LA NEUVILLE-LES-BRAY at 7 p.m.	
"	5-4-16		Weather fine, dull. Take over work on the RANGÉE d' ARBRES from 202nd Field Company R.E.	
"	6.4.16		Weather fine, warm. Nos. 1 and 4 Sections who were stationed in QUERRIEU and had been carrying on work for the 4th ARMY H.Q. relieved by 2 Sections of the 202nd Field Company R.E. arrived in LA NEUVILLE-LES-BRAY at 4.30 p.m.	

2449 Wt. W14957/M90 750,000 1/16 J.B.C. & A. Forms/C.2118/12.

Twenty nine

Instructions regarding War Diaries and Intelligence Summaries are contained in F. S. Regs., Part II. and the Staff Manual respectively. Title Pages will be prepared in manuscript.

WAR DIARY
or
~~INTELLIGENCE SUMMARY~~ 200th Field Company R.E.

(Erase heading not required.)

Army Form C. 2118.

Place	Date	Hour	Summary of Events and Information	Remarks and references to Appendices
LA NEUVILLE LES-BRAY	7.4.16		Weather fine. No 2 Section stationed at CERISY and had been carrying on special work for the 30th Division R.E. On its completion was therefore returned to their unit and rejoined us at LA NEUVILLE-LES-BRAY arriving in billets at 5 p.m. (Copy of march table attached)	Appendix N.
"	8.4.16		Fine, cold. Work on RANGÉE d' ARBRES consisted of the completion of forts that had already been begun, the construction of Machine Gun Emplacements, the excavation of fire trenches, the construction and completion of long lengths of wiring. The laying out and construction of concealed machine gun emplacements; support fire trenches and protective wiring forming a front line to the main position of the RANGÉE d' ARBRES this work was carried out under the aegis of the C.E. 13th Corps. (Tracing and plan)	Appendix O.
"	9.4.16		Weather misty, but fine otherwise. Forward Machine Gun positions on RANGÉE d' ARBRES, selected and work on these commenced.	
"	10.4.16		Weather fine, cold. Hostile air reconnaissance over	

2449 Wt. W14957/M90 750,000 1/16 J.B.C. & A. Forms/C.2118/12.

Thirty

Instructions regarding War Diaries and Intelligence Summaries are contained in F. S. Regs., Part II. and the Staff Manual respectively. Title Pages will be prepared in manuscript.

WAR DIARY
or
~~INTELLIGENCE SUMMARY~~
(Erase heading not required.)

204th Field Company R.E.

Army Form C. 2118.

Place	Date	Hour	Summary of Events and Information	Remarks and references to Appendices
BRAY-SUR Somme	10.4.16		BRAY-SUR-Somme and districts between 10.30 and 11.45 p.m.	
			Lieut. L. A. Hill R.E. returned from leave.	
			No 48822 Sapr. Carter A. transferred to 201st Field Company R.E. Take over work on construction of light tramway SUZANNE to BRONFAY FARM. This railway follows the line of the centre of BILLON VALLEY direct N.E. At the head of the valley sweeping due WEST and by a double S curve mounting the rise through BILLON WOOD. and is taken from there through a deep trench across the open to BRONFAY FARM. joining up to a track already in existence from BRONFAY FARM across the LOOP VALLEY to WATERLOO JUNCTION where it meets the metre gauge railway from BRAY-SUR-SOMME to FRICOURT. (See Appendix O)	
"	11.4.16		Weather very wet. First allotment of leave to England. The following men proceeded on leave from this unit. 14391 A/C.S.M. Harris E. 81527 2nd Cpl Sidebottham A.H. 81904 Spr. Scragge E. 83071 Spr. Dunn A. 99689 Driver W. Hughes.	

2449 Wt. W14957/M90 750,000 1/16 J.B.C. & A. Forms/C.2118/12.

Thirty-one

Instructions regarding War Diaries and Intelligence Summaries are contained in F. S. Regs., Part II. and the Staff Manual respectively. Title Pages will be prepared in manuscript.

WAR DIARY
or
~~INTELLIGENCE SUMMARY~~ 20th Field Company R.E.

(Erase heading not required.)

Army Form C. 2118.

Place	Date	Hour	Summary of Events and Information	Remarks and references to Appendices
BRAY-SUR SOMME	11.4.16		At 7.0 pm. there was considerable Artillery activity to the N.E. of BRAY-SUR-SOMME.	
"	12.4.16		Weather wet.	
"	13.4.16		Weather fine, gloomy. At 3.30 am. hostile Artillery shelled BRAY-SUR-SOMME heavilly. Most of the shells dropping round the junctions of the MARICOURT-BRAY and ALBERT-BRAY Roads. The bombardment ceased at 6.20 am. There was one casualty No 81666 Sapper J. Charlesworth being killed by shell fire. At 9.30 am. hostile shelling recommenced W. of BRAY-SUR-SOMME.	
"	14.4.16		Weather fine, cold. Divisional Orders for men on leave in England to return to their units on the 18th April 1916.	
"	15.4.16		Weather fine, cold. Considerable air reconnaissance by light air-craft. Artillery active at night.	
"	16.4.16		Weather fine, windy. Air reconnaissance continued by Allied air-craft.	

2449 Wt. W14957/M90 750,000 1/16 J.B.C. & A. Forms/C.2118/12.

Thirty two

Instructions regarding War Diaries and Intelligence Summaries are contained in F. S. Regs., Part II. and the Staff Manual respectively. Title Pages will be prepared in manuscript.

WAR DIARY
or
~~INTELLIGENCE SUMMARY~~
(Erase heading not required.)

Army Form C. 2118.

20th Field Company R.E.

Place	Date	Hour	Summary of Events and Information	Remarks and references to Appendices
BRAY-SUR-SOMME	17.4.16		Weather wet. At 3.15 pm a few hostile shells dropped on road W. of BRAY-CORBIE Road. Artillery active at night.	
"	18.4.16		Weather wet, windy. Men return from leave except No. 81904 Spr Scragge E. who was detained at Rest Camp in segregation SOUTHAMPTON.	
"	19.4.16		Weather wet. Hostile Artillery active at FRICOURT N.W of BRAY-SUR-SOMME.	
"	20.4.16		Weather fine, dull. Certain amount of air reconnaissance was carried on by our air craft during the day.	
"	21.4.16		Fine morning turning to wet later.	
"	22.4.16		Weather dull, showery, cold. At 8 pm. our Artillery were active N. of BRAY the bombardment lasting until 11.30 pm.	
"	23.4.16		Weather fine. The day was quiet.	
"	24.4.16		Weather fine. Air reconnaissance by our air craft was carried out during the major portion of the day.	
"	25.4.16		Weather fine, warm. During the day considerable air reconnaissance was carried out by hostile and Allied	

Thirty three

Instructions regarding War Diaries and Intelligence Summaries are contained in F. S. Regs., Part II. and the Staff Manual respectively. Title Pages will be prepared in manuscript.

WAR DIARY
or
INTELLIGENCE SUMMARY
(Erase heading not required.)

Army Form C. 2118.

201st Field Company R.E.

Place	Date	Hour	Summary of Events and Information	Remarks and references to Appendices
Bray-Sur-Somme	25.4.16		aircraft, several encounters taking place.	
"	26.4.16		Weather fine warm. At 4.30 a.m. hostile aeroplane came over BRAY-SUR-SOMME, dropped three bombs on the town very little damage was done and no one was seriously hurt. He proceeded towards SUZANNE dropping 6 more bombs at various points. No damage resulting.	
"	27.4.16		Weather fine warm. We hand over our work on work on the RANGÉE d' ARBRES to the 79th Field Company R.E. Allied aircraft active during the day.	
"	28.4.16		Weather fine warm. We take over from the 79th Field Company R.E. works in the Sectors Z1 & Z2 in that portion of the line in front of MARICOURT. Also workshops and other work that had been carried on by the 79th Field Company R.E. Sections 1 & 2 of the 201st Field Company R.E. proceeding to MARICOURT to carry	

2449 Wt. W14957/M90 750,000 1/16 J.B.C. & A. Forms/C.2118/12.

Thirty four

Instructions regarding War Diaries and Intelligence Summaries are contained in F. S. Regs., Part II. and the Staff Manual respectively. Title Pages will be prepared in manuscript.

WAR DIARY
or
~~INTELLIGENCE SUMMARY~~ 200th Field Company R.E.

(Erase heading not required.)

Army Form C. 2118.

Place	Date	Hour	Summary of Events and Information	Remarks and references to Appendices
BRAY-SUR-Somme	28.4.16		Out work in the front line and MARICOURT DEFENCES. Weather fine, wind N.E.	
"	29.4.16		Weather fine, wind N.W. The day was quiet. Artillery	
"	30.4.16		were active at night.	

200th FIELD COMPANY (COUNTY PALATINE) R.E. No. .... Date ....

Major R.E.
O.C. 200TH FIELD CO. (COUNTY PALATINE) R.E.

2449 Wt. W14957/M90 750,000 1/16 J.B.C. & A. Forms/C.2118/12.

Appendix N

O.C. 200th Field Coy. R.E.

Copy forwarded for information. No moves are to take place pending receipt of further orders.

Lieut. Forbes has been informed direct regarding the N.C.O. and men to be left to complete the laundry.

R.[illegible]

Captain.R.E.

Adjt. 30th Divisional (County Palatine) Engineers.

1/4/1916.

"C" Form (Duplicate). Army Form C. 2123.

MESSAGES AND SIGNALS. No. of Message

DMC GH Co DAK

Cozens

Service Instructions.

Charges to Pay. £ s. d.

Office Stamp. CCB 3 IV 18

Handed in at YCZ (30th Div) Office 7.40 P m. Received 9.0 P m.

TO 200 Fd Co RE.
FRECHENCOURT

Sender's Number R 351 | Day of Month 3rd | In reply to Number | AAA

Relief of 202nd Fd Coy
by 200th Fd Coy will
take place in accordance with
march table issued under this
Office No 1003 of 1st
April aaa 2 Lorries have
been asked for to report
at 7 am to each
Coy on the day on
which Coy HQ move

FROM CRE 30th Div
PLACE & TIME

W 13680—M 151 75,000 Pads. H & S 2/16 Forms/C.2123. (5668)

"A" Form. Army Form C. 2121.

MESSAGES AND SIGNALS. No. of Message

Prefix Code m. Office of Origin and Service Instructions.	Words / Charge	This message is on a/c of	Recd. at m.
D. R 1 S	Sent At m. To By	Service. (Signature of "Franking Officer.")	Date From By

TO ~~202nd Fd Coy RE~~ 200th Fd Coy RE

Sender's Number.	Day of Month	In reply to Number	AAA
R 275	30th		

The 200th and 202nd Fd Coys will exchange duties at an early date. Details of this change will be sent later.

OC 202nd Fd Coy RE will send one officer to the 200th Fd Coy at FRECHENCOURT on 1st April to commence taking over the works on which that Coy is engaged at present

From C R E 30th DIV
Place
Time 12-55 pm.

The above may be forwarded as now corrected. (Z)
Censor. Signature of Addressor or person authorised to telegraph in his name.

R [illegible]
Capt [illegible]

* This line should be erased if not required.

(688-9) —McC. & Co. Ltd., London.— W 14142/641. 225,000. 4/15. Forms C2121/16.

Chief Engineer,

13th Corps.

The attached is a copy of the march table submitted for approval for the relief of the 202nd Field Company by the 200th Field Company.

When these moves have been completed the following Officers, N.C.O's and men will be on detachment for employment as noted :-

200th Field Company, R.E.

One N.C.O. and 4 Sappers. Employed on completing Divisional Laundry.

202nd Field Company, R.E.

2nd Lieut. H.D.Staniar, R.E. On duty at War School.

One N.C.O. Divisional Laundry.

This report is made in accordance with your No.46/278b. of the 31/3/1916, as both Companies are working under your orders.

[signature]

Lieut.Col.R.E.

C.R.E. 30th Divisional (County Palatine) Engineers.

1/4/1916.

RELIEF OF 202nd FIELD COMPANY, R.E. BY 200th FIELD COMPANY, R.E.

TABLE OF MOVES.

	UNIT	From	To	Remarks.
4th April.	Headquarters and 1 Section, 200th Field Coy.	FRECHENCOURT	BRAY	
5th "	1 Section, 202nd Field Coy.	BRAY	QUERRIEUX	
6th "	2 Sections, 200th Field Coy.	QUERRIEUX	BRAY	
7th "	Headquarters and 3 Sections, 202nd Field Coy.	BRAY	FRECHENCOURT and QUERRIEUX	1 Section to go to QUERRIEUX.
7th "	1 Section, 200th Field Coy.	CERISY.	BRAY	

N.B.:- Arrangements are being made for officers from each Company to change over previously in order to take over the work going on at each place.

[signature]

Lieut.Col.R.E.

C.R.E. 30th Divisional (County Palatine) Engineers.

31/3/1916.

FRANCE

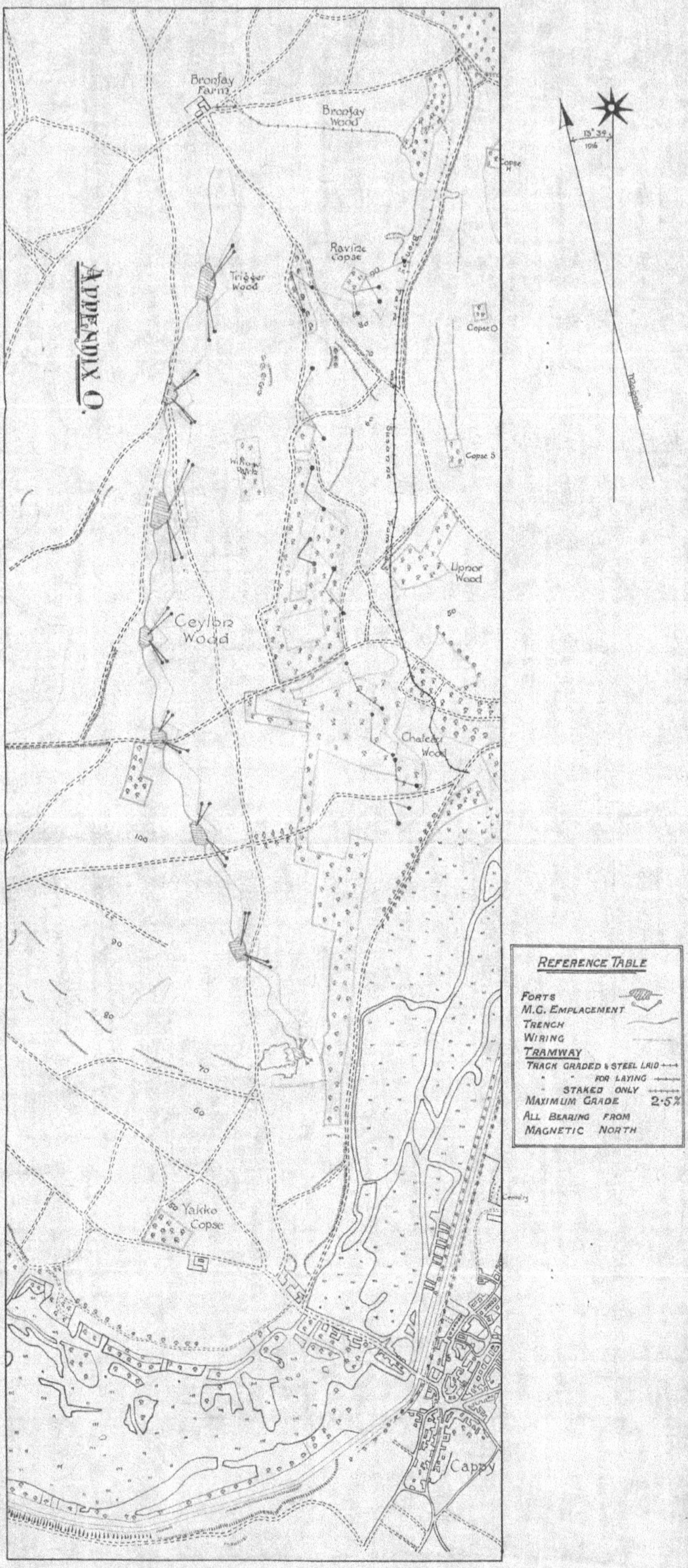

APPENDIX O.
Bronfay Farm
Bronfay Wood
Ravine Copse
Trigger Wood
Copse O
Copse 5
Upnor Wood
Ceylon Wood
Chalet Wood
Yakko Copse
Cappy
REFERENCE TABLE
FORTS
M.G. EMPLACEMENT
TRENCH
WIRING
TRAMWAY
TRACK GRADED & STEEL LAID
FOR LAYING
STAKED ONLY
MAXIMUM GRADE 2·5%
ALL BEARING FROM MAGNETIC NORTH
Scale 1:10000

30th Divisional Engineers

200th FIELD COMPANY R.E.::F: M A Y 1916.

200th Field Company R.E.

Instructions regarding War Diaries and Intelligence Summaries are contained in F. S. Regs., Part II. and the Staff Manual respectively. Title Pages will be prepared in manuscript.

WAR DIARY
or
~~INTELLIGENCE SUMMARY~~
(Erase heading not required.)

200 F.C. R.E. Army Form C. 2118.

XXX Sheet No 1 — Vol 5

Place	Date	Hour	Summary of Events and Information	Remarks and references to Appendices
BRAY and MARICOURT	Month of MAY	}	Coy H.Q and one Section. Running Workshops in BRAY. Steam saw cutting sheeting etc. Carpenters making trench-gratings, notice boards, latrine covers, brackets for gas gongs etc etc. Making a Divisional Bathing place in the lake S.W of BRAY with spring boards, ropes, rafts etc. Water supply in BRAY — pump and engine fitted in a spring in FAUBOURG BETHISY delivering about 13000 gallons daily to a reservoir, and thence to standpipes for water-carts	
			3 Sections in MARICOURT. The keeps in MARICOURT called respectively DONE'S KEEP, CHATEAU KEEP, ROUND POINT KEEP, BREWERY KEEP, OUTER BREWERY KEEP and NAPIER'S REDOUBT were completed, and wired all round. Command posts were provided, and also accommodation for rations and water. Minor work and a good deal of revetting still remains to be done.	
			Water Supply. The pump in BREWERY KEEP was kept running — giving about 3000 gallons daily. A water tower was made in SCHOOL STREET and a pipe taken to it from the BREWERY. It was connected with the tanks in CHATEAU and DONE'S KEEP.	
			Work in Z_1 and Z_2 sectors. 4 large dugouts, connected together, with shell-proof roofs were constructed in the CHATEAU as HQ for Z_2, and the usual supervision and work was carried out in both sectors in revetting etc. etc.	
			Special Work. Forming up trenches were laid out and excavated. 2 Platoons of S. LANCS. PIONEERS were employed in completing them to correct dimensions	

2449 Wt. W14957/M90 750,000 1/16 J.B.C. & A. Forms/C.2118/12.

200th Field Company R.E.

Instructions regarding War Diaries and Intelligence Summaries are contained in F. S. Regs., Part II. and the Staff Manual respectively. Title Pages will be prepared in manuscript.

WAR DIARY
or
~~INTELLIGENCE SUMMARY~~
(Erase heading not required.)

Army Form C. 2118.

Sheet No 2

Place	Date	Hour	Summary of Events and Information	Remarks and references to Appendices
BRAY and MARICOURT			and traversing them. A mined dugout was begun at the junction of BEDFORD ST and LEXDEN ST for a battalion H.Q. a second entrance was made to an existing dugout for another. Forward stores for ammunition were started at two points in the front line, and dugouts in MALDEN ST were strengthened. Pillars in the CHATEAU were strengthened, and shell proofing put on for the Brigade Ammunition Reserve. Three dugouts excavated, connected, and roofed in the N of NAPIERS' REDOUBT for Divisional Ammunition Reserve.	
			MARICOURT AVENUE was cleaned, deepened, and grated, and a start made on that part of STANLEY AVENUE through the village of MARICOURT	
			The following local reliefs were carried out during the month.	
			No 2 Section moved from MARICOURT to BRAY 16/5/16	
			No 3 relieved No 2 from MARICOURT to BRAY 22/5/16.	

200th Field Company R.E.

Instructions regarding War Diaries and Intelligence Summaries are contained in F. S. Regs., Part II. and the Staff Manual respectively. Title Pages will be prepared in manuscript.

WAR DIARY or ~~INTELLIGENCE SUMMARY~~

(Erase heading not required.)

Army Form C. 2118.

Sheet No 3.

Place	Date	Hour	Summary of Events and Information	Remarks and references to Appendices
			CASUALTIES during the Month of May 1916	
BRAY + MARICOURT	12.5.16		Major A. Bishope Lunn R.E. was relieved of the Command of the Company by Capt. R. G. Wright R.E. of the 92nd Field Company Royal Engineers.	
	16.5.16		7 O.R. transferred to No 4 General Base Depot, being the Searchlight personnel of this unit.	
	16.5.16		2 O.R. transferred to this unit from the 92nd Field Company, R.E.	
	18.5.16		2 O.R. transferred from this unit to the 92nd Field Company R.E.	
			HORSES	
	18.5.16		1 Bay Gelding (RIDER) died. Death being due to a bullet wound received at MARICOURT on the night of the 18-5-16.	

R. G. Wright Capt. R.E.
O.C. 200TH FIELD CO., (COUNTY PALATINE) R.E.

200th FIELD COMPANY (COUNTY PALATINE) R.E. No. ___ Date 31.5.16

2449 Wt. W14957/M90 750,000 1/16 J.B.C. & A. Forms/C.2118/12.

30th Divisional Engineers

200th FIELD COMPANY R.E.: ::: JUNE 1916.

200 FC RE Army Form C. 2118.

Sheet 1 Vol 6

June

Instructions regarding War Diaries and Intelligence Summaries are contained in F. S. Regs., Part II. and the Staff Manual respectively. Title Pages will be prepared in manuscript.

WAR DIARY
or
~~INTELLIGENCE SUMMARY~~

(Erase heading not required.)

Place	Date	Hour	Summary of Events and Information	Remarks and references to Appendices
BRAY and MARICOURT	1.6.16 to 11.6.16		COY HQ and No3 Section. Running Workshops – Steam Saw cutting 2" sheeting. Carpenters making Trench gratings, notice boards etc. BRAY Water Supply – a second cellar (capacity 2500 gallons) has been converted for use as a storage tank, and another 1½ stand pipe erected in the RUE CHEVALIER DE LA BARRE. The work on Div. H.Q. Dugouts of BRAY was put under the control of the Company. A lot of excavation had been done, and a great many falls had taken place. Carried on with framing etc.	
			3 Sections in MARICOURT. Maricourt Defences Napiers Keep. Reserve Ration Store completed. Chateau Keep. Reserve Ration Store completed. All work in connection with Maricourt Defences is now complete.	
			WATER SUPPLY All storage in the Keeps completed and filled. The 6000 gallon underground cistern S of the Chateau is being gradually filled as supplies are available.	
			SPECIAL WORK (1) Trenches. MARICOURT AVENUE complete except for widening one or two corners.	
			STANLEY AVENUE The four entrances to the tunnels under the PERONNE ROAD carried about 4 feet in, and the approaches framed and strutted complete. About 60x of the new trench dug. The old trench has been widened - grated etc as far as the barricade on the N edge of the village	

Army Form C. 2118.

Instructions regarding War Diaries and Intelligence Summaries are contained in F. S. Regs., Part II. and the Staff Manual respectively. Title Pages will be prepared in manuscript.

WAR DIARY
or
~~INTELLIGENCE SUMMARY~~
(Erase heading not required.)

Sheet 2

Place	Date	Hour	Summary of Events and Information	Remarks and references to Appendices
BRAY and MARICOURT	1.6.16 to 10.6.16.		MERSEA ST and GROVE AVENUE both well in hand under supervision of O C 11th S. Lancs Pioneers	
			(2) Trench Mortars. N of LEXDEN ST One emplacement for 2" Mortar complete – frames made for the second Heavy Trench Mortar Emplacements N.E of Chateau. Four excavated to depth of 8 feet, and framing made for one emplacement	
			(3) Ammunition Stores Brigade Forward (1) MALDEN ST Complete (2) BEDFORD ST. Dugout mined. 2nd entrance started. (3) Trench A 16/3. About 5' of dugout mined & timbered Brigade Reserve CHATEAU 3 Cellars complete for storage and the fourth half finished. Trenches for access nearing completion. Divisional Reserve NAPIERS KEEP. 3 framed dugouts complete	
			(4) Collecting Station. One dugout 32' x 9' two thirds complete. Second excavated 6'	
			(5) Montauban Road The road clear to N edge of village except for removal of barricades	

2449 Wt. W14957/M90 750,000 1/16 J.B.C. & A. Forms/C.2118/12.

Instructions regarding War Diaries and Intelligence Summaries are contained in F. S. Regs., Part II. and the Staff Manual respectively. Title Pages will be prepared in manuscript.

WAR DIARY
or
~~INTELLIGENCE SUMMARY~~
(Erase heading not required.)

Army Form C. 2118.

Sheet 3

Place	Date	Hour	Summary of Events and Information	Remarks and references to Appendices
BRAY and MARICOURT	1.6.16 to 11.6.16		Other Work. Shell proof dugout nearly completed in WESTON AVENUE a track for handcarts made to give access to ammunition stores in CHATEAU YARD	
			Assistance given as requisite to 148th Bde R.F.A	
			Transport About 300 trench bridges and 400 ladders have been taken up and stored in MARICOURT	
			R.G. Wright Capt RE O.C. 200th Fd Coy RE	

2449 Wt. W14957/M90 750,000 1/16 J.B.C. & A. Forms/C.2118/12.

Instructions regarding War Diaries and Intelligence Summaries are contained in F. S. Regs., Part II. and the Staff Manual respectively. Title Pages will be prepared in manuscript.

WAR DIARY
or
~~INTELLIGENCE SUMMARY~~
(Erase heading not required.)

Army Form C. 2118.

Sheet 4

Place	Date	Hour	Summary of Events and Information	Remarks and references to Appendices
BRAY and MARICOURT.	11.6.16 to 17.6.16		H.Q. and No 3. Section at BRAY running Shops etc Other 3 Sections in MARICOURT (1) Trenches STANLEY AVENUE Completed as far as LEXDEN ST and both tunnels turned under PERONNE RD. WESTON AVENUE Complete as far as N.W. FIRE TRENCH MERSEA ST and GROVE AVENUE completed except for water and latrines (2) Divisional HQ All dugouts roofed except two. Two large splinter proofs complete. and one partly battered (3) Trench Mortars Two emplacements at E end of LEXDEN ST complete Slits in BEDFORD ST made for Stokes ammunition. Ammunition Stores. All completed. (4) Collecting Station One complete for 24 beds. Second about 2/3rds complete (5) Montauban Road Clear as far as GROVE AVENUE. R.G. Wright Capt R.E. O.C. 200th Fd Co R.E.	

2449 Wt. W14957/M90 750,000 1/16 J.B.C. & A. Forms/C.2118/12.

Army Form C. 2118.

Instructions regarding War Diaries and Intelligence Summaries are contained in F. S. Regs., Part II. and the Staff Manual respectively. Title Pages will be prepared in manuscript.

WAR DIARY
or
~~INTELLIGENCE SUMMARY~~
(Erase heading not required.)

Sheet 5

Place	Date	Hour	Summary of Events and Information	Remarks and references to Appendices
BRAY and MARICOURT	11 6 16 to 22 6 16		All special work as shown for previous week in MARICOURT completed as under Down Trench { MARICOURT AVENUE complete WESTON AVENUE carried from DONES REDOUBT to front line via HEAD ST Up Trench STANLEY AVENUE was carried into A.P.3 via LEXDEN ST and WILLIAMS AVENUE Trench Mortars 2 heavy emplacements complete Ammunition Stores all complete. Collecting Station Two dugouts complete and fitted for 40 beds Montauban Road Complete to front trench with all bridges A Mule Track was also made from the sunk lane by DONES REDOUBT down to the 4 Willows, and across the trenches to join the MONTAUBAN ROAD just in advance of front line Divisional H.Q. Complete	
	23 6 16		All Sections returned to BRAY less 2 N.C.Os in the Dumps and the men working the pump in the Brewery	
	23-6-16 to 29 6 16		Company remained at BRAY.	
	30 6 16	5pm	Paraded and moved to points of assembly as under No1 Section Trenches of S face of CHATEAU REDOUBT } MARICOURT No2 Section Copse Valley No3 Section Trenches of S face of NAPIER REDOUBT No4 Section Copse Valley Assembly complete 9pm.	

R G Wright
Capt R.E.
O.C. 200th F Coy R.E.

2449 Wt. W14957/M90 750,000 1/16 J.B.C. & A. Forms/C.2118/12.

Instructions regarding War Diaries and Intelligence Summaries are contained in F. S. Regs., Part II. and the Staff Manual respectively. Title Pages will be prepared in manuscript.

WAR DIARY
or
~~INTELLIGENCE SUMMARY~~
(Erase heading not required.)

Army Form C. 2118.

Sheet 6

Place	Date	Hour	Summary of Events and Information	Remarks and references to Appendices
BRAY & MARICOURT			Casualties during the month of June 1916	
			Lieut. L. J. B. Forbes R.E. of 200th Field Company R.E. struck off the strength of unit having been Medically Boarded in England.	
	21.6.16		1 O.R. wounded by shellfire on the 21-6-16. Struck off the strength having been sent to C.C.S.	
	20.6.16		1 O.R. taken on the strength, reinforcement on the 20.6.16.	
	28.6.16		1 O.R. Killed by Shell fire on the 28.6.16	
			1 O.R. wounded by Shellfire on the 28.6.16 struck off the strength being sent to C.C.S.	
			HOSPITAL	
	25.5.16		1 O.R. to Hospital 25-5-16. (Sickness)	
	7 & 9.6.16		2 O.R. to Hospital 7-6-16 & 9-6-16 (Sickness)	
	13.6.16		1 O.R. to Hospital 13-6-16. (Sickness)	
	16.6.16		1 O.R. to Hospital 16-6-16 (do)	
	16.6.16		1 O.R. to Hospital 16-6-16, since to C.C.S. struck off the strength	
	4.6.16		1 O.R. rejoined from Hospital 4-6-16.	
	14.6.16		1 O.R. rejoined from Hospital 14-6-16.	

2449 Wt. W14957/M90 750,000 1/16 J.B.C. & A. Forms/C.2118/12.

Instructions regarding War Diaries and Intelligence Summaries are contained in F. S. Regs., Part II. and the Staff Manual respectively. Title Pages will be prepared in manuscript.

WAR DIARY
or
INTELLIGENCE SUMMARY
(Erase heading not required.)

Army Form C. 2118.

Sheet 7

Place	Date	Hour	Summary of Events and Information	Remarks and references to Appendices
BRAY			Casualties for June (continued)	
MARICOURT	17.6.16		2 O.R. rejoined from Hospital 17-6-16.	
	21.6.16		1 O.R. to Hospital 21-6-16 (Sickness)	
	27.6.16		1 O.R. struck off the strength, having been sent to C.C.S. 27-6-16	
			REINFORCEMENT	
"	13.6.16		2nd Lieut. J. H. Gledhill R.E. (T.) was taken on to the strength of the unit from 13-6-16.	
			HORSES	
	6.6.16		2 Horses (Riders) arrived on the 6.6.16	
"	18.6.16		2 Mules (L.D.) arrived on the 18.6.16	

R.G. Wright
Capt R.E.
O.C. 200th F. Coy R.E.

2449 Wt. W14957/M90 750,000 1/16 J.B.C. & A. Forms/C.2118/12.

30th Divisional Engineers

200th FIELD COMPANY R.E. :::: JULY 1916.

G118

Headquarters
30th Division

War Diary
Volume 7 for the month of July 1916 forwarded herewith, in accordance with Divisional Routine Order 1722 dated 15th July 1916.

R. G. Wright.
Capt RE
O.C. 200th Fd Co RE

Field
6. 8. 16

Instructions regarding War Diaries and Intelligence Summaries are contained in F. S. Regs., Part II. and the Staff Manual respectively. Title Pages will be prepared in manuscript.

WAR DIARY
or
INTELLIGENCE SUMMARY
(Erase heading not required.)

Army Form C. 2118.

30 Field Coy
200 FCRE
Sheet 1.
Vol 7

Place	Date	Hour	Summary of Events and Information	Remarks and references to Appendices
MARICOURT	1·7·16	8·15a.m.	No1 Section ordered to move into captured trenches, and make Strong Points No1 and 2	
		11 a.m.	No2 Section ordered to move to BRIQUETERIE to consolidate	
		2 p.m.	Received report on MONTAUBA ROAD stating that it was undistinguishable for 200x behind the German front line. No3 Section working on it	
		4 p.m.	Work on No1 Strong point hindered by shelling. Good progress with No2. MONTAUBAN ROAD carried across German front line	
		5·15	Report that No2 section had been hung up by shell fire on way to BRIQUETERIE	
		8 p.m.	No2 Section returned having been unable to work owing to shell fire. The Officer did not come back and the Sergeant was wounded. Ordered the Corporal to take the men back, and have a try at night. The Germans counter attacked during the night and very little work was done – the Sappers helping to man the trench.	
		8·20 p.m.	Full report on area round MONTAUBAN ROAD received	
		9 p.m.	Saw O.C. 19th KLRs and arranged carrying party for BRIQUETERIE. A Convoy of RE. stores and road metal arrived. Saw O.C 2nd Bedfords and gave him a Sergeant to assist in digging a communication trench from DUBLIN TRENCH to the BRIQUETERIE	
		11·45 p.m.	Ordered No4 Section from COPSE VALLEY and 1 platoon of S L Pioneers to proceed with the work on the MONTAUBAN ROAD. ~~They ...~~	

2449 Wt. W14957/M90 750,000 1/16 J.B.C. & A. Forms/C.2118/12.

Army Form C. 2118.

Instructions regarding War Diaries and Intelligence Summaries are contained in F. S. Regs., Part II. and the Staff Manual respectively. Title Pages will be prepared in manuscript.

WAR DIARY
or
~~INTELLIGENCE SUMMARY~~
(Erase heading not required.)

Sheet 2

Place	Date	Hour	Summary of Events and Information	Remarks and references to Appendices
MARICOURT	2.7.16	8am	Ordered No 3 Section to relieve No 4 at 10 am	
			" Lieut Gledhill to collect No 2 Section, and be prepared to move to BRIQUETERIE at 9pm	
		9.30am	Report from No 4 that a road of sorts would be open to MONTAUBAN at 10am	
		12.1pm	Ordered Lieut Hill to collect No 1 Section and proceed to BRIQUETERIE	
		3pm	Ordered men of No 2 Section which had gone up previous night to return	
		4pm	Ordered Lieut Gledhill to get 12 men from No 4 to make up his section and parade at 11pm instead of 9pm.	
		9pm	Carrying party for BRIQUETERIE started after short delay from shelling	
		9.30	20 Waggons road metal arrived and proceeded to GLATZ REDOUBT.	
			No 4 Section relieved No 3 on road	
	3.7.16	9am	Lieut Gledhill with remainder of No 2 Section proceeded to BRIQUETERIE and relieved No 1 Section.	
			No 3 Section proceeded to MONTAUBAN ROAD	
		1pm	Pump in MARICOURT BREWERY reported to be working again	
			Ordered No 1 Section to parade at 9pm with a carrying party of ~~N~~ 50 men	
		4.20pm	Withdrew No 2 section from BRIQUETERIE	

Army Form C. 2118.

WAR DIARY
or
~~INTELLIGENCE SUMMARY~~
(Erase heading not required.)

Instructions regarding War Diaries and Intelligence Summaries are contained in F. S. Regs., Part II. and the Staff Manual respectively. Title Pages will be prepared in manuscript.

Sheet 3

Place	Date	Hour	Summary of Events and Information	Remarks and references to Appendices
MARICOURT	3.7.16.	9pm	Lieut Hill and Richmond and No 4 Section paraded. Their objective was ~~[illegible]~~ To wire the front from the S.E. corner of BERNAFAY WOOD which had just been captured down to the point where the new communication trench to the BRIQUETERIE left DUBLIN TRENCH. A Company of Pioneers arrived at 9.15 to assist, but were in so exhausted a condition that they were not sent out	
		10pm	10 Waggon loads road metal sent to German front line. Convoy of R.E. Stores to MONTAUBAN. Off loading parties from 19th K.L.R.	
	4.7.16	6am	No 4 Section returned. Very little work done owing to heavy shelling. Impossible to work by day	
		8am	No 3 Section proceeded to MONTAUBAN Road.	
		8.30	1 Company South Lancs Pioneers reported. Ordered to (1) Dig new communication trench from point where DUBLIN trench meets GLATZ redoubt to S.E. corner of BRIQUETERIE (2) Dig trench for all-round fire at W. strong point of BRIQUETERIE	
		12 noon	No 2 section sent to complete ~~the~~ Western Strong Point at BRIQUETERIE	
		4pm	Handed over works to C 64th Fd Coy R.E. Withdrew by sections to BRAY	
	5.7.16	5am	No 2 Section returned to BRAY on completion of W. Strong point.	

2449 W. W14957/M90 750,000 1/16 J.B.C. & A. Forms/C.2118/12.

Army Form C. 2118.

WAR DIARY
or
INTELLIGENCE SUMMARY
(Erase heading not required.)

Instructions regarding War Diaries and Intelligence Summaries are contained in F. S. Regs., Part II. and the Staff Manual respectively. Title Pages will be prepared in manuscript.

Sheet 4

Place	Date	Hour	Summary of Events and Information	Remarks and references to Appendices
BRAY	5.7.16 to 8.7.16		Resting at BRAY	
	8.7.16	12 Noon	Sent a party from No 3 Section to make a prisoners enclosure near MARICOURT	
		7 p.m.	Company paraded and moved by Sections to COPSE VALLEY with tool carts and pack ponies	
	9.7.16		Work on accommodation in COPSE VALLEY 4 Shelters 30' x 15' completed.	
		6 p.m.	No 3 Section moved off for work on BRIQUETERIE ROAD.	
	10.7.16	1.30 a.m.	No 3 Section returned.	
		8 a.m.	Company continued work on accommodation in COPSE VALLEY. Knocked off 12 noon	
		8 p.m.	Nos 2.3.4 Sections paraded and moved off to BRIQUETERIE. Nos 2 and 4 Sections wired trench running S from BERNAFAY WOOD. No 3 Section wired trench running N from MALTZ HORN FARM	
	11.7.16.	4 a.m.	No 1 Section arrived at BRIQUETERIE for work in consolidating TRONES WOOD	
		8.30 p.m.	Nos 2 and 3 Sections paraded for putting up wire. Owing to counter attacks all troops stood to all night and no work done.	
	12.7.16	10 a.m.	No 4 Section reported at BRIQUETERIE and ordered to proceed to S corner of TRONES WOOD. Lieut Richmond wounded on the way.	
		8.30 p.m.	Nos 2 and 3 Sections paraded and moved to E end of SUNK LANE and erected wire	
	13.7.16	7 a.m.	Company returned to BRAY after handing over to 80th Fd Coy R.E. (18th Divn)	

2449 Wt. W14957/M90 750,000 1/16 J.B.C. & A. Forms/C.2118/12.

Army Form C. 2118.

Instructions regarding War Diaries and Intelligence Summaries are contained in F. S. Regs., Part II. and the Staff Manual respectively. Title Pages will be prepared in manuscript.

WAR DIARY
or
INTELLIGENCE SUMMARY
(Erase heading not required.)

Sheet 5.

Place	Date	Hour	Summary of Events and Information	Remarks and references to Appendices
	15.7.16.		Company moved to VAUX SUR SOMME	
	16.7.16 to 18.7.16		In camp at VAUX. Carried out training in musketry and pontooning.	
	19.7.16		Marched to HAPPY VALLEY and bivouacked.	
	20.7.16.		Moved to a point ½ mile S.W. of FRICOURT.	
	25.7.16	2 p.m.	No 2 Section moved off to construct a dressing station in CASEMENT TRENCH	
		6 p.m.	No 3 Section moved to make 4 Battalion H.Q Dugouts in MALTZ HORN area.	
		7 p.m.	Supervising a cable trench from BRICK POINT to BRIQUETERIE. Working party of 2nd Bedfords and 17th Kings.	
	26.7.16	7 a.m.	No 1 Section moved off to relieve No 3.	
		8 a.m.	No 2 " " " . Dressing Station	
		11 a.m.	No 4 Section made a model strong point near Bde H.Q	
		2 p.m.	Supervision of cable trench by 1 NCO	
		8 p.m.	No 1 Section returned on completion	
		10.30 p.m.	No 2 returned – work done 2 excavations complete. One 25 x 25 x 8 for cases, " 10 x 8 x 8 for dressing. Work started on roof.	
	27.7.16		Carried on with Dressing Station	
	28.7.16		Dressing Station completed by No 1. Battn H.Q completed	

2449 Wt. W14957/M90 750,000 1/16 J.B.C. & A. Forms/C.2118/12.

Army Form C. 2118.

Instructions regarding War Diaries and Intelligence Summaries are contained in F. S. Regs., Part II. and the Staff Manual respectively. Title Pages will be prepared in manuscript.

WAR DIARY
or
INTELLIGENCE SUMMARY
(Erase heading not required.)

Sheet 8

Place	Date	Hour	Summary of Events and Information	Remarks and references to Appendices
	29.7.16	9 pm	Paraded and moved into Oxford Copse. 1 Coy 17th Lancs Fusiliers reported at TALUS BOISÉ at 11.30	
	30.7.16	6 am	Hill and Gledhill with parties of N.C.O.s proceeded to follow up attack on FALFEMONT FARM to lay out the support line should the objective be reached	
		12 noon	Report that above parties were hung up S of MALTZ HORN FARM.	
		3 pm	Ordered above parties to return	
		6 pm	Ordered to send back Coy of 17th Lancs Fusiliers to their Battalion	
	31.7.16	1.30 am	Ordered to move back	
		6.30 am	Company moved back to point ¼ mile S W of FRICOURT.	
		6.30 pm	Company moved back to BRAY.	

R J Wright
Capt R.E.
O.C. 200th Fd Coy R.E.

2449 Wt. W14957/M90 750,000 1/16 J.B.C. & A. Forms/C.2118/12.

Instructions regarding War Diaries and Intelligence Summaries are contained in F. S. Regs., Part II. and the Staff Manual respectively. Title Pages will be prepared in manuscript.

WAR DIARY
or
~~INTELLIGENCE~~ SUMMARY
(Erase heading not required.)

Army Form C. 2118.

Sheet 7

Place	Date	Hour	Summary of Events and Information	Remarks and references to Appendices
			Casualties during the month of July 1916	
BRAY	1-7-16		1 O.R. Wounded in Action (At duty) 1-7-16	
			3 O.R. -do- (Hospital) 1-7-16 } Struck off the strength of the Unit.	
	2-7-16		1 O.R. Killed in Action (Shellfire) 2-7-16 }	
	3-7-16		1 O.R. Wounded in Action (Hospital) 3-7-16 }	
	6-7-16		1 O.R. Injured Accidental (do) 6-7-16 }	
	10-7-16		1 O.R. Wounded in Action (Shellfire) 10-7-16 Struck off Strength.	
	12-7-16		2 O.R. Slightly wounded (At duty) 12-7-16	
	"		2nd Lieut. F. A. D. Richmond R.E. Wounded in Action (Bullet) 12-7-16 Struck off the strength of the unit.	
			– HOSPITAL –	
	2-7-16		1 O.R. to Hospital (Sickness) 2-7-16. Since to C.C.S. Struck off strength	
	3-7-16		1 O.R. to Hospital (-do-) 3-7-16 – do – – do –	
	5-7-16		1 O.R. to Hospital (-do-) 5-7-16	
	11-7-16		1 O.R. to Hospital (do) 11-7-16	
	23-7-16		1 O.R. to Hospital (do) 23-7-16	
	26-7-16		2 O.R. to Hospital (do) 26-7-16	
	27-7-16		1 O.R. to Hospital (do) 27-7-16	
	29-7-16		3 O.R. to Hospital (do) 29-7-16	

2449 Wt. W14957/M90 750,000 1/16 J.B.C. & A. Forms/C.2118/12.

Instructions regarding War Diaries and Intelligence Summaries are contained in F. S. Regs., Part II. and the Staff Manual respectively. Title Pages will be prepared in manuscript.

WAR DIARY
or
~~INTELLIGENCE SUMMARY~~
(Erase heading not required.)

Army Form C. 2118.

Sheet 8.

Place	Date	Hour	Summary of Events and Information	Remarks and references to Appendices
			Casualties for July Continued.	
BRAY	8.7.16		1 O.R. rejoined from Hospital 8.7.16.	
			– REINFORCEMENTS –	
	11.7.16		5 O.R. Arrived from No 4 General Base Depot on 11-7-16 and taken on the strength of the unit from that date.	
	16.7.16		2nd Lieut C. J. Barker R.E. was taken on the strength of the unit from 16-7-16.	
	18.7.16		3 O.R. Arrived from No 4 General Base Depot on 18.7.16 and taken on the strength of the unit from that date.	
			– HORSES &c. –	
	29.7.16		2 Mules (L.D) arrived on the 29.7.16. to replace 2 Mules (L.D) evacuated to the Base for Veterinary reasons.	

R G Wright
Capt R.E.
O.C. 200th Fd Coy R.E.

30th Divisional Engineers

200th FIELD COMPANY R. E.

AUGUST 1 9 1 6A

Instructions regarding War Diaries and Intelligence Summaries are contained in F. S. Regs., Part II. and the Staff Manual respectively. Title Pages will be prepared in manuscript.

200th Field Company R.E.

WAR DIARY
or
~~INTELLIGENCE SUMMARY~~
(Erase heading not required.)

Army Form C. 2118.

Sheet I

Place	Date AUG	Hour	Summary of Events and Information	Remarks and references to Appendices
BRAY.	1st		Transport left BRAY at 9.30 a.m and proceeded to CARDONNETTE.	
	2nd	3a.m	Company left BRAY marching via MORLANCOURT.	
		6.30a.m	Arrived MERICOURT.	
		6.p.m	Entrained	
		10.45p.m	Arrived at LONGPRÉ and detrained.	
		11 p.m	Transport arrived HOCQUINCOURT.	
	3rd	4.a.m	Company arrived HOCQUINCOURT and bivouacked.	
	4th	7p.m	Company marched to PONT RÉMY arriving at 9 p.m. Entrained and left at midnight	
	5th	8a.m	Company arrived at MERVILLE, detrained, and went into billets 1 mile N.W of the town	
	10th	2p.m	Company marched via LOCON to GORRE arriving at 7p.m.	
	11th to 31st		Took over work in FESTUBERT SECTOR held by the 93rd Infantry Brigade. The following work was put in hand.	
			(a) <u>Communications</u>. Relaying floor boards and clearing out drain underneath, revetting and thickening parapets in SHETLAND ROAD East of RICHMOND TERRACE, PIONEER ROAD, BARNTON ROAD and LOOP ROAD.	
			(b) <u>Defences</u>. Improving Island No5. Rebuilding No12 and joining 30A and 30B. Providing Parados, traverses etc in RICHMOND TERRACE. Work on derelict breastwork between OBL and LE PLANTIN EAST Keep	
			Other Work. Construction of two brick O.P.s in FESTUBERT and LE PLANTIN. Supervision of work at Gun Positions	

R G Wright
Capt R.E.
O.C. 200th Fd Coy R.E.

2449 Wt. W14957/M90 750,000 1/16 J.B.C. & A. Forms/C.2118/12.

200th Field Company / RE

WAR DIARY
or
INTELLIGENCE SUMMARY
(Erase heading not required.)

Army Form C. 2118.

Sheet II

Instructions regarding War Diaries and Intelligence Summaries are contained in F. S. Regs., Par. II. and the Staff Manual respectively. Title Pages will be prepared in manuscript.

Place	Date	Hour	Summary of Events and Information	Remarks and references to Appendices
			Casualties for month of August 1916	
			- HOSPITAL -	
BRAY	30.7.16		1 O.R. to Hospital (Sickness) 30.7.16	
HOCQUINCOURT	3.8.16		1 O.R. to Hospital (do) 3.8.16	
MERVILLE	9.8.16		1 O.R. to Hospital (do) 9.8.16	
"	10.8.16		4 O.R. to Hospital (do) 10.8.16	
GORRE	14.8.16		1 O.R. to Hospital (do) 14.8.16	
"	15.8.16		2 O.R. to Hospital (do) 15.8.16	
"	24.8.16		1 O.R. to Hospital (do) 24.8.16	
BRAY	30.7.16		1 O.R. rejoined from Hospital 30.7.16.	
MERVILLE	3.8.16		1 O.R. - do - 3-8-16	
GORRE	13.8.16		1 O.R. - do - 13-8-16	
"	18.8.16		1 O.R. - do - 18-8-16	
"	20.8.16		2 O.R. - do - 20-8-16	
	11.7.16		1 O.R. to Hospital (Sickness) 11-7-16	
	23.7.16		1 O.R. - do - 23-7-16	
	27.7.16		1 O.R. - do - 27-7-16	
	29.7.16		3 O.R. - do - 29-7-16	
	15.8.16		1 O.R. - do - 15-8-16	
	21.8.16		1 O.R. - do - 21-8-16	

(Bracketed against the last six entries:) These men having been sent to C.C.S. are struck off the strength of this unit.

2449 Wt. W14957/M90 750,000 1/16 J.B.C. & A. Forms/C.2118/12.

200th Field Company R.E.

Instructions regarding War Diaries and Intelligence Summaries are contained in F. S. Regs., Part II. and the Staff Manual respectively. Title Pages will be prepared in manuscript.

WAR DIARY
or
~~INTELLIGENCE SUMMARY~~

(Erase heading not required.)

Army Form C. 2118.

Sheet III

Place	Date	Hour	Summary of Events and Information	Remarks and references to Appendices
			Casualties for August continued	
			– REINFORCEMENTS –	
GORRE	19.8.6		1 O.R. Arrived from No 4 General Base Depot on the 19.8.16 and taken on the strength of unit from that date.	
"	21.8.16		6 O.R. Arrived from No 4 General Base Depot on the 21.8.16 and taken on the strength of unit from that date.	
			– TRANSFERS –	
"	23.8.16		1 O.R. Transferred to Base Depot ROUEN 23.8.16. MEDICAL BOARD. Authority: A.D.M.S. 30th Div. A/158/3 dated 21.8.16 Marked P.B.	
			– HORSES &c –	
"	21.8.16		1 Mule (L.D.) Transferred from this unit to 30th Divl. Signals on 21-8-16.	

R. G. Wright Capt R.E.
O.C. 200TH FIELD CO., R.E.

2449 Wt. W14957/M90 750,000 1/16 J.B.C. & A. Forms/C.2118/12.

30th Divisional Engineers

200th FIELD COMPANY R.E. ::: SEPTEMBER 1916.

200th Field Company R.E.

Instructions regarding War Diaries and Intelligence Summaries are contained in F. S. Regs., Part II. and the Staff Manual respectively. Title Pages will be prepared in manuscript.

WAR DIARY
or
~~INTELLIGENCE SUMMARY~~
(Erase heading not required.)

Army Form C. 2118.

Sheet I

Place	Date	Hour	Summary of Events and Information	Remarks and references to Appendices
GORRE	1.9.16		Work continued in FESTUBERT SECTOR.	
"	12.9.16	9.30 a.m.	Left GORRE and marched to BRUAY.	
BRUAY	13.9.16	9 a.m.	" BRUAY and marched to ECOIVRES	
ECOIVRES	14.9.16	8 a.m.	Three sections went up to SECTOR opposite VIMY RIDGE for following work which was commenced — The construction of Ammunition Dumps along Parapets of Support, and other Trenches.	
"	16.9.16	8 a.m.	Received orders to move and left ECOIVRES marched to ACQ	
ACQ	17.9.16	9.45 a.m.	Marched to CAMBLIGNEUL.	
CAMBLIGNEUL	19.9.16	10 a.m.	" " SAVY STATION and entrained for DOULLENS, detrained at DOULLENS and marched to GEZAINCOURT	
GEZAINCOURT	21.9.16	7.30 am	Left GEZAINCOURT and marched to VIGNACOURT	
VIGNACOURT	27.9.16	2 p.m.	" VIGNACOURT and marched to ALLONVILLE.	
ALLONVILLE	28.9.16	7.30 a.m.	" ALLONVILLE marched to Camp about 1 1/2 miles S of ALBERT.	
CAMP	29.9.16	11 a.m.	" Camp marched to S 26 d 8.8 W of MONTAUBAN	
MONTAUBAN	30.9.16		Commenced work on Road running between MONTAUBAN and BAZENTIN-LE-GRAND at point S.15 a 8.8	

[illegible signature]
Capt. R.E.
& O.C. 200th F. Coy R.E.

2449 Wt. W14957/M90 750,000 1/16 J.B.C. & A. Forms/C.2118/12.

200th Field Company, R.E.

Instructions regarding War Diaries and Intelligence Summaries are contained in F. S. Regs., Part II. and the Staff Manual respectively. Title Pages will be prepared in manuscript.

WAR DIARY

or

~~INTELLIGENCE SUMMARY~~

(Erase heading not required.)

Sheet II

Army Form C. 2118.

Place	Date	Hour	Summary of Events and Information	Remarks and references to Appendices
			Casualties for the month of September 1916	
			- HOSPITAL -	
GORRE	29.8.16		2nd Lieut. R.W.R. RANKIN R.E. admitted to Hospital 29-8-16. (Sickness)	
"	2.9.16		Capt. R.G. Wright R.E. - do - 2-9-16. (do)	
			- REINFORCEMENTS -	
"	11.9.16		7 O.R. Arrived from No 4 General Base Depot on the 11-9-16 and taken on the strength from that date.	
VIGNACOURT	25.9.16		2 O.R. Arrived from No 4 General Base Depot on the 25-9-16 and taken on the strength of the unit from that date.	
CAMBLIGNEUL	17.9.16		Capt. W. Guise Tucker R.E. Joined the 200th Field Coy. R.E. on the 17-9-16, and was taken on the strength from that date.	
VIGNACOURT	24.9.16		2nd Lieut. J.O. Leslie R.E. Joined the 200th Field Coy R.E. on the 24.9.16 and was taken on the strength from that date.	
			- TRANSFERS -	
GORRE	11.9.16		81776 L/Cpl. Berry R.C. from 200th Field Coy. R.E. to H.Q. 30th Divisional Engineers 11-9-16.	Authority O/c R.E. Base Records No X/1089/980 dated 14/9/16
			81794 L/Cpl. Unwin R. from H.Q. 30th Divisional Engineers to 200th Field Company, R.E. 11-9-16.	

2449 Wt. W14957/M90 750,000 1/16 J.B.C. & A. Forms/C.2118/12.

200th Field Company R.E.

Instructions regarding War Diaries and Intelligence Summaries are contained in F. S. Regs., Part II. and the Staff Manual respectively. Title Pages will be prepared in manuscript.

WAR DIARY
or
INTELLIGENCE SUMMARY
(Erase heading not required.)

Sheet III

Army Form C. 2118.

Place	Date	Hour	Summary of Events and Information	Remarks and references to Appendices
			Casualties for September. Continued.	
			- TRANSFERS -	
CAMBLIGNEUL	19.9.16		66199 Sapr. Chaney H. Transferred to Base Depot ROUEN MEDICAL BOARD, Marked P.B. Authority: A.D.M.S. 30 Div. A/207/3 dated 15/9/16.	
VIGNACOURT	26.9.16		83094 L/Cpl. Morley J.A. Sent to Home Establishment for Munition Work on the 26/9/16 Authority: War Office letter No. 19/M/730 A.G.5 dated 6-9-16 and D.A.G. G.H.Q. 3rd Echelon letter C.R. No. 25300/670/A dated 23-9-16. (MUNITIONS WORKERS)	
"	26.9.16		108130 Driver Craven W.A. Transferred from 200th Field Company R.E. to 215th (A.T.) Company R.E. on the 26-9-16. Authority: O/c R.E. Base Records. X/1689/1022 dated 22-9-16.	
	12.9.16		Capt. R.G. Wright R.E. To England on 12-9-16. Struck off the strength of the unit. Authority: 30th Division letter No. A 2202 dated 25-9-16. "Extract from List No 494 A dated 24/9/16 of officers transferred to ENGLAND.	
			Chas. [signature] Capt. O.C. 200TH FIELD CO., R.E	

2449 Wt. W14957/M90 750,000 1/16 J.B.C. & A. Forms/C.2118/12.

30th Divisional Engineers

200th FIELD COMPANY R.E.:::: OCTOBER 1916.

Army Form C. 2118.

Instructions regarding War Diaries and Intelligence Summaries are contained in F. S. Regs., Part II. and the Staff Manual respectively. Title Pages will be prepared in manuscript.

WAR DIARY
or
~~INTELLIGENCE SUMMARY~~
(Erase heading not required.)

200th Fd Co R.E.

Place	Date	Hour	Summary of Events and Information	Remarks and references to Appendices
MONTAUBAN (S 26. d 8.8)	1-10-16	7-45 Am	Time put back 1 hour.	
		-4pm	2, 3 & 4 Sections ~~Company~~ employed repairing road BAZENTIN-le-GRAND. - Weather "Fine"	
			A/C.S.M. HARRIS returned from No. 4 G.B.D.	
"	2-10-16	"	Work as for 1-10-16. Weather - Fine at first - Later Very wet.	
"	3-10-16	"	Road work continued. Weather : Morning Fine - afternoon wet.	
"	4-10-16	"	Road work continued. Carpenters & Blacksmiths making Stokes Bomb carriers. - Weather wet.	
"	5-10-16	"	Road work continued. Stoke Bomb carriers continued. Weather Fine turning wet	
"	6-10-16	"	Work as on 5-10-16 continued. Weather Fine - cold.	
"	7-10-16	"	Work as on 6-10-16 continued. No. 1 Sect under Lieut HILL returned from 4th Army School. Weather: wet.	
"	8-10-16	"	3 Sections Roads & Stoke Bomb carriers. No. 1 on advanced D.H.Q.* Weather: wet.	* Map ref: S.16.d.3.4.
"	9-10-16	"	Same work as before. Weather Fine.	
"	10-10-16 to 13-10-16	&	Operations. Report attached.†	† (marked) A
	11-10-16		Moved camp to S 21 a 8.4. Weather. Fine.	
	14-10-16	7-45 Am	2 Sections & all carpenters on Advanced D.H.Q. Remainder on LONGEVAL-HIGHWOOD Road. Weather Fine & cold.	
	15-10-16	"	2 Sections on shelters at D.H.Q. 1 Section improving B.H.Q in FERRET TRENCH (M 36 c 4½.2). 1 Section on LONGEVAL-HIGHWOOD Road with 250 Infantry. Weather Fine & cold.	
	16-10-16	"	2 Sections all day on D.H.Q. 1 Section LONGEVAL-HIGHWOOD Road with 350 Infantry. 1 - ½ day. 1 Section ½ day on Public latrines at LONGEVAL. Weather Fine & cold.	
	17-10-16	"	2 Sections + 35 RA on D.H.Q. 1 Section Public Latrines LONGEVAL. 1 Section + 2 Cos S Lancs Pioneers on LONGEVAL-HIGHWOOD Rd. Weather Fine & cold.	

2449 Wt. W14957/M90 750,000 1/16 J.B.C. & A. Forms/C.2118/12.

Instructions regarding War Diaries and Intelligence Summaries are contained in F. S. Regs., Part II. and the Staff Manual respectively. Title Pages will be prepared in manuscript.

2

WAR DIARY
or
~~INTELLIGENCE SUMMARY~~
(Erase heading not required.)

200th Fd Co R.E.

Army Form C. 2118.

Place	Date	Hour	Summary of Events and Information	Remarks and references to Appendices
MONTAUBAN S.21.a.9.4.	18-10-16		1 Section all day, 1 Section finished 1.45 pm + 40 ORA on D.H.Q. (This section was 3 hours in by till 1 pm) 2 Sections attached to O.C. 202 Fd Co & marched to SWITCH TRENCH at 2 pm. Weather. Fine & cold.	
	19-10-16		1 Section + 30 Infantry D.H.Q. 1 Section + 250 Infantry LONGUEVAL-HIGHWOOD Road. 2 Sections attached to 202 Fd Co Returned to Camp 5.30 A.m. worked all night. Weather very wet. The 2 Sections attached to 202 Co went out again 5.30 pm, returning 6 a.m. 20-10-16.	
	20-10-16		No 1 Section (1 NCO & 3 men only) + 12 RFA on D.H.Q. No 1 Section (less 1 NCO 13 men), No 2 Section & 200 R. Scots Fus: on LONGUEVAL HIGHWOOD Rd. 2 Sections attached to 202 Co night work. 5.30 - 4.45 am. Fine & cold.	
	21-10-16		No 1 Section on 1st Field Survey Co Dug Out at S.5.d.7.4. No 2 Section + 350 Infantry on LONGUEVAL-HIGHWOOD Road. No 3 & 4 Sections went out for work under O.C. 202 Fd Co at 6 pm & returned at 5.30 A.m. They were not employed. Weather. Fine - cold (some frost). Orders to hand over to Australian Fd Co received.	
	22-10-16		Handed over to 15 Australian Fd Co RE left camp 10.30 A.m. marched via BAZENTIN to MAMETZ WOOD S.19.d.9.7. Co: arrived 12.15 pm. Transport held up owing to road repairs for 2 hours, arrived about 3 pm. Bivouacs. Weather:- Fine & cold.	
MAMETZ WOOD (S.19.d.9.7)	23-10-16		Awaiting Orders to move. Weather: day Fine & good - night wet.	
	24-10-16		Left camp 9.30 A.m. marching via MAMETZ, BECORDEL-MEAULTE-DERNANCOURT to BUIRE, arriving 1.30 pm. Weather wet.	
BUIRE	25-10-16		Transport under Capt IRWIN left at 6.45 AM for TALMAS. Weather warmer - inclined to rain.	

2449 Wt. W14957/M90 750,000 1/16 J.B.C. & A. Forms/C.2118/12.

Instructions regarding War Diaries and Intelligence Summaries are contained in F. S. Regs., Part II. and the Staff Manual respectively. Title Pages will be prepared in manuscript.

WAR DIARY
~~or~~
~~INTELLIGENCE SUMMARY~~

(Erase heading not required.)

Army Form C. 2118.

200th Field Co. R.E.

Place	Date	Hour	Summary of Events and Information	Remarks and references to Appendices
BUIRE	26-10-16		Left camp at 2-40 pm. marched to EDGEHILL Station, arriving about 3-10 pm. Entrained 6-30 pm. Remained in train till arriving next morning at DOULLENS at 7.0 am.	
DOULLENS	27-10-16	7 AM	Marched to GRENAS (where Transport had already arrived) getting in about 9 am, & went into billets. O.C. (Capt. TUCKER) & 2nd Lieut. LESLIE, left about 12-30 pm for BAVINCOURT for a guide to conduct them to POMMIER the H.Q. of 1/1 N. Midland Field Co. R.E., from whom work in hand, billets &c had to be taken over. Weather wet.	
POMMIER	28-10-16		Major McGrath, O.C. N. Midland Field Co., ~~[illegible]~~ took O.C. & 2nd Lieut. LESLIE round the large portion of line & ~~[illegible]~~ principal work in hand. No. 2 Section ~~marched~~ marched with 2nd Lieut. GLEDHILL to BAVINCOURT for work under C.R.E. 30th Div. No. 3 Section marched to BIENVILLERS (via POMMIER) for work in the line. 2nd Lieut. LESLIE in charge. Weather wet.	
GRENAS BIENVILLERS	29-10-16		Sunday Church parade 11-45 AM. C of E. (10 AM R.C.) 1 & 4 Sections. Transport overhauled. ~~No~~ No. 3 Section taking over left Sector of line.	
	31-10-16		Took over 1/1 N. Midland Field Co. R.E.'s camp at POMMIER, billets at BIENVILLERS, billets & horse lines at LA HERLIERE. No. 1 Section marched from GRENAS to BIENVILLERS, H.Q. & 4 to POMMIER, & Transport to LA HERLIERE. No. 2 Section under C.R.E. at BAVINCOURT. No. 3 Section work on line.	
BIENVILLERS BAVINCOURT POMMIER	31-10-16		No. 1 Section N.C.O. going round trenches, sappers settling into billets. No. 3 work on C.T. & front line. No. 2 Section work on A.S.C. Camp, C.R.E.'s office, A & Q office &c. Miscellaneous minor work by No. 4 Sect.	

W. Ernest Tucker Capt. R.E. Cdg.

2449 Wt. W14957/M90 750,000 1/16 J.B.C. & A. Forms/C.2118/12.

SECRET.

(A) (1.)

C.R.E. 30th Div.

Report on Operations on 12-13 October 1916.

200th Field Co: R.E.

Ref: Map GUEUDECOURT-LONGEVAL 1/10000.

PRELIMINARY.

10-10-16

1. In accordance with C.R.E. 30th Div: No. 11 of 9-10-16, directing Field Companies of 30th Div to take over commencement with work in hand by 41st Div, and ordering 200th Field Co to take over from 233rd Field Co by 4 pm 10-10-16, accompanied by Lieut. HILL R.E. I went over a portion of the line, as he considered necessary, with Captain THWAITES R.E. O.C. 233rd Co R.E. on 10-10-16, and took over from him.

2. Advanced copy of distribution of Technical Troops (C.R.E. 128 of [illegible]) received.

11-10-16.

3. Reported at B.H.Q. 89th Brigade between 1.30 & 2 pm. The G.O.C. 89th Brig: sent me out to reconnoitre & site 2 assembly trenches capable of holding 350 men each.
4 officers & 16 N.C.O's of 19th K.L.R. (to act as guides to the 20th K.R.R. who were to dig & occupy the trenches) were detailed to assist me.
We went out about 4 p.m.
Sited two trenches running at right angles due west out of GOOSE ALLEY. They were about 120-130 yards apart, & being on a reverse slope were practically free from enemy observation. They were about 200 yards in length.
Their position was approximately:-
(1). From M [illegible] to M [illegible]
(2). " M [illegible] to M [illegible]

I heard, after the attack, that there was only one casualty in these trenches.

Returned to B.H.Q. about 5.30 p.m., and then came back to Camp.

OPERATIONS.

11-10-16

1. CRE S No. 129 of 11-10-16 covering extract from 30th Div. Operation Order No. 40 received.

12-10-16.

2. No. 3 Section 200th Field Co R.E. paraded at 9.0 am under 2nd Lieut: LESLIE R.E. at Co: H.Q. with digging tools & marched to B.H.Q; where they arrived at 11 a.m. and reported. They were ordered to find accommodation in a neighbouring trench M 30 C 0 1½, and await orders from the G.O.C. 89th Brig:

3. Nos 1. 2 & 4 Sections paraded at 1 p.m. and in accordance with orders, marched to FIGTRENCH (S6 a 4 7) under the Command of the Senior officer - LIEUT. HILL. R.E.

The following were in charge of Sections:-

No. 1. LIEUT: HILL.
2. Sergt. PEACOCK (2nd Lieut: GLEDHILL sick)
4. 2nd Lieut: BARKER R.E.

4. I proceeded to and reported at B.H.Q about 1.30 p.m., & found that the 2 platoons Infantry detailed in Appendix C 1(a) had not been sent to FIGTRENCH to meet Lieut: HILL, and arranged for their immediate despatch.

5. As the Co had to be ready to follow up the attack and commence constructing Strong points by 6 p.m. on the "Green" line, I instructed Lieut: HILL to bring Nos 1, 2 & 4 Sections with him & meet me at M 30 C. 9.7 by 5 p.m., which he did leaving the 2 platoons of Infantry (v. previous para) to bring on material.

6. I had ascertained by this time (5 pm) that our objective had not been obtained, & therefore left Nos 1, 2 & 4 Sections under 2nd Lieut. BARKER in FACTORY TRENCH (M 30 a 8.3½) and taking Lieut. HILL and 5 N.C.Os with me proceeded towards the Front line to see if these sections could be employed.

7. We went via GOOSE ALLEY, which we found to be crowded with wounded men & others coming in the opposite direction, and we were held up frequently by numerous checks. I was endeavouring to push on & became separated from the rest of the party. When I arrived at the top of GOOSE ALLEY, which was difficult to pass owing to dead men lying in the trench, and to men resting, I waited for Lieut. Hill & party to come up. I waited ½ to 3/4 hour, and as they didn't come went back to find them.

And after proceeding down the trench (GOOSE ALLEY) for some 500x came across them, & found that they had been forced back, by men going down the trench.

8. We then went forward again and arrived at the H.Q. of the 17th K.L.R, where I saw their C.O. Lt Col: PECK, I found that this Regiment was back in the trenches from which it started, but that no assistance was required.

9. On leaving the H.Q. 17th K.L.R. we endeavoured to reach H.Q. 2 Bedford Regt, which we eventually found, after losing our way. Here I saw the C.O. Lieut Col: POYNTZ, and gathered that, as far as he was concerned, his right flank had advanced, though it had not reached its objective, but that his left had had to come back to its starting point. I asked if any R.E. assistance was required, and Lieut-Col POYNTZ said that there was a trench, which he intended to have dug, and I said that I would see if I could send him some help. We then returned to FACTORY TRENCH, where we picked up Nos 1, 2 & 4 Sections. We arrived back without casualty.

10. I went on to B.H.Q. 89th Brigade, & found that no orders for me had come through, and that No 3 Section was not required by the G.O.C. 89th Infantry Brigade, ~~On returning to the Co with No 3 Section I [illegible] was going up~~ and sent it to join the other 3 Sections. I followed & was with the Co when a message was brought to me saying that I was required to speak to the Adjt (Capt STONE). I sent the Co on under Lieut HILL to report to Col: POYNTZ, & went back to B.H.Q. where I received orders to withdraw the Co immediately, to Camp, but that I personally was to remain at B.H.Q. and go out in the early morning to reconnoitre the front line and report to C.R.E. at 10 A.M. 13-10-16 at 21st B.H.Q.

11. I sent a message to Lieut HILL, who on his return informed me that Lieut: Col POYNTZ considered that on account of the moonlight it was impracticable to dig the trench, so he took the Co to GOOSE ALLEY which he had just started improving, when my message to withdraw reached him. He stated that everything was then very quiet (2–2.30 am 13.10.16)

12. I went out at 5.0 am. 13-10-16 to reconnoitre arriving back about 9 a.m. & was commencing to write my report when a message arrived at 89th B.H.Q. (where I was) saying that the C.R.E. would meet me there, and he arrived very shortly after.

W. Gerrard Tucker
Capt R.E. S.R.
O.C. 200th Fd Co R.E.

18.10.16

83/

COMMANDING ROYAL ENGINEERS
No. 118
9 OCT 1916
30th DIVL. (COUNTY PALATINE) ENGINEERS

O.C. 200th Field Co. R.E.
~~O.C. 201st Field Co. R.E.~~
~~O.C. 202nd Field Coy.R.E.~~

Field Companies will tomorrow make themselves conversant with work in hand by 41st Division Field Companies with a view to carrying on the work as soon as the Brigade to which they are affiliated goes into the line.

200th Field Company which will be working in the left brigade section of the front will be relieving 233rd Field Company.

201st Field Company which will be working in the right brigade section of the front will be relieving 237th Field Company.

202nd Field Company in reserve brigade area will be relieving 228th Field Company.

R.P.

Captain.R.E.
Adjt. 30th Divisional
(County Palatine) Engineers.

9-10-1916.

P.S. work will actually be taken over from 4 pm tomorrow

RP

24

SECRET.

O.C. 200th Field Co. R.E.

~~O.C. 200th Field Co. R.E.~~
~~O.C. 201st Field Co. R.E.~~
~~O.C. 202nd Field Co. R.E.~~
~~O.C. 11th Bn. South Lancs.~~

COMMANDING ROYAL ENGINEERS
No. 128
10 OCT 1916
30th DIVL. (COUNTY PALATINE) ENGINEERS

Herewith advanced copy of table shewing distribution of technical troops for forthcoming operations. You will make all necessary arrangements as regards stores, and equipment of your parties.

The C.R.E. will be at MONTAUBAN Church at 12 noon tomorrow when you should bring up any points which are not clear.

Map shewing Strong Points, Communication Trenches, Green line, etc., will be forwarded with Operation Order later.

Captain. R.E.
Adjt. 30th Divisional
(County Palatine) Engineers.

10-10-1916.

Secret

DISPOSITION OF R.E. AND PIONEERS.

Affiliation	Strength &c. of Parties	Place and time of Assembly	Objective	Remarks.
	1. CONSOLIDATION PARTIES.			
90th Inf: Bde:	(a) 1 Section 201st Field Coy. R.E.	Under Brigade orders.		These Parties to move under Brigade orders.
89th Inf: Bde:	(b) 1 Section 200th Field Co. R.E.	" " "		
Division.	X(c) 201st Field Coy. R.E. (less 1 Section). 2 Platoons Infantry.	Switch trench, (astride TURK LANE) 2-30 pm. 12th Oct	Consolidation of Green line, on 90th Inf: Bde: Front. Strong Points to be made as shewn on attached map. Sites are provisional, O.C. Coy being responsible for actual siting after necessary R.E. reconnaissance.	To move forward in time to commence work on Green line by 6 pm.
	X(d) 200th Field Co. R.E. (less 1 Section) 2 Platoons Infantry.	FIGT RENEW (NEAR FERRETT TR ~~Switch~~ trench, (astride FISH ALLEY) 3 - 0pm. 12th Oct	ditto on 89th Infy: Brigade Front.	Amended 11-10-16 CRE 12/1
	2. COMMUNICATION TRENCH PARTIES.			
"	X(a) 2 Coys 11th S.Lancs	Switch trench (West of 201st Field Coy.) 2-30 pm. 12th Oct	Continuation of FISH ALLEY to Front line as shewn on attached map.	To move forward in time to commence work (from both ends of trench) by 6 pm.
	X(b) 2 Coys 11th S.Lancs	Switch trench (East of 200th Field Coy.) 2-30 pm. 12th Oct	Continuation of GOOSE ALLEY to Front line as shewn on attached map.	
	3. DIVISIONAL RESERVE.			
"	202nd Field Coy. R.E.	BAZENTIN LE GRAND	In Divisional Reserve.	To be in readiness to move at 15 minutes notice.

X Subject to approval of 21st Infy Bde

10-10-1916.

Lieut-Col. R.E.
C.R.E. 30th Divl. (C.P) Engineers.

S E C R E T.

O.C. 200th Field Co. R.E.
~~O.C. 201st Field Co. R.E.~~
~~O.C. 202nd Field Co. R.E.~~
O.C. 11th South Lancs.

With reference to this Office No.128 of the 10-10-16, the following amendments to "Distribution of R.E. & Pioneers" will be made:-

Unit	Place of Assembly
201st Field Co.	FLERS TRENCH. (Portion East of FISH ALLEY)
200th Field Co.	FIG TRENCH. (Near FERRET TRENCH).
11th S. Lancs.	CREST TRENCH.

You will send Officer and small party on ahead to reconnoitre the above and guide Company to place of Assembly.

Dauker details 1 NCO & 3 sappers

R J Stone

Captain.R.E.
Adjt. 30th Divisional
(County Palatine) Engineers.

11-10-1916.

S E C R E T.

COMMANDING ... L ENGINEERS
No. 129/3
12 OCT 1916
30th DIVL. (COUNTY PALATINE) ENGINEERS

O.C. 200th Field Co. R.E.
O.C. 201st Field Co. R.E.
O.C. 202nd Field Co. R.E.

In connection with Extracts from Operation Order No.40 forwarded under this Office No.129 yesterday, herewith Extracts from "Amendments & Addenda to O.O. No.40" and "Appendix 'B'" and complete Appendices 'C', 'F' and 'H'.

Please acknowledge.

12-10-1916.

Captain.R.E.
Adjt. 30th Divisional
(County Palatine) Engineers.

SECRET.

Appendix "B".

Extract from "System of Liaison and Communication.

ALTERNATIVE METHODS OF COMMUNICATION.

(a) Visual (continually manned) Divl. Lamp and Helio Station at Advanced Divl. H.Q., CARLTON TRENCH to communicate with station at M.36.b.6.2. (West of FLERS) via transmitting stations at S.6.c.6.6. and S.5.d.3.8.

Advanced Divl. Lamp and Helio (receiving) station at S.6.c.1.7. where messages can be received from GIRD SUPPORT in N.19.a. & b. and LIME TRENCH in M.18.d.
All ranks will be warned of positions whence messages can be sent to Advanced Divl. Lamp Station.

24 Light Morse Discs, 6 Venetian Shutters and 2 electric torches are in possession of every unit.

x x x x x x

(c) Orderlies. Divl. H.Q. runners will be employed in relays. Relay stations will be maintained at Advanced Divl. H.Q. in CARLTON TRENCH to Brigade H.Q. (Runners). A half-way post will be established in this stage probably at junction of SWITCH TRENCH with main C.T.

Divl. H.Q. FRICOURT to CARLTON TRENCH (mounted orderlies and runners).

In front of Brigade Headquarters runners will be employed in pairs.

x x x x x

COMMUNICATION WITH ARTILLERY.

(i) Tin Discs. Every infantryman in the Division will wear a tin disc shiny side outwards. Observers must understand that as all infantry wear these, they do not (like flags and flares) represent only the front line.

(ii) Flags. Every Company and every Platoon will carry one coloured Flag. These flags will mean nothing unless waved and they are to be waved only by the front line. They are not to be stuck in a parapet and the utmost care must be taken not to lose them, as great harm may result. They mean when waved like flares "we are here and so far as we know we are the leading infantry or within 50 yards of the leading infantry".

30th Div. flags are blue and yellow, halved diagonally.

12th and 9th Div. are not using flags but 9th Div. wear tin discs.

They will be waved

(a) On reaching first and second objectives (GREEN and BROWN lines).

(b) If checked before reaching line given, or if specially desired at any time to make position of Company known.

(c) Whenever flares are lit in the same unit.

(iii) S.O.S. rocket signal - one special.

SECRET.

Extract from "Amendments and Addenda to O.O. No.40".

Appendix "C".

Brigadiers Commanding 89th and 90th Infantry Brigades will please issue the necessary orders for the assembly with the R.E. of parties detailed to work with them.

30th Division.

(sd). W.F.WEBER, Lieut-Col.
General Staff.

DISPOSITION OF R.E. AND PIONEERS.

Affiliation	Strength &c. of Parties	Place and time of Assembly 12th instant.	Objective	Remarks.
	1. CONSOLIDATION PARTIES.			
90th Inf:Bde:	(a) 1 Section 201st Field Coy.R.E.	Under Brigade Orders.		These parties to move under Brigade Orders.
89th Inf:Bde:	(b) 1 Section 200th Field Coy.R.E.	" " "		
Division	(c) 201st Field Coy.R.E. (less 1 Section) 2 Platoons Infantry. ⊗ (from 90th Bde)	FLERS TRENCH (Portion East of FISH ALLEY) ~~Switch Trench (astride TURK LANE)~~ 2.30 p.m. ✱	Consolidation of green line, on 90th Inf:Bde: Front. Strong points to be made as shown on attached map. Sites are provisional. O.C. Coy. being responsible for actual siting after necessary R.E. reconnaissance	To move forward in time to commence work on green line by 6 p.m.
"	(d) 200th Field Coy.R.E. (less 1 Section) 2 Platoons Infantry ⊗ (from 89th Bde)	FIG TRENCH (near FERRET TRENCH) ~~Switch Trench, (astride FISH ALLEY)~~ 3-0 p.m. ✱	ditto on 89th Infy: Brigade Front.	
	2. COMMUNICATION TRENCH PARTIES.			
"	(a) 2 Coys: 11th S.Lancs.	~~Switch Trench (West of 201st Field Coy)~~ 2-30 p.m. ✱	Continuation of FISH ALLEY to Front Line as shown on attached map.	To move forward in time to commence work (from both ends of trench) by 6-0 p.m.
	(b) 2 Coys: 11th S.Lancs.	~~Switch Trench (East of 200th Field Coy.)~~ 2-30 p.m. ✱	Continuation of GOOSE ALLEY to Front Line as shown on attached map	
	3. DIVISIONAL RESERVE.			
"	202nd Field Coy:R.E.	CREST TRENCH BAZENTIN-LE-GRAND	In Divisional Reserve.	To be in readiness to move at 15 minutes notice

✱ Subject to arrangements between C.R.E. and G.O.C., 21st Inf:Bde:

⊗ orders for assembly will be sent later.

Appen[dix]

APPENDIX "F."

RATIONS & WATER SUPPLY.

RATIONS.

(i). Every man will carry his iron ration on his person in addition to the unexpended portion of the day's ration.

(ii) Rations will be taken by Supply Wagons to First Line Transport Lines in the usual way.

First Line Transport will meet ration parties at appointed places and times which will be arranged by Brigades.

WATER.

(iii) Every man starts with a full water bottle. Great importance is attached to the supervision by Regimental Officers and N.C.Os. of the use of water bottles.

(iv) Water can be drawn at the following points:-

S.21.d.5.0.	for horses.
S.27.c.5.2.	for water carts.
S.17.c.7.0.	for horses and water carts.
F.9.b.3.9.	for water carts.
F.4.d.	for horses.
F.3.d.6.7.	for filling petrol tins only.

There are also seven good wells in FLERS and one at FACTORY Corner.

(v) Carriage from Water points by petrol tins and on mules 8 mules per Battalion carrying 12 gallons each (6 petrol tins).

400 petrol tins per Brigade for hand carriage and storage, in addition to the 48 per Battalion carried on mules.

Water carts will go up to the line with rations.

(vi) A petrol tin dump is being formed at the Advanced Divl: Grenade Dump at T.1.a.16. Application for tins should be made to the Divisional Bombing Officer.

APPENDIX H.

MEDICAL ARRANGEMENTS.

1. Wounded will be carried from the Regimental Aid Posts, which will be in the neighbourhood of Battalion Headquarters, to a Relay Post at M.36.a.6.7. thence via TURK LANE and the open c ountry to the Collecting Station. The long carry will be done by a succession of Relay Posts and horsed Ambulance Wagons will be sent as far forward as circumstances will allow to meet the Stretcher Bearers.

2. COLLECTING STATION.

at S.16.a.2.8. - evacuation by Horsed Ambulance Wagons to

3. ADVANCED DRESSING STATION.

at FLAT IRON COPSE, S.14.c.4.2. - evacuation from here by Motor Ambulances (busses for lightly wounded) to the Main Dressing Station and the Lightly Wounded Collecting Station.

4. MAIN DRESSING STATION.

at BECORDEL, F.7.a.central.

5. LIGHTLY WOUNDED C OLLECTING STATION.

at F.7.b.5.2.

From (4) and (5) wounded are evacuated by Motor Ambulance Convoy to 36 and 38 Casualty Clearing Stations at HEILLY.

S E C R E T.

33

O.C.200th Field Co. R.E.
O.C. 201st Field Co. R.E.
O.C. 202nd Field Co. R.E.
O.C. 11th South Lancs.

The attached extract from 30th Division Operation Order No.40, dated 11th October, '16, is forwarded for your information and guidance.

You have already received in advance a copy of Appendix 'C'.

Please send an Orderly to be at Headquarters, R.E., FRICOURT CHATEAU at 9 am. tomorrow. He should bring two days rations and will remain at H.Q.R.E. probably for a couple of days.

It is hoped that a telephone will be put in today at one of the Field Company Camps between BAZENTIN and MONTAUBAN.

For sending messages the nearest Signal Office should be used. This will be to start with Advanced Div. H.Q. at CARLTON TRENCH, S.16.b.2/3, at which place you should keep a runner for delivery of messages sent to you there.

Other Signal Offices will be 21st Infantry Brigade, S.16.b.2/3, till 9 am. October 12th and afterwards at FERRET TRENCH, S.6.a.5/9; 89th Infantry Brigade, M.30.c.3/1; 90th Infantry Brigade FERRET TRENCH, S.6.a.5/9, till 9 am. October 12th and afterwards in ABBEY ROAD, M.36.b.3/7.

The hour of Zero will be notified later. From that time you will report to this Office every 4 hours location by map reference of all portions of your unit and any work which has been done.

H.Q.R.E. will be with Div. H.Q. at FRICOURT CHATEAU and may later be established at Advanced Div. H.Q., CARLTON TRENCH.

Please acknowledge.

R.G.Hunt

Captain.R.E.
Adjt. 30th Divisional
(County Palatine) Engineers.

11-10-1916.

S E C R E T.

30th Division Operation Order No.40.

11th October, 1916.

Reference attached plan 1/10,000.

1. The Fourth British and Sixth French Armies will continue the attack tomorrow, 12th October, at an hour zero to be notified later.

The whole XV Corps is attacking. The 30th Division will have on its Right 12th Division, on its left the 9th Division of the III Corps. Boundaries are shown on the attached plan.

The troops believed to be opposite us are 6th Bavarian Reserve Division and the 6th Active (Brandenburg) Division.

2. The 30th Division will capture and consolidate the objective indicated by the brown line on the attached plan.

The operation is to be conducted in three stages:-

(i) At Zero the Artillery barrage will begin and the Infantry will advance to the attack and establish itself on the Green line.

(ii) At Zero + 20 the Infantry will advance to the Brown line which will be consolidated.

(iii) After the capture of the Brown line, every effort will be made to establish posts on the approximate line marked Red. —○—○—○— , so as to obtain observation to the North. It is intended later to join up these posts so as to form a trench of departure for subsequent operations.

2. The 90th Inf. Brigade will be on the Right, the 89th Inf. Brigade on the left and the 21st Inf. Brigade in Divl. Reserve.

Boundary between Brigades is shown on the attached plan.

Consolidation.

4. The first objective will be consolidated by the R.E. by a series of strong points, approximate position shown on attached

The second objective will be consolidated, by the Infantry in the first instance, by the conversion of the Northern portion of GIRD SUPPORT and LIME TRENCH and the construction of a series of posts across the interval between.

Exploiting a success.

5. Every effort is to be made to establish posts on the Red line to which detachments of Infantry and Lewis guns will be pushed out.

Approximate positions to be occupied

M.18.a.8.3. (To command trough running through M.12.c.)

M.18.b.8.5. (Observation over S.edge of LE BARQUE)

M.13.b.4.4.

Method of attack.

6. The Brigades will be assembled by dawn 12th October in accordance with instructions and plan issued under this Office G.159 of 10th October.

Each Brigade will have two Battalions in the front line, one in support, and one in reserve.

x x x x x

(c) Artillery Bombardment. Lift arrangements are as follows:-

(i) The barrage will commence without previous warning at Zero and will be on, and some distance in front of the enemy first line trench. The Infantry must get in as close as possible to it.

(ii) From 0.2 it will gradually creep back until it is on the enemy front line trench only (between 0.4 and 0.6).

(iii) At 0.6 it will lift off the Green line altogether to a general line about 150 to 200 yards North of it.

4. (iv) At 0.20 it will again begin to creep back at the rate of 50 yards a minute until it reaches the final barrage beyond the Brown line.

7. x x x x x

Artillery. 8. The attack of the 30th Division will be supported by 21st and New Zealand Divl. Artilleries.

Communications.

9. Contact aeroplanes will be in the air from Zero until dark on 12th and from 6-30 am. till 8-0 am. on 13th.

Flares will be lit:-

(a) On reaching the Green line.
(b) On reaching the Brown line.
(c) At certain stated times on 12th instant to be notified later.
(d) At 7-0 am. on 13th October.

No.3 Kite Balloon will be prepared to receive messages during the night 12/13.

Technical Troops.

10. One Section 201st Field Coy. R.E. will be attached to 90th Inf: Bde: and one Section 200th Field Coy. R.E. to 89th Inf: Bde;

BARKER attached.

The remainder of the Technical Troops will be kept in Divl. Reserve under C.R.E.

They will be assembled in 21st (Reserve) Brigade area under arrangements to be arrived at between C.R.E. and 21st Inf: Bde; and will be employed for consolidation purposes and for cutting new C.T's as opportunity occurs.

Further details as to Technical Troops and working parties required from the Infantry will be contained in Appendix "C."

x x x x x

30th Division.

(sd). W.F.WEBER, Lieut-Col.
General Staff.

33/1

SECRET.

O.C. 200th Field Co. R.E.
O.C. 201st Field Co. R.E.
O.C. 202nd Field Co. R.E.

With reference to Para: 1(c). of Appendix 'C' to Operation Order No.40, the 21st Infantry Brigade have now arranged for the 201st Field Co. R.E. to assemble at FLAG ALLEY instead of FLERS TRENCH.

R.G. Hart
Captain.R.E.
Adjt. 30th Divisional
(County Palatine) Engineers.

12-10-1916.

SECRET. Copy 12

21st INFANTRY BRIGADE ORDER No.4.

October 11th 1916.

Reference Sheet 57.c.S.W. 1/20,000.

1. On October 12th, the British Fourth Army and French Sixth Army will resume the offensive. The whole of the XVth Corps will be attacking. 30th Division will attack with the 89th and 90th Brigades in the front line and the 21st Brigade will be in Divisional Reserve. The 12th Division will be attacking on the right of the 30th Division and the 9th Division on its left.

2. The 89th and 90th Brigades are attacking two lines of German trenches and consolidating along a line which will run roughly as follows:- N.18.a.1.4., N.18.c.7.7., N.13.c.5.8., N.13.b.6.2., with an advanced line of outposts holding approximate positions at N.18.a.8.3., N.18.b.8.5., N.13.b.4.4.

3. Zero hour will be given later.

4. The 89th and 90th Brigades are each free to call upon 4 guns of the 21st Machine Gun Company. The Officer Commanding 21st Machine Gun Company will arrange to send an orderly to each of the above Brigade Headquarters to receive instructions for the movements of these guns.

5. At 9 a.m. tomorrow Brigade Headquarters closes at CARLTON TRENCH and opens FERRET TRENCH, S.6.a.5.9., at the same hour.

6. The Lewis Guns of the 11th Bn South Lancashire Regiment will tonight move into a trench in the neighbourhood of FERRET TRENCH, sending an orderly to Brigade Headquarters at 9 a.m. tomorrow.

7. The following technical troops will move into the 21st Brigade area under arrangements made with the C.R.E. and will be accommodated as follows:-

200th Field Company R.E. (less one section).} FLERS TRENCH
201st Field Company R.E. (less one section).} East of FISH ALLEY.

202nd Field Company R.E. FIG TRENCH.
11th Bn South Lancs. Regt. (Pioneers) in unnamed trench South of CREST TRENCH.

8. Battle Headquarters will be as follows:-

30th Division FRICOURT CHATEAU (on October 12th at a time to be notified later an advanced 30th Division may be established in CARLTON TRENCH S.16.b.2.3.)
21st Brigade after 9 a.m. October 12th FERRET TRENCH S.6.a.5.9.
89th Brigade N.30.c.3.1.
90th Brigade after 9 a.m. October 12th in ABBEY ROAD N.36.b.3.7.
35th Infantry Brigade, 12th Division S.12.d.8.8.
Right Brigade, 9th Division BAZENTIN-le-GRAND.

Each unit will send an officer to reconnoitre the positions of the Battle Headquarters of 89th and 90th Brigades.

J. L. Hobson Captain,
Brigade Major 21st Infantry Bde.

Issued to Signals at:- 230pm

Copy No.	1	War Diary.
	2	30th Division 'G'.
	3	30th Division 'Q'.
	4	18th Liverpools.
	5	2nd Yorkshires.
	6	2nd Wiltshires.
	7	19th Manchesters.
	8	21st M.G.Company.
	9	21st T.M.Battery.
	10	202nd Field Coy R.E.
	11	201st Field Coy R.E.
	12	200th Field Coy R.E.
	13	11th Bn Sth. Lancs.
	14	89th Brigade.
	15	90th Brigade.
	16	Staff Captain.

30th Divisional Engineers

200th FIELD COMPANY R.E. ::: NOVEMBER 1916.

Army Form C. 2118.

Instructions regarding War Diaries and Intelligence Summaries are contained in F. S. Regs., Part II. and the Staff Manual respectively. Title Pages will be prepared in manuscript.

WAR DIARY
~~or~~
~~INTELLIGENCE SUMMARY~~

(Erase heading not required.)

200th Field Company RE.

November 1916.

Place	Date	Hour	Summary of Events and Information	Remarks and references to Appendices
BIENVILLERS	1-11-16		No 1 Section Revetting Trenches. Dugouts.	
			3 " Trench Trenches Dugouts. — 2nd Lieut LESLIE surveying [illegible] of Decauville Track to W 17.c.2.1 (RANSART 1/10,000)	
POMMIER			4 " Repairing billets. Officers' Club (29th Brigade)	
BAVINCOURT			2. " Miscellaneous work under CRE	
	2-11-16		1, 3, 4, 2 } Continued as yesterday.	
	3-11-16		as per yesterday.	
	4-11-16		as per yesterday	
	5-11-16		as per yesterday	
	6-11-16		as per yesterday.	
	7-11-16		as per yesterday — 2nd Lieut BARKER. Surveying Divisional Line	
	8-11-16		as per yesterday — do —	
	9-11-16		as per yesterday — do —	
	10-11-16		as per yesterday — do —	
	11-11-16		as per yesterday — do —	
	12-11-16		as per yesterday	
	13-11-16		as per yesterday.	
	14-11-16		as per yesterday.	
	15-11-16		as per yesterday.	
	16-11-16		as per yesterday. Handed over subsector LULU LANE - NITRATE St to ½ WR. PCRE	
	17-11-16		as per yesterday Took over NITRATE St to 121 from 202 Coy.	
	18-11-16		No 1.3 [illegible] Sections moved to BERLES (relieved by ½ WR 2 Coy RE at BIENVILLERS) -	
			No 4 on Dug Outs (Ball[illegible]) FARNBOROUGH Rd	
BERLES	19-11-16		No 4 Section as per yesterday.	
			No 1, 3 } Trench work.	
BAVINCOURT			2 under CRE	
LA CAUCHIE			Head Quarters of Co moved from POMMIER.	

2449 Wt. W14957/M90 750,000 1/16 J.B.C. & A. Forms/C.2118/12.

Army Form C. 2118.

WAR DIARY

~~or~~

~~INTELLIGENCE SUMMARY~~ 200th Fd Coy RE

(Erase heading not required.)

Instructions regarding War Diaries and Intelligence Summaries are contained in F. S. Regs., Part II. and the Staff Manual respectively. Title Pages will be prepared in manuscript.

Place	Date	Hour	Summary of Events and Information — November 1916.	Remarks and references to Appendices
BERLES	20-11-16		as per yesterday.	
	21-11-16		as per yesterday.	
	22-11-16		as per yesterday.	
	23-11-16		as per yesterday.	
	24-11-16		as per yesterday.	
	25-11-16		as per yesterday	
	26-11-16		as per yesterday.	
	27-11-16		as per yesterday.	Works Report for Month attached
	28-11-16		as per yesterday	
	29-11-16		as per yesterday	
	30-11-16		as per yesterday. Captain N. W. NAPIER-CLAVERING R.E. arrives.	

[illegible signature]
Capt R.E.
O.C. 200th Fd Coy

2449 Wt. W14957/M90 750,000 1/16 J.B.C. & A. Forms/C.2118/12.

Works Report from 6p.m. 2.11.16 1916 to 6 p.m. 3.11.16 1916. Field Co.R.E.

Section.	Locality.	Description of work.	Progress.	Numbers employed. R.E. NCO.	R.E. Sprs.	Infy.	R.A. R.A.M.C.	Remarks.
A 1911	Cross Street	Clearing, draining, revetting	Continued		2	72		
	Left Comp: Trench	" " "			1	6		
	79 Street	" " "		1	4	36		
	Centre Comp H.Q.	Repairs to dugout	Roof finished		2			
	Cross Street Dugouts	" " "	Continued	1	4	10		
	~~Wedding Arch~~ Rosenthal X St	Wedding Arch Type	Slow work	(1)	(2)	6		
	Brewery	Pumping Station, Guard, Tool Cart, Orderly, Cooks, Painter,		1	8	26		
	80 Street	Revetting, Clearing			1	6		
[illegible]	[illegible]	Inspecting Pumps, Clearing & Revetting	Continued	1	13	21		
	[illegible]	" "		1	3	18		
	[illegible]			1	1	5		
	[illegible]	Digging Shaft	Start		1	5		
	Junction [illegible]	Clearing [illegible]	Continued	1	1	10		
	[illegible]	Clearing [illegible]	Cleared		1	10		
	[illegible] Street	[illegible]	[illegible]		1	5		
	Pumps	Repairing			1			
	[illegible]				3			
	[illegible]				4			
	[illegible]				2			
	[illegible]				2			

Works report [illegible] Coy R.E.

Section	Locality	Description of work	Progress	Numbers Employed: NCO	Sappers	Infy	RAMC	Remarks
No 4	[illegible]	[illegible]	[illegible]		2			
	[illegible]	[illegible] Drying Room	[illegible]	1				
	[illegible]	[illegible] No 1		1	2			
	[illegible]	[illegible] No 77			4			[illegible]
		[illegible]	Continued		13	6	10	[illegible]
	HQ	[illegible]	—	1	2			
		[illegible]	—		2			
	C.R.E.	—	—		2			
		[illegible]	—	1	1			
		[illegible]	—		1			
		[illegible]	—		1			
	[illegible]	[illegible]	[illegible]		3			

[illegible] R.E.

To O.C 200th Field Coy RE

Report on Work – Section No 4

NCO	Sappers	Work.
	2	Repairing billets Town Mayor
	3	Workshops Bienvillers
1		Drying Room Bienvillers
1	8	Officers' Club Pommier
	2	Well near Billet 97 Pommier
1	5	With Section No 1
1	2	Gas guard
	2	Cooks
	3	With CRE
1	1	With transport Laherliere
	1	Supply wagon
	1	Hospital
	7	Sick

C J Barker

2Lieut RE

4/11/16.

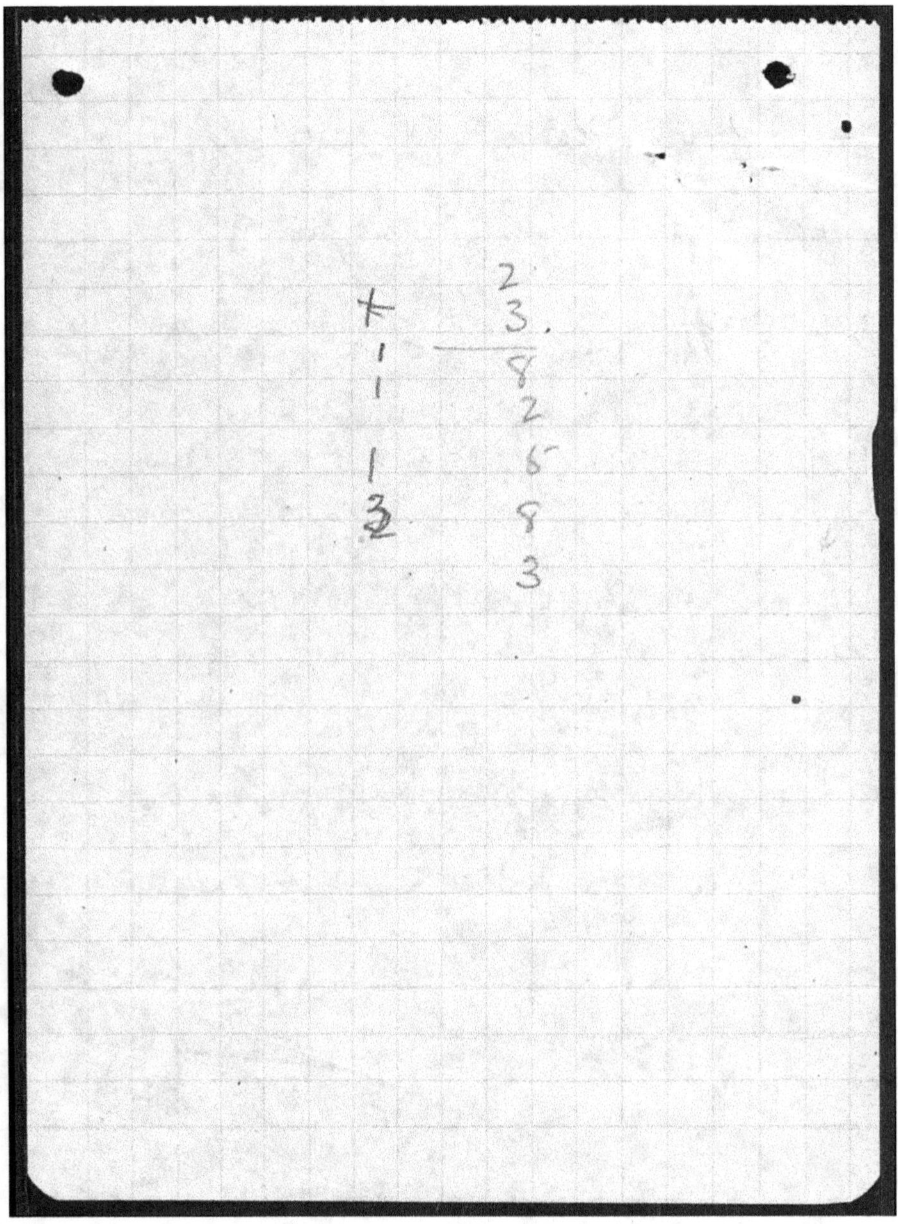
2
+ 3
1 8
1 2
1 5
3 8
3

Works Report from 6 p.m. 3-11-16 to 6 p.m. 4-11-16 [illegible]

Section	Locality	Description of work	Progress	Nos.	Sappers	Infantry	R.A.	Remarks
1	[illegible]	[illegible]	[illegible]	1	7			
			[illegible]	1	[illegible]			
		[illegible]		3	4	Nil.	Nil.	
2	[illegible]	[illegible]	[illegible]		2			
	[illegible]	[illegible]	[illegible]	1	3			
	[illegible]	[illegible]	[illegible]	1	3			
	[illegible]	[illegible]		1	2			
		[illegible]		1	7			
		[illegible]						
		[illegible]			6.			
		[illegible]	Completed.		2. [illegible]			
4	Buirelles	Repairing Billets Town Major	Continued.		2			
	"	Workshops.	"		3			
		Drying Room 89th Brigade	"	1				
	Pommier	Officers' Club	"	1	8			
	"	Well near billet 97	"		2			
	Cross Street	Well Section 1801	"	1	5			
		Gas guard Cooks with transport / Supply Wagon Hospital / Sick Sergt		3	8			
		with CRE			3			

C J Barker
2 Lieut RE
5/11/16

R. E. 46th. DIVISION.

DAILY WORK REPORT.

From 6-0 p.m. / / / . to 6-0 p.m. / / . UNIT 200 Field Coy RE

R. E. Offrs.	R. E. O.R.	R. E. Section.	WORKING PARTIES Offrs.	WORKING PARTIES O.R.	WORKING PARTIES Regiment.	WORK CARRIED OUT	Hours	REMARKS.
	8	1	—	—	—	Fire stepping 80, 81, ^	—	Completed
	5	1	—	—	—	Cross Street Dugouts	—	Shaft blown in Cork House dugout
1	14	1	—	—	—	Cooks, Orderly, Dump duties, Tool Cart duties, Batt^n Pump man, Pump House man, Sergt. Cover Coy HQ	—	
	2	(3)	–	–	–	Naked Street (Bridge)	–	Revetting Continue
	4	(3)	–	–	–	90 Support.		
	4	(3)				90 Street & 47 Firebays		
	3	(3)				Junction Support		
1	4/14 2 (included above)	(3)				Workshops, Dump Duties, Gas guard, Pumps, Cooks		
						Repairs to Brigade OP		Completed

L Hill
Lt RE
4.11.16

Works Report from 6 PM 4-11-16 1916 to 6 PM 5-11-16 1916 2nd [illegible] Field Coy RE

Section	Locality	Description of Work	Progress	Numbers Employed RE NCO	RE Sap	Inf	RA Band	Remarks
	St Cronstat	Clearing & Revetting	continued	1	2	56		
	Dugouts	Repairs & Air Shaft	8'-6" near completion	1	4	10		
	79 Support	Clearing & Revetting		1	3	40		
	General Support Salient	"			1	10		
					1	10		
	88th Support Left Coy	[illegible] Repairs			2			
	Pump Water	Pump Repairs		1	2	10		
		Cooks Orderlies [illegible]						
		and Water Pumping Sta			8			
				4	23			
	96 Support	Clearing & Revetting	Continued	1	3	20		
	90 Street	"			1	10		
	Machine [illegible]	Clearing Trench	"		2	10		
	[illegible] O.P.	Sinking Shaft	9 feet deep finished		1	5		
	Junction Support	Pumping of [illegible] & Draining	Complete	1	4	2		
	90 Fir Bay	Instructing Spl Rqds RE Revetting	Continued	1	1	–		
	Dump Duties	Gas Guard, Cooks, Stores, Workshops & Transport Sgt.	"	1	11			
				4	23			

J. Hill

Works Report from 6 pm. 4/11 1916 to 6 pm. 5/11 1916. 200th Field Co.R.E.

Section.	Locality.	Description of Work.	Progress.	Numbers employed. R.E. NCO.	Sprs.	Infy.	R.A. RAMC.	Remarks.
A	Pommiers [illegible]	[illegible]	"	1	9			
	[illegible]	[illegible]		—	2			
	[illegible]	[illegible]	Completed	1	—			
	[illegible]	Attached to No/ Section		[illegible]	[illegible]			
	[illegible]			—	3			
	[illegible]	[illegible]	———	1	2			
		[illegible]	———	—	2			
	[illegible]	[illegible]	———	1	1			
	[illegible]	[illegible]	———	—	1			
	[illegible] C.R.E.	———	———	—	5			
	[illegible]	———	———	—	4			
	[illegible]	———	———	—				
	[illegible]	———	———	1				
	[illegible]		———	—	1			
		[illegible] Section		6	31			[illegible] Capt. R.E. 5-11-16

Weekly Report from ... 6.9.16 ... 200

Section	Locality	Description of Work	Progress	Numbers Employed R.E. N.C.O.	Sprs	Inf.		Remarks
1	Cross Street	Clearing & revetting.	11 U frames 700 cub. ft excavated.	1	2	34		
	" Dugouts							
	79 Support	Clearing & revetting	3 Wedding Arches 600 Cu. Ft Earth excavated	1	3	40		
	88 "	" "	2 U frames 160 cub. ft excavated		1	8		
	Support Salient	" "	200 cu. ft earth excavated.		1	10		
	Dump duties, Orderlies etc	Pump House, Cooks	– – – – – –	1	9	20		
	Cross Street	No 2 Cook-house air shaft finished & steps completed No 7 Mined dugout 3 drives		1	4		22	
3.	90 Support.	Revetting	8 Frames with Hurdles & Trench boards	1	3.	20.		
	90 Street	do			1	10.		
	Naked Street.	do.	6 " "					
	94 Mined OP.	Sinking shaft.	2 Wedding arches with hurdles & T.board.		2	5.		
			4 feet dug. Now 13' deep.		1	5.		
	92 Street.	Clearing & Draining.	Cleared to 91 Street.	1	2	54.		
	90 Fire bay.	Instructing "Special" Bgde R.E.	5 Frames.	1	1	—		
	Nobs Walk.	Anchoring back pickets	—	X	1	5.		
	Dump Duties, Workshops, Cooks, Gas Guard. Pumps.			1	12			

J. Hall ... 6/9/16

WORK REPORT from 6 PM 5/11 to 6 PM 6/11 1916 200th Field Coy RE

Section	Locality	Description of Work	Progress	Numbers Employed R.E. N.C.O.	R.E. Sprs	Infy	R.A. [illegible]	Remarks
4	[illegible] Officers Club	[illegible] Field [illegible] [illegible] [illegible] [illegible] [illegible] [illegible] [illegible] [illegible]	[illegible] completed	1	8	6		Infantry employed [illegible]
	[illegible]	Repairs [illegible] of Bath House	Completed	—	2			
	[illegible]	[illegible] to [illegible] Billet No 97	[illegible] to complete	1	1			
	[illegible]	Workshops	—	—	3			
	Cross Street	Work Section No 7	—	1	6			
	[illegible] HQ	Guard	—	1	2			
	"	Cooks	—	—	2			
		Camp orderlies	—	—	1			
	[illegible]	Workshops	—	1	1			
	"	Supply wagon	—	—	1			
		Work C.R.E.	—	—	3			
		Hospital	—	—	1			
		England	—	1	—			

Strength of Section 6 31

[illegible]
[illegible]

[illegible] 6/11 [illegible] 7/11 [illegible] 200[illegible]

1	Cross Street	Clearing & revetting & [illegible]	[illegible] frames fixed & [illegible]	1	2	16	
	"		[illegible] fixed & [illegible]	1	5	10	
	"	Dug outs	[illegible] frames [illegible] steps [illegible] dugout [illegible]			*22	
		H.Q. Dugout	Four frames fixed			* 7	
	79 Support	Clearing & revetting	[illegible] frames fixed 7 firesteps fixed 20 x [illegible] cleared	1	4	23	
	88 "	" "	4 frames fixed & revetted & [illegible]		1	10	
	General Support Salient	" "	30 yds trench cleared		1	10	
	Left Comp. Dugouts	Framing.	[illegible] re propped & [illegible]		2		
	Cooks, orderlies	water supply, pump men, [illegible] dump	----------		12		
				3/5	27	27.	
3	90 Support	Revetting & excavating	One frame & Trench Cleared.	1	3	20	
	90 Street	" " & carrying	1 " " "		1	10	
	91 & 92 Support	Clearing Trench.	[illegible] Returned by [illegible]	1	2	60	
	Naked	Revetting & excavation	1 [illegible] arch		1	10	
WD.	Newark Street	Clearing trench	Slow		1	10	

Work Report from 6 PM 6/11 1916 to 6 PM 7/11 1916 200 Field Coy RE

Section	Locality	Description of Work	Progress	Numbers Employed: N.C.Os	R.E. [illegible]	Infantry	R.E. [illegible]	Remarks
3 (cont)	90 Fire Bay	Preparing Trench	Slow	1	1	—		Still Special C. of RE.
	New Street TMB	x Dugout [illegible]			1	8x		
	44 Mud OP.	Sinking Shaft	Pumping Shaft		1	8x		All work very much retarded owing to the rain & progress made very poor.
	Newark Street OP.	Rebuilding OP.	Complete		2			
	Billet B1	Dugout Shaft	Half finished		1	10x		
	Cooks Hse Comp. Pumps Sergt	Camp [illegible]		1	9	14x		x Attached to RE for dugout work.
				4/5	[illegible]/26			

Report from 6PM [illegible] 1916 to 6PM [illegible] 1916 Field Coy RE

Section	Locality	Description of Work	Progress	Numbers Employed N.C.O.	Sprs	Inf	R.A.M.C.	Remarks
	[illegible]	[illegible]		1	2			
		[illegible]			3			
	"	[illegible]			1			
	"	[illegible]		—	1			
	Pommier Officers Club	[illegible]	[illegible]	1	5			
	Divisional Line	Survey	———	1	1			
	Pommier	[illegible] Bde 97 [illegible] H.Q.	Completed	—				
	"	[illegible]			1			
	Cross Street	Well Section No 1		1	3			
	Pommier H.Q.	Gas guard	———	1	2			
	"	Cellar	———		2			
	[illegible]	[illegible]	———	1	1			
		Supply [illegible]	———		1			
	With C.R.E.	———	———	—	3			
	[illegible]	———	———	1	1			
		[illegible]						

WORK REPORT from 6am 7-11 to 6am 8-11 1916 [illegible] Field Coy

Section	Locality	Description of Work	Progress	Numbers Employed R.E. N.C.O.	R.E. men	Infy.	[illegible]	Remarks
[illegible]	[illegible] Cross St	Fixing frames [illegible]	17 [illegible] frames [illegible]	1	2	32		
[illegible]	[illegible]		[illegible]					
[illegible]	[illegible]	[illegible] tunnel	[illegible]	1	3	6		
[illegible]	28 "	[illegible] tunnel	20 yds [illegible]		4	10		
[illegible]	[illegible] Support [illegible]	do do	30 "		1	0		
	Camp [illegible] Cooks. Orderlies. Company [illegible]			21	11			
	[illegible] St	No 1 Dug out Completed No 2 " " No 3 " " No 6 " " No 7 " "	[illegible] + [illegible] slips Repair to roof [illegible] [illegible] frames [illegible] slips Made 5 slips [illegible] 3'-0" [illegible]		4	22		
3	[illegible]	[illegible]	50 [illegible] 20 [illegible]	1	5	20 10		
	[illegible]	[illegible]	[illegible]		2	60		
	[illegible]	[illegible]			1			
	[illegible]	[illegible]		1	1	–		
	[illegible]	[illegible] Gulls	3 frames [illegible]	1	1 2	10		
	[illegible]	[illegible]	2 [illegible]		1	6		
	[illegible]	[illegible]			1	6		
	[illegible]	[illegible]			1	2		
	[illegible]	[illegible]				4		

J. Hill

Works Report from 6 pm. 7/11 1916 to 6 pm. 8/11 1916. Field Co.R.E.

Section.	Locality.	Description of Work.	Progress.	Numbers employed R.E. NCO.	Numbers employed R.E. Sprs.	Infy.	R.A. RAMC.	Remarks.
4	Bienvillers.	Repairing Billet No 89 for Town Major.	Nearly Completed	—	2.			
	" "	Workshops.		—	3			
	" "	Workshops - preparing Sashes for. Officers Club.	Completed tomorrow	—	2			
	Cross Street	With Section No 1.		1	5			
	89 Street.	With Section No 1		—	2			
	Pommier Officers' Club.	Panelling upper room - Repairing windows damaged by Shell fire - Clearing Yard		1	3			
	Pommier HQ.	Camp duties		—	1			
	" "	Repairing Billets		—	1			Excused Equipment
		Sick	——	—	1			Assisting at Officers' Club afternoon.
	Divisional Line	Survey	——	1	1			
	With CRE	——	——	—	3			
	[illegible]	Workshops	——	1	1			
	"	Supply wagon	——	—	1			
			——	—	2			
	Pommier HQ.	Cooks						
	" "	Gas guard		1	2			
		Hospital.		—	1			
	89 Street.	Heavy Trench Mortar Emplacement		1				
				6	31			

C J Barker
2/Lieut RE

8/11/16.

Work Report from 6th Nov 1916 to 10th Nov 1916 20th Field Co. R.E.

Section	Locality	Description of Work	Progress	Numbers employed: N.C.O.	Spr.	Inf.	Att.	Remarks
[illegible]	[illegible]	[illegible]	[illegible]	1	2	30		
[illegible]	[illegible]		[illegible]	[illegible]	3	6		
[illegible]	[illegible]		[illegible]	1	4	10		
[illegible]	[illegible]	Clearing up Trench & Draining	[illegible]		1	10		
[illegible]	[illegible]	[illegible]			2			
	[illegible]	[illegible]		2	10			
	[illegible]	[illegible]			1	[illegible]	6	
	[illegible]	[illegible]			4		4	
	[illegible]	[illegible]			2		10	
	[illegible]	[illegible]			1		6	

[illegible]

9/11/16

WORKS REPORT [illegible] [illegible] Field Coy R.E.

Section	Locality	Description of Work	Progress	Numbers Employed R.E. N.C.O.s	Numbers Employed R.E. men	Numbers Employed Infy	Numbers Employed [illegible]	REMARKS
3	Ao Support	[illegible]	5 U frames [illegible]	1	2	20	[illegible]	
	[illegible]	" "	[illegible]		1	10		
	[illegible]	[illegible]	[illegible]		1	24		
	[illegible]	[illegible]	7 frames [illegible]	1	1	40		
	[illegible]	[illegible]	2 [illegible]	1	8	8		
	[illegible]	[illegible]	[illegible]		1	–	2	
	[illegible]	[illegible]	11 frames [illegible]		1	15		
	[illegible]	[illegible]	[illegible]		1		8	
	[illegible]	[illegible]	[illegible]				8	
	[illegible]	[illegible]	[illegible]		1		6	
	[illegible]	[illegible]	[illegible]		1		2	
	[illegible]	[illegible]	[illegible]	1	10		4	

[illegible signature]

WORK'S REPORT from [illegible] /11 up to [illegible] 9/11 1916 Field Coy R.E.

Section	Locality	Description of Work	Progress	Numbers Employed R.E. NCOs	R.E. Sprs	Infy	R.A. R.A.M.C.	Remarks
1	[illegible]	Repairs to Billet-89 for Town Major	Nearly Complete	–	2			
	"	Workshops.		–	3			
	"	" preparing [illegible] for Officers' Club [illegible]	Nearly Complete	–	1			
	"	Repairing Pumps, Factory		–	2			
	Cross Street	Well [illegible] No 1		1	7			
	89 Street	Trench Mortar [illegible]		1	–			
	[illegible] Officers Club	Repairing windows [illegible] [illegible] Billiard [illegible] [illegible]		1	3			
	[illegible]	[illegible]		1	1			
	[illegible] H.Q.	Cooks.		–	2			
		Camp [illegible]		–	1			
		[illegible] Camp		–	1			
		[illegible] Guard		1	2			
	[illegible]	Workshops.		4	1			
		Supply wagon		–	1			
	With C.R.E.			–	3			
	Hospital			–	1			
				6	31			

[illegible signature]
Lieut. R.E.
9/11/16.

WORKS REPORT from 6 pm. 9th Nov 1916 to 6 pm. 10th Nov 1916 200th Field Coy R.E.

Section	Locality	Description of Work	Progress	Numbers Employed R.E. NCO's	Sappers	Infy.	Digger	Remarks
[illegible]	77 Fire Trench	Shelter [redacted]	Completed	1	4			no Infantry
[redacted]	St. Cross St	Fixing the frames & Revetting	12 frames fixed & revetted	1	6			
[illegible]		Fixing Building Shelter & Revetting	2 [illegible] fixed & revetted 2 yds [illegible] revetted	1	6			
[illegible]	Pump Duties Orderlies	Cooks, Tool Cart, Pumping Station		2	9			
	[illegible] St	[illegible] No 2 Cookhouse repaired [illegible] [redacted] [illegible]	[illegible]	1	4		[illegible]	

Shell St Decauville Track was completed last night

[illegible signature]

Works Report [illegible] Field Coy R.E.

Section	Locality	Description of Work	Progress	Number Employed R.E. NCOs	Sappers	Infantry	Other	Remarks
3	[illegible]	[illegible]	[illegible]	1	2	—	[illegible]	No Infantry [illegible]
					1	—		
	[illegible]	[illegible]	[illegible]	1	2		2	
	[illegible]	[illegible]	[illegible]		1		6	
	[illegible]	[illegible]	[illegible]		1		[illegible]	
		[illegible]	[illegible]					
					1		2	4-14
	[illegible]	[illegible]	[illegible]	1	4			
	[illegible]	[illegible]	[illegible]					
	[illegible]	[illegible]	[illegible]	1	1		2	
	[illegible]	[illegible]			1			
	[illegible]	[illegible]						
	[illegible]	[illegible]	[illegible]		1		[illegible]	
	[illegible]	[illegible]			7		[illegible]	
	[illegible]	[illegible]						

[illegible]

Works Report from 6 pm. [illegible] 1916 to 6 pm. [illegible] 1916. [illegible] Field Co.R.E.

Section.	Locality.	Description of Work.	Progress.	Numbers employed R.E. NCO.	Numbers employed R.E. Sprs.	Infy.	R.A. RAMC.	REMARKS.
[illegible]	[illegible]	[illegible]		[illegible]	[illegible]			[illegible]
		[illegible]		[illegible]	[illegible]			
		[illegible]	[illegible]	-	2			
		[illegible]		-	2			
	[illegible]	[illegible]		1	[illegible]			
	[illegible]	Signing		1	1			
	[illegible]	[illegible]		1	-			
	[illegible]	[illegible]		[illegible]	[illegible]			
	[illegible]	[illegible]		[illegible]	1			
	[illegible]	[illegible]		[illegible]	[illegible]			
	[illegible]	[illegible]		[illegible]	[illegible]			
	[illegible]				[illegible]			

[illegible]

Works Report from 6 pm. 1916 to 6 pm. 1916. Field Co.R.E.

Section.	Locality.	Description of Work.	Progress.	Numbers employed				REMARKS.
				R.E.			R.A.	
				NCO.	Sprs.	Infy.	RAMC.	

Works Report from 6 pm. [illegible] 1916 to 6 pm. [illegible] 1916. [illegible] Field Co. R.E.

Section.	Locality.	Description of work.	Progress.	Numbers employed R.E. NCO.	R.E. Sprs.	Infy.	R.A. RAMC.	REMARKS.
2	90 Support	Excavating & Revetting	[illegible]	1	2	12	[illegible]	
	90 Street	" "	Complete		1	20		
	91 Support	" "	[illegible]		1			
	92 Support	" "	[illegible]	1	1	20		
4	New Street	Clearing trench & [illegible]	[illegible]	1	4	—		
3	Newmarket Street	Excavating & revetting	[illegible]		1	15		
	93 Support	Clearing trenches	Complete	1	—	40		
	Nairne St Bridge	Completed, erecting bridge			1	—		
	[illegible] O.P.	Timbering & [illegible]	[illegible]		1		6	
	[illegible] H.Q.	[illegible]	[illegible]		1		2	
	New Street [illegible]	[illegible]	[illegible]		1		6	
	Right Coy H.Q.	"	[illegible]		1		6	
	96 Lewis Gun [illegible]	Repairing	[illegible] Complete		1		3	
	Pump [illegible]				1			
	Bde [illegible]	[illegible]					2	
	Dump [illegible]	[illegible] Gas [illegible]	Transport & [illegible]	10			4	
	Leave						1	

[illegible]

Works Report from 6 pm. [illegible] 1916 to 6 pm. [illegible] 1916. [illegible] Field Co.R.E.

Section.	Locality.	Description of Work.	Progress.	Numbers employed R.E. NCO.	Numbers employed R.E. Sprs.	Infy.	R.A. RAMC.	REMARKS.
[illegible]	[illegible]	[illegible]		–	2			
		[illegible]		–	3			
		[illegible]	[illegible]	–	1			
		[illegible]		–	2			
	[illegible]	[illegible] Section No 1		1	6			
		[illegible] Section No 3		1	4			
	[illegible]	[illegible]	Completed.	–	1			
	[illegible]	[illegible]		1	1			
	[illegible]	[illegible]		–	1			
		[illegible]		1	2			
		[illegible]		–	2			
	[illegible]	[illegible]		1	1			
		[illegible]		–	1			
	With C.R.E.			–	3			
	Hospital			–	1			
	[illegible]	[illegible]		1	–			[illegible]
				6	31			[illegible]

Works Report from 6 pm. [illegible] 1916 to 6 pm. [illegible] 1916. [illegible] Field Co.R.E.

Section.	Locality.	Description of Work.	Progress.	Numbers employed R.E. NCO.	Numbers employed R.E. Sprs.	Infy	R.A. RAMC.	REMARKS.
[illegible]	[illegible]	[illegible]	[illegible]		7			
		[illegible]	[illegible]		1		6	
		[illegible]	[illegible]		1		6	
		[illegible]	[illegible]		1		6	
	[illegible]	[illegible]	[illegible]		1		4	
	[illegible]	[illegible]	[illegible]		1		4	
[illegible]	[illegible]	[illegible]	[illegible]	[illegible]	[illegible]	[illegible]	[illegible]	[illegible]

Works Report from 6 pm. 11/11/16 1916 to 6 pm. 12/11/16 1916. [illegible]th Field Co. R.E.

Section.	Locality.	Description of Work.	Progress.	Numbers employed R.E. NCO.	R.E. Sprs.	Infy.	R.A. RAMC.	REMARKS.
4	Brasseries.	Preparing Billets for Town Major No 56.			1			
		Workshops.			3			
	"	Preparing shelves for Officers' Club [illegible]	completed		1			
	[illegible] St.	[illegible] Section No 1		1	6			
	New St.	" " No 3		1	5			
	Brasseries.	Repairs to pump factory.			2			
	Divisional Lines.	Survey.			1			
	[illegible] HQ	Camp duties			1			
		Gas guard		1	2			
		Locks.			2			
		Camp repairs.			1			Light duty
	[illegible]	Workshops		1	1			
		Supply wagon			1			
	Attd CRE				3			
	Hospital [illegible]				1			
	29 Street	Trench Mortar Emplacement		1	—			
	[illegible] Chiswick avenue	advising Artillery as to clearing & reconstructing		1	—			
				6	31			

C G [illegible]
Lieut RE
13/11/16.

Works Report from 6 PM 11-11-1916 to 6 PM 12-11-1916 [illegible] Field Coy RE

Section	Locality	Description of Work	Progress	R.E. NCO	R.E. Sprs	Inf	Att'd	Remarks
No 1	St Cross St	Fixing Frames & Revetting	160 frames fixed 80 yds of Trench Revetted & Sumps	1	8	40		Inf 30 carrying material
No 4	do do		[illegible] 4 yds of Trench Revetted	1	6	10		6
No 1	Dump	Dump Duties		1	2	10		
No 1	Pumping Sta. Sick & Sergt	Cooks, [illegible] orderlies, Painting		2	7			
	Cross St	Dugouts	[illegible]					
	No 1 [illegible]	[illegible]	[illegible]					
	[illegible]	[illegible]	[illegible] finished					
	RE Dugout	[illegible]						
	[illegible] St. S.	[illegible]	Chamber [illegible]	1	4		27	
		Cooks & Gas Picket					3	
No 3	91-92 Support	Excavating & revetting	Fixed 24 U frames	3	14	40		
	94 [illegible] O.P.	Finishing & excavating	Shaft, bottom chamber complete.		1	–	6.	
No 2	[illegible] Support Dugout	Retimbering Dugout	Lined 2 [illegible] Cross & 3 Supports	1	4		9.	
No 3	[illegible]	Clearing entrances & Dugout	20 yards of trench cleared.		1		9.	
	40 [illegible]	Instruction [illegible] Bde RE Revetting.		1	–	–	–	
	Dump	Store Guard, Gas Guard, Pumps, Cooks, & Transport of material			7		4	
							1	Sick

[illegible signature]

Works Report from 6 pm. 12/11 1916 to 6 pm. 13/11 1916. 20th Field Co. R.E.

Section.	Locality.	Description of Work.	Progress.	Numbers employed R.E. NCO.	R.E. Sprs.	Infy.	R.A. RAMC.	REMARKS.
4	Bienvillers	Repairs to Billet 456	Almost completed		2			
		Town Major			1			
	" "	Workshops erecting beds in Factory	4 erected.		1			
	Cross Street	Wells Section No 1		1	6			
	Middle Street	Wells Section No 3		1	5			
	Pommier	Repairs to well opposite Church			1			
	Bienvillers	Repairs to pump in Factory			2			
	Pommier HQ	Camp duties			1			
		Gas guard		1	2			
		Cooks			2			
	Laherlière	Workshops		1	3			
		Supply wagon			1			
	With CRE				3			
	Hospital Sergeant				1			
		Heavy Trench Mortar		1				
		Emplacement (Supervision)		1				
				6	31			C J Barker Lieut RE 13/11/16.

Works Report from 6 pm. 1916 to 6 pm. 1916. Field Co.R.E.

Section.	Locality.	Description of Work.	Progress.	Numbers employed R.E. NCO.	Numbers employed R.E. Sprs.	Numbers employed Infy.	Numbers employed R.A. RAMC.	REMARKS.
				2	7			

Works Report from 6 pm. 13/11/16. 1916 to 6 pm. 14/11/16 1916. 2nd Field Co. R.E.

Section.	Locality.	Description of Work.	Progress.	Numbers employed R.E. NCO.	R.E. Sprs.	Infy.	R.A. RAMC.	REMARKS.
4	Bienvillers.	Repairing Billets for Town Major No 5b.			2			
	" "	Repairs to pump in factory			2			
	St. Cross St.	Work - Section No 1		1	6			
		Work - Section No 3		1	5			
	Pommier.	Repairs to well opposite Church.			2			
	" HQ	Cooks			2			
		Gas guard		1	2			
		Camp duties.			1			
		Repairs to Cycles.			1			
	Lattre	Workshops		1	3			
	"	Supply wagon			1			
	With CRE				3			
	Hospital				1			
	89 Street.	Trench Mortar Emplacement Supervision.		1				
	Sergeant.			1				
				6	31			C J Barker 2/Lieut RE 14/11/16

Works Report from 6 pm. [illegible] 1916 to 6 pm. [illegible] 1916. [illegible] Field Co.R.E.

Section.	Locality.	Description of work.	Progress.	Numbers employed R.E. NCO.	Sprs.	Infy.	R.A. RAMC.	REMARKS.
[illegible]	[illegible]	[illegible]	[illegible]	1	5	~~7~~6		
		[illegible]	[illegible]					
[illegible]	Dump	[illegible]	[illegible] material to [illegible]	1		6		
	Pumping Sta		[illegible]	1	3		12	
	[illegible]	[illegible] Painting	[illegible]	1	1			
	[illegible]	[illegible]	[illegible]					
			[illegible]	1	1		15	
			[illegible]				3	
No. 3	91 + 92 support	[illegible] frames and [illegible]	[illegible] 20 frames and	2	1	40		
	94 mined O.P.	[illegible] shaft and [illegible] gallery	[illegible] and excavated [illegible]		1		2	
	Noodle Ave [illegible]	Repairs	[illegible] ~~[illegible]~~		1		4	
	Noodle Ave support dug out	Repairs	[illegible] 3 [illegible] and [illegible]	1			6	
	pump	Repairs to pumps	Repairs to pumps					
	pumps & billets	pumps, cooks & gas			1			
					6			

[illegible signature]

Works Report from 6 pm. 13/11 1916 to 6 pm. 14/11 1916. 2nd Field Co.R.E.

Section.	Locality.	Description of Work.	Progress.	Numbers employed R.E. NCO.	R.E. Sprs.	Infy.	R.A. RAMC.	REMARKS.
4.	Cross Street	with Section No 1		1	6			
	Pommier.	Repairs to well near Clinic.	Winding gear fixed grappling for rubbish in bottom		1			
	Farnborough Rd. Pommier HQ.	Dugouts for B.H.Q.		1	2			
		Cooks.			2			
		Gas guard			2			
		Camp duties.			1			
	[illegible]	Day off		2	[illegible]			
	– " –	Workshops.		1	[illegible]			
		Supply wagon			1			
	With C.R.E.				3			
	Hospital.				1			rejoined to-night 15/11/16
	Leave.			1	1			
					2			
				6	32			

[signature]
Lieut R.E.
15/11/16.

WORKS REPORT from 6 a.m. [illegible] to 6 a.m. [illegible] 1916 [illegible] Field Coy. R.E.

Section	Locality	Description of Work	Progress	Number Employed: R.E. Mos	R.E. Sprs	Infy	R.A.M.C.	Remarks
[illegible]	[illegible]	[illegible]	[illegible]	1	2			
	[illegible]	[illegible]	[illegible]	1	3			
	[illegible]	[illegible]	[illegible]	2	7			[illegible]
	[illegible]		[illegible]	1	2	12		[illegible]
	[illegible]	[illegible]				3		
	[illegible]					5		
	[illegible]				1			
	[illegible]	[illegible]			5			[illegible]
	[illegible]				1			
	[illegible]				1			[illegible]
					1			[illegible]
				5/5	27/29			
[illegible]	[illegible]	[illegible]	[illegible]					
	[illegible]	[illegible]	[illegible]		1	3		
	[illegible]	[illegible]	[illegible]		1	2		
		[illegible]	[illegible]	1	1	4		
	[illegible]	[illegible]			6	4		
	[illegible]	[illegible]				18		
	[illegible]	[illegible]			5			[illegible]
					1			
				1	1			
	[illegible]	[illegible]			2			[illegible]
		[illegible]			1			[illegible]
		[illegible]		1				[illegible]
	[illegible]			1	1			
				5/5	28/27	2		[illegible]

[illegible]

Works Report from 6 pm. 15/11/ 1916 to 6 pm. 16/11/16 1916. 2nd Field Co. R.E.

Section.	Locality.	Description of Work.	Progress.	Numbers employed R.E. NCO.	Numbers employed R.E. Sprs.	Infy.	R.A. RAMC.	Remarks.
4.	Fanborough Road Batt. Dug-outs	Cleaning out rubbish & falls in dug-outs & drawing new sleeping.	2 dugouts & 5 entrances cleared.	2	8	15		15 Special dug-out party
	" "	Do & retimbering		2	9	15		15 Special dug-out party. This party commenced work 4 p.m.
	Pommiers HQ.	Cooks			2			
		Gasguard			2			
		Camp duties			1			
	Laberliere	Workshops		1	3			
	"	Supply wagon			1			
	With CRE				3			
	On leave			1	1			
	Bienvillers	repairs to pump.			2			
				6	32			

16/11/16.

C J Barker
2 Lieut RE

Work Report from 6PM 16th Nov 1916 to 6PM 17th Nov 1916 200th Field Coy R.E.

Section	Locality	Description of Work	Progress	Numbers Employed R.E. NCOs	R.E. Sprs	Inf.	RA RAMC	Remarks
No 1	Cross St	Fixing & Revetting 11 Frames	11 frames fixed & 30 yds of trench revetted	1	4	30	[illegible]	23 carrying material
	"	Dug outs	Drove 3'0" fixed frames 6'0" Revetted & made 5" steps	1	3	-	9	
	Billet 165	Dug outs	Drove 3-0 & fixed frames				3	
	Dump	Dump Duties	Cooks for Pickets & Sick				4	
	Pumping Station	Repair to Pump	Transport & repair to Pumps & Hose	1	3	10		
		Toolcart Duties		1	1	—		Sep Boys [illegible] Section
		Orderlies			1			
		Cooks			2			
		H.Q. 200th Fd Coy RE Workshops			2			
		Sick			5			one [illegible]
		Hospital			2			[illegible]
		At Rest in Billets			1			
		On Leave			3			
		Sergeant		1	1			
				5/5	28/28			
No 3	91 & 92 Support	Frames & Revetments	14 fixed	1	7	54		7
	New Street	Repairs to Trench	Trench cleared	x	1	6		
	91 Mine P.	Driving gallery	Excavated 2'6" [illegible]	1			5	
	Support Dugout	Timbering	Reframed 6 props [illegible]		1		4	
	Attachs: Cooks Gas Guard				6		4	
	Pump man				1			
	Attached to HQ. 200 Workshops				5			(one Farrier)
	" " Divl HQ				2			
	" " 11th Borders						14	
	" " AHQ 18 Corps			1.	1			
	On Leave			1	1			
	At Rest (1 day per week)			1	2.			
	Hospital				1		1	
	Sick (1 Excused only light duty)							
				5/5	25/25			

A Mould [illegible] RE

WORKS REPORT from 6 PM 1916 to 6 PM 1916 Field Coy RE

Section	Locality	Description of Work	Progress	Numbers Employed				Remarks
				RE NCOs	RE Sprs	Infr	RA RAMC	

WORK REPORT from 6 PM 17/11/ 1916 to 6 PM 18/11/ 1916 203rd Field Coy R.E.

Section	Locality	Description of Work	Progress	Numbers Employed: A NCOs	E Sprs	Inf	RA RAMC	Remarks
4	Battle Dugouts Farnborough Road	Framing entrance passage.						
		Reframing 2 Staircases.	Roof Sheeting 4 frames fixed 6 frames fixed.					
		Framing Chamber at end of first Staircase on the right & propping roof.	1 frame fixed	2	8	13		Night Party
		Clearing of floor in two large dug outs & [illegible] recesses for [illegible].		2	9	15		Day Party
		Framing in 5th Staircase & repairing	2 frames taken out & refixed.					had to be abandoned owing to very heavy [illegible]
		Clearing away rubbish, &c.						
	Pommiers HQ	3 Cooks.						
		Gasguard						
		Camp duties.			2			
	Salvage.				2			
		Workshops.			1			
	With C.R.E.	Supply wagon		1	3			
	On Leave				1			
					3			
	Brummers.	Repairs to Pump		1	1			
					2			

C J Barker
2nd Lieut R.E.
18/11/16.

Works Report [illegible] 19th [illegible] 20th Field Coy RE

Section	Locality	Description of Work	Progress	Numbers Employed: RE NCOs	RE Sappers	Inf.	RA / Infantry	Remarks
[illegible]	[illegible]	[illegible]	[illegible]		[illegible]			
	[illegible]	[illegible]	[illegible]	1	1	[illegible]		
		[illegible]			1			
		[illegible]			2			
	[illegible]	[illegible]		1	1			
	[illegible]	[illegible]			1			
[illegible] No. 5	93 Support	[illegible] Frames and [illegible]	Fixed 5 Frames	1	4	30		
No. 5			Fixed 5 Frames	2	2			
	[illegible]	[illegible]	[illegible]		1		6	
	99 [illegible]	[illegible]	Excavated and [illegible]					
	[illegible]	[illegible] M.G. [illegible]	[illegible]	1	1	12		
		[illegible]	Repairs to [illegible]		1		2	
	[illegible]		[illegible] 6 [illegible] 2 frames		2		6	
	[illegible]	[illegible]	Excavation [illegible]				5	
	[illegible]						14	
		Pumps		1	4			
	[illegible]	[illegible]			1			
	[illegible]				6		4	
	[illegible]						2	
							1	
	[illegible]			1	1			
					2			

[illegible]

Works Report from 6 pm. 18/11/16 1916 to 6 pm. 19/11/ 1916. 200th Field Co.R.E.

Section.	Locality.	Description of Work.	Progress.	Numbers employed R.E. NCO.	Sprs.	Infy.	R.A. RAMC.	REMARKS.
4.	Battn. Dug outs Farnborough Road.	1st Staircase on left all frames refixed perpendicular to Slope 2 Entrance frames fixed Roof Sheeted.		2	9	15		Day party
		1st Staircase on right.	2 entrance frames fixed & Sheeted Sandbag revetment built	2	8	15		Night party
		Entrance passage	Framed & revetted.					
		2nd Staircase on right.	Frames re-erected square with Slope. Steps half finished					
		Small dug-out at end of 1st Staircase on right.	2 frames fixed Cavity in roof propped & partly filled in.					
		Cleaning out falls &c						
	Laluliere.	Workshops.		1	3			
		Supply wagon			1			
	With C.R.E.				3			
	Brenvillers	Repairs to Pump	———		2			Handed over
		Cooks	———		2			
	Berles H.Q.	Gas guard	———		2			
		Camp duties	———		1			
	On leave			1	1			
				6	32			C J Barker Lieut RE 19/11/16.

WORK REPORT. From 6pm 19th/11/16 to 6pm 20/11/16. 200 Field Coy RE.

SECTION	LOCALITY	DESCRIPTION OF WORK	PROGRESS	Numbers Employed. RE NCO's	Sappers	Inf.	Dugouts	REMARKS.
No 1	Nuts Road	Revetting	6 yds revetted		3	10		Infantry Carrying
	Farn Boro Rd		5'0"	1	6	20		" "
	200th Field Co	Workshops	Vlast, Doors & Pins fixed		5			
	La Bauchie Dump	Erecting Nissen Hut			2			
		Dump Duties		1	3.	10		(One No 4 Section).
		Cooks			2			
		orderly			1			
		Tool Cart Duties			1			
		On Leave			1			
		At Rest in Billets		1	2			
		Sergt		1				
	Nutt Road HQ	Dug outs	Excavated 3-0' Fixed 3 frames Drove 2'-0'	1	1		12	
	Attached	to Lt Barker	2 Cooks 1 Gas Guard				3 15	
No 3.	93 Support.	Frames & Revetting	Fixed 8 frames	2	5.	30		
	94 Mines OP.	Driving Gallery.	(Fixed 5 Mining frames (Driven Gallery 4'.		1	x	4.	
	Newark Street	Repairs to dugout Signallers	Not Complete.		1		6.	
	99 Trench	Preparing frames for [illegible].	Excavated.		1	12.		
	Attached	to Headquarters		1	9.			
	Pumpman				1			
	~~[illegible]~~ NEVERENDING St	[illegible] M.G.E.	Two frames for Instruction		1			
	Special Bge RE.			1.				
	Dump Loading Gas Rocket.				6.	x	4.	
	Attached	to Lt Barker					14	
	Hospital & Sick.						3.	
	Leave			1	1.	[illegible]		
	Resting (one day per week)							

J Leslie [illegible] RE.

Works Report from 6 pm. 19/11/16 to 6 pm. 20/11/16 — 205th Field Co. R.E.

Section	Locality	Description of work	Progress	Numbers Employed: R.E. NCO	Numbers Employed: R.E. Spr	Numbers Employed: Infy	Numbers Employed: RA RAMC	Remarks
4	Battn H.Q. Tamborough Road.	Small room at end of 1st passage on right.	Two frames erected and roof packed					
		Passage leading to room	2 frames erected	2	9			Day-party
		4 staircases leading into dug-outs.	forming steps					
			5 frames erected in Entrances	2	10			Night-party
			Revetting sides commenced in two					
			Strutting between frames					
		Entrance Passage	Frames erected roof & sides revetted.					
		Cut & cover dug-outs	Framing commenced in one. Sills placed 6 props ready for framing					
	Berles H.Q.	Cooks			2			
		Gasguard			2			
		Camp duties			1			
	Laherlière	Workshops		1	3			
		Supply wagon			1			
	With C.R.E.				2			
	On leave			1	1			
	With section No. 1				1			
				6	32			

C J Barker
2 Lieut R.E.

20/11/16.

Copy

WORK REPORT from 6pm 20th 11/1916 to 6pm 21st 11/1916 200 Field Coy RE

Section	Locality	Description of Work	Progress	NCO's	R.E. Saprs	Infy	RA RAMC	Remarks
No 1	Nuts Road	Revetting & Picketting back	20x Completed	1	4	14		Dugouts
	Farnborough "	"	12x " 25x anchored	1	3	16		
	~~Hersin~~ La Cauchie	Nissen Hut "	No material		2	-		
	Attached to No 4	Dugouts			2		15	
	RE Dump Berles	Dump duties		1	2	10		(1 at La Cauchie Dump)
	Orderly (2) cooks (4) Attest (3) Gasguard				6		3	
	Att to HQ workshops				5			
	On Leave				1			
	Hospital				1			
	Nuts Road	Dugout Coy HQ	Drove 5' fixed 3 frames	1	1		9	
	Sick No duty						3	
	Sergt			1				
No 3	93 Support	Revetting & Clearing	7 frames	2	4	22		
	94 Upper OP	Gallery excavation	4 frames fixed Drove 1ft		1	·	6	
	99 Trench	Shelter in traverse	fixed 4 frames		2	12		
	Signalers Dugout	Newark Street	Completed Repair		1	8	3	
	Attached to HQ	Workshops & Coy HQ		1	9			
	Pumpman				1			
	Neverending St	Anti aircraft Position	Excavating complete		1	3		
	Special Bde RE			1				
	Att to Lt Barker						14	
	Dump Cooks	gasguard			6		4	
	Hospital						3	
	On Leave			1	1			
	Rest				2			

[illegible] Lt RE

Copy

WORK REPORT from 6PM 20/11/1916 to 6PM 21/11/1916 200th Field Coy R.E.

Section	Locality	Description of Work	Progress	Numbers Employed R.E. NCO's	R.E. Sappers	Infy	RA Regmt	Remarks
4	Batt'n HQ in Farnborough Road	Shutting frames in entrance staircases. Reveting sides. Fixing frames in passage to small dug-out. Shuttering roof to do. Fixing frames in Signal Office	3 frames completed. One frame fixed	2	11	15		Night party
		Fixing bedding arch (?) in Main entrance. Sandbagging	One fixed.					
		Driving heading into small dug-out.	heading broken in one frame fixed.	2	10	14		Day party
		Cut cover dug-out.	Sills fixed & props erected in one dug-out ready for girders					
		Clearing away excavated material.						
	Billets HQ	Cooks.			2			
		Gas guard			2			
		Wheelwright			1			
	Lahoussière (?)	Workshops		1	3			
		Supply wagon			1			
	With CRE				2			
	On leave			1	1			
	With Section No 1				1			
			Including 2 sappers attached from No 1 Sect	6.	34			

C J Barker (?)
2 Lieut RE
21/11/16.

WORK REPORT from 6 PM 21st 11/1916 to 6 PM 27th 11/1916 200 FIELD Coy RE

Section	Locality	Description of Work	Progress	Numbers Employed RE NCOs	RE Sappers	Inf.	WA Admr	REMARKS.
No 1.	Huts Road.	Revetting	24 yards revetted	3	8	–		
	Lalcuchie	Nissen Hut	Sand boards & curb partly fixed 5.		2			
	200 FC workshops				5			
	Attached to No 4 Section				1		15.	
	At Rest.				3			
	Corps Dump Duties Orderly Tool Cart.				5.		3	
	On Leave				1			
	Sick				1		2	
	Sergt.			1				
	Dugout Huts Road Coy HQrs		Driven 4' fixed 1 frame	1	2	20*	10	*Emptying sandbags at night.
No 3	93 Support.	Revetting & Frames	5 fixed & revetted	3	2	–	–	
	94 Annex OP	Driving Gallery	Driven 2ft.		1		9.	
	99 Trench	Firing shelter.	Shelter erected but not complete		4		–	(2 at night.
	Ravelsberg Rd	Antiaircraft Emp.	Fixed 6 frames		2			
	Pumps				1			
	Att. Special Coy.			1				
	Dump Corps gasguard				6		4.	
	Att to Lt Barker.						14.	
	Hospital						3	
	On Leave			1	1.			
	Resting				2			
	Att HQrs workshops			1	9			

[signature]
11 RE

Works Report from 6PM 21/11/1916 to 6PM 22/11/1916 [illegible] Field Coy R.E.

Section	Locality	Description of Work	Progress	Numbers Employed: R.E. Nos Off.	Numbers Employed: R.E. men	Numbers Employed: Inf.	Numbers Employed: for [illegible]	Remarks
4.	B.H.Q. [illegible] Road.	Signal Office fixing frames & [illegible] sides.	[illegible] frames fixed	2	9/114	14		night party
		[illegible] for [illegible] [illegible] frames	Frames finished.					
		[illegible] Sheeting roof [illegible] sides & [illegible] between frames.		2	10/75	15		Day party
		[illegible] to [illegible] fixing frames & Sheeting roof.	4 frames fixed					
		Main Entrance fixing [illegible] frames.	3 fixed					
		Cut & Cover dug out	Frames & [illegible] & [illegible] 3 [illegible] erected. Sills laid & 3 posts erected.					
	Details H.Q.	Cooks.			2			
		Gas Guard			2			
		Wheelwright.			1			
	[illegible]	Workshops		1	3			
		Supply Wagon			1			
	[illegible] C.R.E.				2			
					1			
		attached to No 1 Section		1	1			
	On leave				1			
		attached from No 1 Section						
				6	33			

[illegible signature]
Lieut R.E.
22/11/16.

WORKS REPORT from 6pm 22nd 11/1916 to 6pm 23rd 11/1916 200 Field Coy R.E.

Section	Locality	Description of Work	Progress	Numbers Employed R.E. NCOs	Numbers Employed R.E. Sappers	Numbers Employed Inf.	Numbers Employed R.A. / Other	Remarks
No 1	Nuts Road	Revetting.	22 yds revetted & cleared	1	4	10	— Dugouts	
	Farnborough Road hr Cauchie	Erecting Nissen Hut. False roof.	2½ completed. frames ready for sheeting	2	4	8.		
	First aid Post Valley NE Berles.				5.			
	Company HQ workshops				2		15	
	Attached to No 4 Section				6		3.	
	Dump duties to	Cooks gasguard. Toolcart Orderly.					2	
	Sick.				3	10.		
	At Rest.				1			
	In Hospital							
	Nuts Road Dugout.	Mining.	Drove 3' timbers 1 frame	1	2		10.	
	Sergt.			1				
	Leave							
No 3	93 Support.	Frames & revetting	15 Frames	3	7	18	x	
	94 Mined OP.	Driving Gallery.	1½ yards excavated		1		6.	
	99 Trench	Shelter	Complete.		2.			
	~~Ged~~ Neverending St	Frames & Revetting	6 Frames fixed.		1	5		
	Attached to Special Bde R.E.			1.				
	Attached to HQ workshop.			1	9			
	Attached to R.H. Barker. Dugouts.						14.	
	Ravine Tubular Dugouts.						3.	
	Dump duties Cooks gasguard.				6		4.	
	Hospital			1	1		3.	
	On Leave							

M Leslie
Lt R.E.

Works Report from 6 pm 22/11/1916 to 6 pm 23/11/1916 200th Field Coy R.E.

Section	Locality	Description of Work	Progress	Numbers Employed R.E. N.C.Os	Numbers Employed R.E. men	Numbers Employed Infy	Numbers Employed RA RAMC	Remarks
4	Baths HQ	Cooks			2			
		Gas Guard			2			
		Blacksmith			1			
	Interpreter	Workshops		1	1			
		Supply Wagon			1			
	Under C.R.E.				2			
	Attached to Section No 1				1			
	On leave			1	1			
	B. H.Q. [illegible] Road	Entrances. Strutting between frames [illegible] sides & cross bracing. Large dug-out framing additional frames	2 frames	2	9	15		Day party
		Smoke dug-out. Excavating for [illegible] framing frames in [illegible]	3 fixed	2	10	14		Night party
		Signal Office framing frames & props & [illegible] sides	all frames fixed					
		Main entrance framing [illegible]	2 fixed					
		Extra Cover dug-out	frames fixed in one [illegible] sheeted [illegible] [illegible] sheeted sides & 16 props fixed in No 2.					
	attached from No 2 Section				2			
				6	34			

[illegible]
[illegible] R.E.
23/11/16.

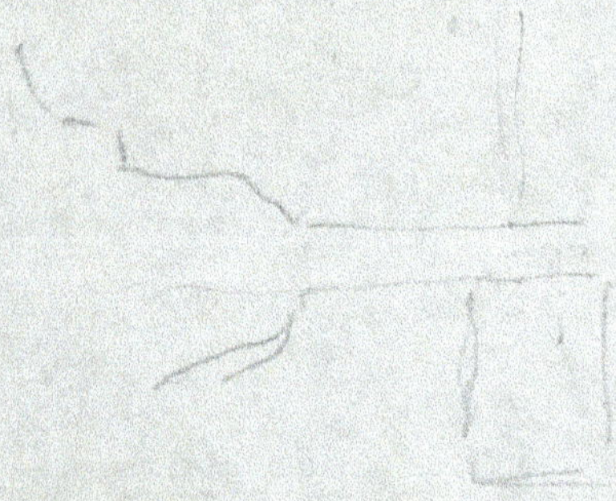

1

WORKS REPORT from 6PM 23rd [illegible] 1916 to 6PM 24th [illegible] 1916 [illegible] Field Coy R.E.

Section	Locality	Description of Works	Progress	Numbers Employed R.E. NCOs	R.E. Sappers	Infy	RA RAMC Orderlies	REMARKS.
No 1.	N018 Road	Revetting	20 [illegible]	1	3	5		
	[illegible] Road		Wired up pickets	1	6	10		
	[illegible] Road	Dugout Coy HQ	[illegible]	1	1		10	
	First aid Post	[illegible]	Half roofed		1	6		
	Attached to No 4 Sect				2		15	
	Coy HQ [illegible]	[illegible]	[illegible] completion		1			
	Dump. Cooks Orderly, Tool[illegible]			[illegible]	6	10	3	
	HQ [illegible] Workshops				6			
	At Rest			1	2			
	[illegible]				1			
	Sick & Hospital				1		2	
	[illegible]			1				
No 3	[illegible] Support	Frames & Revetting	7 frames [illegible]	2	7	21	–	
	[illegible]	[illegible] Gallery	[illegible]		1		6	
	[illegible]	[illegible] approach	[illegible]		1	8	8	
	[illegible]	[illegible] position	[illegible]		1	5		
	[illegible]	[illegible]	Excavating	1			5	
	[illegible]				1			
	[illegible]	[illegible]		1				
	[illegible]	[illegible]					14	
	[illegible]	[illegible]		1	9		4	
	[illegible]	[illegible]			6		3	

[illegible signature]

WORKS REPORT from 6PM 23/11 1916 to 6PM 24/11 1916 200th Field Coy RE.

Section	Locality	Description of work	Progress	Numbers Employed: R.E. NCOs	Numbers Employed: R.E. Sapps	Numbers Employed: Infy	Numbers Employed: RA RAMC	Remarks
4	[illegible]	Cooks.			2			
		Gasguard			2.			
		Wheelwright			1			
	[illegible]	Workshops		1	3			
		Supply wagon			1			
	[illegible]			1	1			
	[illegible]				1			
	[illegible]				2			
	[illegible]	Signal Office revetting sides	completed.	2	9	15		Day party
		Large Dug-out: fixing frames & strutting outs		2	10	14		Night party.
		Small dug-out foot of 1st Staircase on right. Excavating for extension Passage leading to small dug-out fixing frames & sheeting roof.						
		4 entrances revetting sides extending.						
		Offices Entrance to small dug-out excavating & fixing frames	2 frames fixed.					
		"& Cover dug-outs".						
		No1 Fixing struts & sheeting sides						
		No2 Sills fixed. Sill frames fixed one side sheeted						
		No3 Sills fixed						
		No4. Sills fixed.						
	attached from Section No1.				2			
				6	34			

C J Barker
2Lt RE
24/11/16.

Report of work from 6pm 29/11/16 to 6pm 30/11/16 [illegible]

Section	Locality	Description of Work	Progress	MEN RE NCO's	MEN RE Sappers	MEN Inf.	MEN Dugouts	Remarks
No 1	Nuts Road	Revetting	10 Hurdles	2	7	10	–	
	Nut Road HQ	Dugouts Excavating	Done 3' into 2 frames	1	1	x	11	
	First Aid Post	False Roof	Completed		2	4.		
	Coy HQ Front Line	Beds	Completed		1			
	HQ Workshops				5			
	Attached to No 4 Sect				2		15.	
	Cooks Toolcart Dump Duties Gas guards				5	10	3	
	Orderly				1			
	On leave			1			1	
	Sick				1			
	Hospital			1	2			
	At Rest				1			
	Pumpman			5/5	27/27			
No 3.	93 Support	Framing & Revetting	Fixed 5 frames	1	6.	6.		
	Carrying to all working parties					12		
	74 Trench	Fixed [illegible]	Fixed 18 of timbers					
	Noodles Av.	Revetting approach	Driven 11*	2	1		6.	
		to MG Dugout	One side complete		1	5.		
	[illegible]	Anti Aircraft post	Revetted		1	4		
	Ravine	Tubular Dugout	Excavating	1	–		3	
	Pumps				1			
	Special Bgd RE			1	2			
	Attached to Pt Barker						14.	
	"	RE Workshops & Div. works		1	9.			
	Dump duties	Cooks Gasguard			6		4	
	Hospital						3	
	On leave			1	1			
	Resting			6/6	27/27			

[signature] Lt RE

Work Report from 6pm 24/11/1916 to 6pm 25/11/1916 200th Field Coy RE

Section.	Locality	Description of Work.	Progress	Numbers Employed RE NCO	Sprs.	Infy	RA RAMC	Remarks.
4.	Bde. HQ.	Cooks.			2			
		Gasguard.			2			
		Wheelwright			1			
	Laherliere.	Workshops.		1	3			
		Supply Wagon			1			
	With CRE				2			
	On leave			1	1			
	Attached to No 1 Section				1			
	Batt. HQ. Farnborough Road.	Small dug-out Excavating for enlargement.						
		Passage leading to Small dug-out. fixing frames & Sheeting roof & fixing new heads.		2.	9	15		Day party.
		Signal Office revetting Sides	almost completed.	2.	10	14.		Night party.
		Large Dug-out fixing extra frames.						
		4 entrances Sheeting roof revetting sides & forming steps.						
		New Staircase. Refixing frames with cleats & Clearing fall in trench.	2 frames fixed					
		Cut & Cover dug-outs. ① Bridging & strutting	completed					
		② Fixing stretchers & bearers.						
	Attached from Section No 1.	Preparing Sills for Small dug-out.			2			
				6/6	[illegible]/32			

C. J. Barker.
2/Lieut RE.
25/11/16.

Work Report from 6pm 25th 11/16 to 6pm 26th 11/16. 200 Field Coy R.E.

Section.	Locality	Description of Work	Progress	Numbers Employed RE NCOs	Men	Inf.	Dugouts	Remarks
No 1	Nuts Road	Fixing U Frames	16 fixed	2	4.	8.		
	Decauville Track Ravine.	Clearing way for Track.	About 30^x Clear	1	3.	2.		{120^x of Track laid and unbolted for removing to a new position.
	Nuts Road	HQ Dugout.	Holed thro' Entrance 2 Fixed 2 Frames	1	1	10^x	12.	^x Night Party, emptying sandbags
	First aid Post.	False Roof.	Preparing Gutter.		2.			
	Attached to No 4 Section				2		15	
	Dump Orderly Cooks gasguard Toolcart				5	10.	3	
	HQ 200th Workshops				5			
	On leave				1			
	Hospital				1			
	At Rest				3.			
	Sergt. Dumps			1.				
				5/8	28/27			
No 3.	93 Support.	Revetting & Frame & Clearing falls	3 Frames & cleared Trench	2.	24.	8		
	94 Trench	Mined O.P.	Fixed Frame 1^x Excavated		1	8.	6.	
	Neverending St.	Antiaircraft.	Revetting, Fixed frame & Trench boards		1	4.		
	Ravine	Tubular Dugout.	Excavating	1			3.	
	Noodles Av.	Centre Coy HQ.	Material prepared		2			
	Carrying to all faces					12.		
	Pumps				1			
	Attached to Lt Barker						14	
	" "	HQrs workshops & Div workshops		1	4			
	Dump Duties Cooks gas guard				6.		4	
	Hospital						5	
	Leave.			1	1			
	Rest.			6/6	5/ 2/27			

[signature] Lt R.E.

6pm 6pm
Work Report from 25/11/1916 to 26/11/1916 — 200th Field Coy RE

No.	Locality	Description of Work	Progress	RE NCOs	RE Spr	[illegible]	RA [illegible]	Remarks
1	Brdе HQ.	Cooks			2			
		Gas Guard			2			
		Wheelwright			1			
	Interpreters	Workshops		1	3			
		Supply Wagon			1			
	With CRE				2			
	On leave			1	1			
	With Section No 1				1			
	Batt HQ	[illegible] for [illegible]						
	[illegible] Road	[illegible] same [illegible] & [illegible] frames.		2	9	15		Day party
		[illegible] Stairs	[illegible] completed	2	10	14		Night party
		4 [illegible] Stairs & [illegible]	[illegible] completed					
		[illegible] frames.	2 frames fixed.					
		[illegible] & clearing [illegible]	One frame fixed					
		[illegible]						
		(1) [illegible]						
		(2) [illegible] & [illegible]						
		[illegible]						
	Attached from No 1							
					2			
				66	34 32			

[illegible]
26/11/16

Works Report from 6 a.m. 25/11 – 1916 to 6 p.m. 26/11/1916. Field Co. R.E. 200

Sect	Locality	Description of Work	Progress	R.E. NCOs	R.E. Sprs	Inf	R.A.	REMARKS.
No 1	Nuts Road.	Clearing Trench & Driving frames.—	6 Frames fixed & 20' Cleared	1	4	10		
	Decauville track Ravine	Clearing & laying track	130x track laid & ballasted	2	3	20		
	Nuts Road	Coy HQ. Dugouts	Drove 2' fixed 1 frame		1	8	8.	
	First Aid Post.	Roof completed and gutter fixed.			2.			
	Attached to No 4.				2		15	
	Dump Orderly	Cooks Toolcart Gasguard.						
	Coy HQ Workshops.				5	10	3.	
	At Rest.				5			
	Sick			1	2		2	
	Leave				1		2	
	Hospital				1.			
	Sergt				1			
No 3.	93 Support.	Frames & Revetting	Fixed 5 frames & cleared falls	2.	4	8.	4.	
	94 Trench	Mined O.P.	2 Frames fixed & Sheeting.		1			
	Neverending St.	Anticraft position	Revetting Traverse & Excavating		1	2		
	Ravine	Tubular Dugout	Excavating ~~[illegible]~~	1		2.	6.	
	Noodles Av N.E.	Clearing Trench after falls.			1	4.		
	Noodles Av	Centre Coy HQ. Repairing	Servants Quarters fixed 2 girders		2		2	
	Carrying to all works					12		
	Pumps				1			
	Special Bge R.E.			1				
	Attached to HQ & new workshops			1	9.			
	" to Lt Barker.				6.		~~9~~ 4	
	Dump Cooks Gasguard						3	
	Hospital			1	1			
	On Leave							
	Resting				1		2	

[signature] Lt R.E.

Works Report from 6 pm. 26/11/ 1916 to 6 pm. 27/11/ 1916. 200 Field Coy R.E.

Sect.	Locality.	Description of Work	Progress.	R.E. N.C.O.	R.E. Sprs	Inf	R.A.M.C.	REMARKS.
4	Rivers H.Q.	Cooks			2			
		Gas guard			2			
		Wheelwright.			1			
	Laberlière	Workshops.		1	3			
		Supply wagon			1			
	On leave			1	1			
	With CRE				2			
	attached to Section No 1.				1			
	Divisional HQ Divisional Line Survey.	Cookery Course			1			
	B.HQ Farnborough Road.	Large dug-out fixing extra frames.	1 frame fixed		1			
		Small dug-out Excavating for enlargement.		2	11	15		Day party
		Passage leading to same fixing frames & sheeting roof		2	6	9		Night party
		Entrance to large dug-out on the right fixing frame & sheeting roof	1 frame fixed					
		Entrances revetting sides & sheeting roof.						
		New Entrance, fixing frames	4 frames fixed					
		Cut & Cover dug-out. (1) Bridging between posts (2) Fixing end posts Centre girder & bridging (3)(4) Sills drilled for dowels	Completed.					
		Shelter in French Road fixing sills	fixed					
		CO's dugout Clearing falls.						
	attached from No 1 Section				2			
				6	34			

C J Barker
2 Lieut RE
27/11/16.

Works Report from 6 pm. 27th 11/ 1916 to 6 pm. 28th/11/1916. 2nd Field Co. R.E.

Sect.	Locality.	Description of Work	Progress.	R.E. NCO.	R.E. Sprs.	Infy.	R.A. RAMC.	REMARKS.
3	93 Support.	Fixing Frames & Revetting	8 Frames fixed	2	4.	—	Dugouts.	
	94 Mined OP.	Mining work fixing frames	Fixed 1 frame & sheeting		1		4	
	Centre Coy HQ Cookhouse	Fixing supports & revetted	Ends of dugout		1		2	
	Woodess M.G. dugout.	Revetting Entrance	Cleared Entrance		1			
	Ravine	Tubular dugout 1 1st aid dugout.	Set 2 frames Excavated 20 [illegible]	1	1		3.	
	Pumps				1			
	Attached to Special Bgd R.E.			1				
	Attached to HQ & Div Workshops			1	9.			
	Attached to No. 4 Section.						4.	
	Dump Duties	Cooks Gasguard.			6.		4	
	Hospital						3.	
	Resting.				2			
	Sergt.							
	Leave			1				
				4/6	1 25/27			
1	Ravine	Decauville Track	250 yards track laid.	3	8	—	—	
	Nutt Road	Comp. H.Q.	4' felt driven 3 frames fixed	1	1	—	11	
	Attached No. 4 Section				2	—	13	
	Dump. Cooks. Orderly. Tool Cart etc.				4	—	6	
	Sick. Rest. Leave. Gas guard. Comp. H.Q.			1	17	—		
				5/5	25/27			

L. Hill 2/Lt RE
28/11/16

Works Report from 6 pm. 27/11/ 1916 to 5 pm. 28/11/ 1916. 200 Field Co. R.E.

Sect.	Locality.	Description of Work	Progress.	R.E. NCO.	R.E. Sprs.	Inf.	R.A. RAMC.	REMARKS.
A.	Brdes. H.Q.	Cooks			2			
		Gas Guard.			2			
		Wheelwright			1			
	Laberliere	Workshops		1	3			
		Supply Wagon			1			
	with CRE.				2			
	On leave				1			
	Divisional H.Q.	Cookery Course			1			
	In hospital			1				
	Sick				1			
	Batt^n H.Q. Farnborough Road.	Cut & Cover Dug-outs. CO's dugout. Cills fixed posts prepared for fixing. (2) Sides & roof completed Bridging completed fixing diagonal bracing. (3) Sides posts & girders fixed. New Entrance to dug-outs	6 steps fixed. Sandbag revetment to entrance, Sheeting roof frames all fixed.	2	9	17		Day party
		Large dug-out fixing extra frames. Small dug-out Excavating for enlargement. Entrance passage to Small dug-out & Big out on right fixing frames & Sheeting roof 4 Entrances, Sheeting roof levelling sides & forming Steps.	1 frame fixed Frames completed	2	7	10		Night party.
	Survey Divisional line				1			
	attached to No/ Sect				1			
	attached from No1				2			
				6/6	34/32			

C J Barker
2 Lieut RE
28/11/16.

Works Report from 6 pm. 28/11/ 1916 to 6 pm. 29/11/ 1916. 20 Field Co. R.E.

Sect.	Locality.	Description of Work	Progress.	R.E. NCO.	R.E. Sprs.	Infy.	R.A. RAMC.	REMARKS.
4	Billets. HQ.	Cooks			2			
		Gas Guard			2			
		Wheelwright & assistant			2			
	[illegible]	Workshops		1	3			
		Supply wagon			1			
	Divisional HQ	Cookery Course			1			
	On leave				1			
	In hospital Sick			1				
	With CRE				1			Light Duty
	attached to No 1.				2			
					1			
	Batt HQ Farnborough Road.	Large dug-out fixing extra frames.	All fixed		10			
		Small dug-out excavating for enlargement.		2		15.		
		Sheeting roof & revetting sides in passage leading to ditto. Entrances revetting sides & forming steps.		1	5	10		night party
		New entrance strutting & sheeting roof. Sandbag revetment to entrance revetting sides						
		Cut & Cover dug-outs						
		COS dug-out posts & girders fixing	All fixed					
		① finished but for interior work						
		② do						
		③ All posts & girders fixed and given to fix						
	Assisting A Survey Coy Sergeant	⑤ 7 Sides fixed.		1	1			
				6/6	32/32			

C J Barker 2/Lt RE
29/11/16

Works Report from 6 pm. [illegible] 1916 to 6 pm. 9 1916. Field Co. R.E.

Sect.	Locality.	Description of Work	Progress.	Numbers employed: R.E. NCO.	R.E. Sprs.	Infy.	R.A. RAMC.	REMARKS.
	[illegible]	[illegible]	[illegible]		2			
	[illegible]	[illegible]	[illegible] completed		2			
	[illegible]	[illegible]	[illegible]		2			
	[illegible]		[illegible] complete		2			
	[illegible] Road	[illegible]	All [illegible] completed	1	1		11	
	[illegible] Road	[illegible]					14	
	[illegible]				5			
	[illegible]			2	11		5	
	[illegible]	[illegible]	[illegible]	5/5	27/27			
		[illegible]	[illegible]	2	3	10		
No 3	[illegible]		[illegible]		2		2	
	[illegible]	[illegible]	[illegible]		1	2		
	[illegible]	MG [illegible]	[illegible]	1	1	5	5	
	[illegible]	[illegible]	[illegible]	1	1	2		
	[illegible]			1				
	[illegible]				1			
	[illegible]			1	7			
	[illegible]						4	
	[illegible]				6		2	
	[illegible]						3	
	[illegible]				2		2	
	[illegible]					12		
	[illegible]				1			
	[illegible]							

1

6/6 27/27

[illegible]

Works Report from 6 pm. [illegible] 1916 to 6 pm. [illegible] 1916. [illegible] Field Co. R.E.

Sect.	Locality.	Description of Work	Progress.	R.E. NCO.	R.E. Sprs.	Infy.	R.A. AMC.	REMARKS.
1	[illegible]	[illegible] Track	[illegible]	2	3	18		
	121 Street	Repair dugout	Work finished		2	2		
	18 A		Dugout cleared of earth.		2	3		
	O.P. [illegible] Road	O.P.	[illegible] prepared [illegible]		2			
	[illegible] Street	Repairs "	[illegible] cleared of [illegible]		2	6		
	[illegible] Road	Coy. H.Q. Dugout	[illegible] dugout [illegible]	1	1		10	
	Coy. H.Q. Workshop	— Rest — [illegible] — Orderly — [illegible] — [illegible]		2	[illegible]	10	20	
	Dump — Leave — Sick — Hospital — [illegible] Attached [illegible]							
				8/5	27/27			
2	93 Support	[illegible]	[illegible]	2	[illegible]	10		
	[illegible]	M.G. Emplacement [illegible]	[illegible]		1	2		
	[illegible]	[illegible] Dugout	[illegible]	1		10	3	
	[illegible]	[illegible] Dugout	[illegible]		2	4		
	[illegible]	[illegible] Coy. H.Q. [illegible]	[illegible]					
	94 [illegible] Trench	[illegible] O.P.	[illegible]		1		2	
			[illegible]		1		4	
	Attached to Special [illegible]			1			4	
	[illegible]						2	
	[illegible]						3	
	[illegible]			1	2			
	[illegible]				6		20	
	[illegible]				8			

1/1/6 27/27

[illegible signature]

Works Report from 6 pm. 29/11/16 1916 to 6 pm. 30/11/16 1916. Field Co. R.E.

Sect.	Locality.	Description of Work	Progress.	Numbers employed R.E. NCO.	R.E. Sprs.	Infy.	R.A. RAMC.	REMARKS.
4.	Bertes H.Q.	Cooks 2. Gas Guard 2. Wheelwright 1.			5			
	Labeuvrière.	Workshops.		1	3			
		Supply Wagon			1			
	With CRE				2			
	attached to No 1 Sect.				1			
	On leave.			1	1			
	Hospital.			1	–			
	Sick.				1			
	'Q' Survey Coy.	Assisting in construction dug-out.			1			
	Batt. HQ Fairborough Road.	Large dug-out. Strutting between frames.						
		Dug-out on right. fixing frames. (extra)	2 fixed.	3	16	24.		
		Small dug-out. Excavating for extension & fixing frames	2 fixed.					
		Passage leading to same revetting sides.						
		New entrance – Sandbagging entrance & revetting sides.						
		Cut & cover dug-out.						
		Co's dug-out. Side posts & girders fixed.						
		(2) Ventilation pipes fixed						
		(3) End posts & centre girder fixed Sides revetted						
		Main shelter & fixing frames	8 fixed.					
		Loading & carrying material.			1	4		
				6	32.			
				6.32				

[signature]
2Lieut-RE
30/11/16.

30th Divisional Engineers

200th FIELD COMPANY R.E. ::: DECEMBER 1916.

Army Form C. 2118.

WAR DIARY
or
~~INTELLIGENCE SUMMARY~~

(Erase heading not required.)

Instructions regarding War Diaries and Intelligence Summaries are contained in F. S. Regs., Part II. and the Staff Manual respectively. Title Pages will be prepared in manuscript.

Vol. XII.

200th Field Company, R.E.

Place	Date	Hour	Summary of Events and Information 1/10.000 Map. RANSART 51c S.E. 3+4 Ed. 3A.	Remarks and references to Appendices
BERLES.	1.12.16		No 1 Section, Lieut HILL, employed in Front-Line System in B2 ~~Subsector~~ between W 23 b 0.0 and W 18 a 2.5. ~~employed on~~ new dugouts (3) for left Co H.Q. at W 17 d 85.75. and repairs to other dugouts.	
			No 3 Section, 2Lieut LESLIE, employed in Front Line System in B1 Subsector between W 29 c 25.80 and W 23 b 0.0. on revetting Support line, new dugout for C.O. at W 22 d 7.4. repairs to dugouts, MG emplacements.	
and			No 4 Section, 2Lieut BARKER employed behind Nos 1, 3, sections on new Bn HQ. at W. 17 c 9.4 reconstructing 3 mined dugouts and making 5 cut & cover dugouts and 1 shelter: also one cut & cover dugout for Q Survey Co, R.E.	
BAVINCOURT			No 2 Section, Lt GLEDHILL, employed at RE Div. HQ under orders of C.R.E.	
	2.12.16		as above	
	3.12.16		No 3 Section started to assist in construction of mined dugout for Stretcher Bearers at W 17 c 9.4.	
	4.12.16		CAPT. W. GUISE TUCKER having handed over command to CAPT. N.W. NAPIER-CLAVERING left to report to C.E. 4th Army for duty.	
	5.12.16			
	6.12.16		as above	
	7.12.16			
	8.12.16			
	9.12.16			
	10.12.16		No 1 Section moved to BAVINCOURT, exchanging work with No 2 Section which moved into BERLES.	
			No 3 Section engaged in making emplacements for Stokes guns.	
	11.12.16		as above. 1 NCO and 6 men in training with a raiding party of 20th Bn KING'S LIVERPOOL Regt. for use of Bangalore Torpedo for cutting wire, should the Trench Mortars and guns fail.	
	12.12.16			
	13.12.16		Bombardment of GERMAN LINES near MONCHY-AU-BOIS. Wire successfully cut so RE. Party were not used in raid.	
			No working parties	
	14.12.16		Work as usual.	
	15.12.16		Owing to continued frost, rain & snow. FARNBOROUGH RD at W 16 c 7.5, began to fall in. Revetment taken in hand by No 4 Sec.	
	16.12.16		work continued	
	17.12.16			
	18.12.16			
	19.12.16		The enemy dropped a shell in the RE. Dump at BERLES, and henceforth shelled BERLES on most days. 1 NCO. wounded.	
	~~20.12.16~~		A party of 300 infantry employed at night on digging out the support line between ~~W 23 b 3.0 and~~ W 17 d 7.0 and W 18 a 00.25 which was for the most part only 2' deep. On subsequent days parties were employed on the completing of the excavation and the revetment of the trench.	
	20.12.16		Started work with RAMC working parties on Regimental Aid Post at W 17 c 05.30. and on Relay Post at W 16 c 9.8.	
	21.12.16		Started work on T heads from FOX LANE at W 18 c 05.30, and W 18 c 10.35. as part of the support line. This work was done in consequence of the proposals now approved to abandon & hold in portions of the front line trenches.	

Instructions regarding War Diaries and Intelligence Summaries are contained in F. S. Regs., Part II. and the Staff Manual respectively. Title Pages will be prepared in manuscript.

FIELD COMPANY R.E. COUNTY PALATINE

WAR DIARY
or
~~INTELLIGENCE SUMMARY~~
(Erase heading not required.)

Army Form C. 2118.

200th Field Company RE

Place	Date	Hour	Summary of Events and Information 1/10.000 Map RANSART 51c S.E. 3+4 Ed 3A	Remarks and references to Appendices
BERLES and BAVINCOURT	22.12.16		Det of 1 NCO & 5 men sent to HUMBERCAMPS to work on the repair and refitting of hutment camps for occupation by Divisional Draft training DEPOT. 6 men attached from 202nd Field Co.	
	23.12.16 24.12.16		Work continued. On the afternoon of the 24th the enemy shelled heavily the N.W. portion of BERLES. He also shelled at intervals on these & other days the Divisional Line along the SE. outskirts of BERLES.	
	25.12.16		Christmas Day. No work done. All the men had a good dinner.	
	26.12.16 27.12.16 28.12.16 29.12.16		Work continued as usual. The 29th was very wet and a very heavy fall of rain occurred during the early hours of the 30th.	
	30.12.16		The heavy rain caused extensive damage to the trenches and movement was very difficult and in many cases impossible. NEWARK ST was absolutely blocked the revetment on both sides giving way and meeting in the middle. The Left Co HQ in the SUNKEN RD were flooded. All available labour was turned onto the task of reestablishing the communications with the front line.	
	31.12.16		Owing to the weather no infantry working parties were available and all the RE labour was concentrated on the urgent work of repairing the damaged trenches, dugouts etc.	

M. [illegible] Major RE

J.C. 200TH FIELD CO., R.E.

2449 Wt. W14957/M90 750,000 1/16 J.B.C. & A. Forms/C.2118/12.

Instructions regarding War Diaries and Intelligence Summaries are contained in F. S. Regs., Part II. and the Staff Manual respectively. Title Pages will be prepared in manuscript.

WAR DIARY
or
~~INTELLIGENCE SUMMARY~~
(Erase heading not required.)

Army Form C. 2118.

200th Field Company, R.E.

Place	Date	Hour	Summary of Events and Information	Remarks and references to Appendices
			Casualties for the month of December 1916.	
			– HOSPITAL –	
BERLES	3.12.16	–	1 O.R. to Hospital (Sickness) 3-12-16.	
and	8.12.16	–	1 O.R. -do- do 8.12.16	
LAHERLIERE	14.12.16	–	2 O.R. -do- do 14.12.16	
	19.12.16	–	1 O.R. -do- do 19.12.16.	
	23.12.16	–	1 O.R. do do 23.12.16	
	26.12.16	–	1 O.R. do do 26.12.16.	
	3.12.16	–	1 O.R. Rejoined from Hospital 3.12.16.	
	8.12.16	–	1 O.R. -do- 8.12.16.	
	10.12.16	–	1 O.R. do 10.12.16	
	17.12.16	–	1 O.R. do 17.12.16	
	10.12.16	–	1 O.R. to Hospital (Sickness) 8/12/16.	
	16.12.16	–	1 O.R. do do 14/12/16.	
	20.12.16	–	1 O.R. do do 19/12/16	
	24.12.16	–	1 O.R. do do 23/12/16.	
	19.12.16	–	1 O.R. WOUNDED by Shellfire 19/12/16	
			} These men having been sent to C.C.S. are struck off the strength of the unit.	

2449 Wt. W14957/M90 750,000 1/16 J.B.C. & A. Forms/C.2118/12.

Army Form C. 2118.

WAR DIARY
or
~~INTELLIGENCE SUMMARY~~
(Erase heading not required.)

Instructions regarding War Diaries and Intelligence Summaries are contained in F. S. Regs., Part II. and the Staff Manual respectively. Title Pages will be prepared in manuscript.

200th Field Coy. R.E.

Place	Date	Hour	Summary of Events and Information	Remarks and references to Appendices
			Casualties for December continued	
			— REINFORCEMENTS —	
BERLES	2.12.16		1 O.R. Arrived from No 4 Gen. Base Depot 2/12/16.	These men have been taken on the strength of Coy. from dates shown.
and	7.12.16		1 O.R. do do 7/12/16	
LAHERLIERE	15.12.16		4 O.R. do do 15/12/16	
	20.12.16		1 O.R. do do 20/12/16	
			— TRANSFERS —	
	5.12.16	-	Capt. W. GUISE TUCKER R.E. (S.R.) Transferred from 200th Field Coy Royal Engineers to C.E. 4th Army - 5-12-16.	

M.W. Draper Clavering
Major

H.Q. 200TH FIELD CO. R.E

2449 Wt. W14957/M90 750,000 1/16 J.B.C. & A. Forms/C.2118/12.

SECRET

Ab

Vol 13

- WAR DIARY -

OF THE 200th Field Company, Royal Engineers.

FOR THE

month of January 1917.

(VOLUME XIII)

Instructions regarding War Diaries and Intelligence Summaries are contained in F. S. Regs., Part II. and the Staff Manual respectively. Title Pages will be prepared in manuscript.

WAR DIARY
or
~~INTELLIGENCE SUMMARY~~
(Erase heading not required.)

Army Form C. 2118.

Vol. XIII

200th Field Company R.E.

Place	Date	Hour	Summary of Events and Information Map 1/10000 TANSART 51c S.E. 3 & 4 Ed 3A.	Remarks and references to Appendices
BERLES and BAVINCOURT and HUMBERCAMPS	1.1.17 / 2.1.17		Work continued on the clearing the communication trenches, NEWARK ST, FARNBOROUGH ROAD and on the repair of the dugouts also on the repair of the camps at HUMBERCAMPS for the Divisional Depot. Lt HILL proceeded on leave 2nd.	
	3.1.17 / 4.1.17		Work continued as above, except that the work on the hutment camps at HUMBERCAMPS was stopped and begun on the huts for a Field Ambulance at the same place.	
	5.1.17	10 am	No 4 Section under Capt IRWIN [2Lt BARKER being on leave] moved from BERLES through SOMBRIN to IVERGNY, exchanging places with a section of 57th Field Co. R.E. Work continued as above.	Map FRANCE 1/40000, 51c.
	6.1.17		2Lt BARKER returned from leave and proceeded to IVERGNY. Work continued.	
	7.1.17		Capt IRWIN returned from IVERGNY to LA CAUCHIE. Work continued.	
	8.1.17		The company moved to the rear area the 57th Co. RE taking over. Capt IRWIN with No1 Sec. No2 Sec. and the Transport left the wagon lines at LA HERLIERE at 10 am. moving by SAULTY, SOMBRIN, SUS-ST LEGER to IVERGNY. No 2 Sec proceeding further to REBREUVIETTE. No 3 Sec under 2Lt LESLIE moved by TOMMERA to HALLOY.	
HALLOY IVERGNY REBREUVIETTE	9.1.17		Work started at HALLOY on the site of Field Ambulance hutments at Work started at IVERGNY on the putting of bunks into barns	
	10.1.17		Work started at REBREUVIETTE on the site of a hutment camp at M12 c 6.6.	
			Work started at OPPY on bunking of barns by 1 platoon of 11th S. Lancs Pioneers under 2Lt STRUTHERS	
	11.1.17		Working party of 2 officers 50 men of 2nd Bn Royal Scots Fusiliers joined at IVERGNY.	
	12.1.17 / 13.1.17		No 3 Section under 2Lt LESLIE moved from HALLOY (leaving 3 O.R. to continue work) to REBREUVIETTE for work on water supply.	
	14.1.17		Work continued as above.	
	15.1.17		Work continued. Work begun on pipe line of water supply to M12 Camp. No 1 Section moved from IVERGNY to BEAUDRICOURT. 1 Officer and 52 men of 2nd Bn. Yorkshire Regt arrived at BEAUDRICOURT as working party.	
BEAUDRICOURT	16.1.17		Work continued. Work begun on erection of bunks at BEAUDRICOURT. Working party of 5 Officers and 100 O.R. arrived at REBREUVIETTE for work on water supply.	
	17.1.17		Lt HILL rejoined from leave. Snowfall 3-4 inches interfered with transport of material.	
	18.1.17 / 19.1.17		Work continued.	
	20.1.17		Work on camp at M12 c 6.6. being stopped No 2 Section moved to BEAUDRICOURT to work on huts and bunking there.	
	21.1.17		Work continued – very sharp frost	
LUCHEUX GROUCHES SUS-ST-LEGER LECAUROY	22.1.17		Lt HILL and No1 Section moved to LUCHEUX and GROUCHES taking over work in LUCHEUX area hitherto done by the 201st Fld Co. RE. Work in SUS-ST-LEGER and LECAUROY also taken over by No 3 Section	
	23.1.17 / 24.1.17 / 25.1.17		Work continued. Frost severe and continuous	

2449 Wt. W14957/M90 750,000 1/16 J.B.C. & A. Forms/C.2118/12.

Army Form C. 2118.

WAR DIARY
or
~~INTELLIGENCE SUMMARY~~
(Erase heading not required.)

Instructions regarding War Diaries and Intelligence Summaries are contained in F. S. Regs., Part II. and the Staff Manual respectively. Title Pages will be prepared in manuscript.

VOL XIII Cont.

200th Field Company R.E.

Place	Date	Hour	Summary of Events and Information (Maps. FRANCE 1/40000 51c S.E. / FRANCE 1/100 000 LENS 11.)	Remarks and references to Appendices
IVERGNY	26.1.17		Work continued. Details brought to H.Q. from HALLOY. Work handed over to 202nd Fd Co. RE.	
	27.1.17		Lieut HILL and No 1 Section moved from GROUCHES and LUCHEUX to IVERGNY. No 3 Section from REBREUVIETTE to IVERGNY. No 2 Section from BEAUDRICOURT to IVERGNY. 2Lt CHIDGEY joined as reinforcement from Base.	
SIMENCOURT	28.1.17	9.30am	Transport with transport of 1 Section of 202nd Fd Co attached, proceeded by march route to SIMENCOURT. Remainder of	
ACHIECOURT		1.0 pm 4.0 pm 7.0 pm	Company proceeded by motor lorry to WARLUS and thence by march route to ACHIECOURT. 2Lt FROST with 1 section of 202nd Co. joined at IVERGNY and proceeded with company.	
	29.1.17 30.1.17 31.1.17		Taking over work in G sector from 201st Field Company.	

31 Jan 1917.

Mr Napier Clavering
Major RE.
OC. 200th Field Company RE.

2449 Wt W14957/M90 750,000 1/16 J.B.C. & A. Forms/C.2118/12.

Army Form C. 2118.

Instructions regarding War Diaries and Intelligence Summaries are contained in F. S. Regs., Part II. and the Staff Manual respectively. Title Pages will be prepared in manuscript.

WAR DIARY
or
~~INTELLIGENCE SUMMARY~~

(Erase heading not required.)

200th Field Coy. RE.

Place	Date	Hour	Summary of Events and Information	Remarks and references to Appendices
			Casualties for month of January 1917	
			– HOSPITAL –	
BERLES and LAHERLIERE	2.1.17		2 O.R. To Hospital (Sickness) 2-1-17	
	3.1.17		1 O.R. do do 3.1.17	
	4.1.17		1 O.R. do do 4.1.17	
	16.1.17		2 O.R. do do 16.1.17	
	19.1.17		1 O.R. do do 19.1.17	
	31.12.16		1 O.R. Rejoined from Hospital 31.12.16	
	2.1.17		1 O.R. do do 2.1.17	
	3.1.17		1 O.R. do do 3.1.17	
	6.1.17		1 O.R. do do 6.1.17	
	12.1.17		1 O.R. do do 12.1.17	
	15.1.17		1 O.R. do do 15.1.17	
	6.1.17		1 O.R. To Hospital (Sickness) 2.1.17 } These men having been sent to C.C.S.	
	24.1.17		2 O.R. do do 16.1.17 } are struck off the strength of Company.	
			– REINFORCEMENTS –	
	3.1.17		1 O.R. Arrived from No 4 Gen. Base. Depot. 3-1-17 } These men having joined	
	11.1.17		1 O.R. do do 11.1.17 } on dates shown are taken	
	20.1.17		1 O.R. do do 20.1.17 } on the strength of the Coy.	

Army Form C. 2118.

Instructions regarding War Diaries and Intelligence Summaries are contained in F. S. Regs., Part II. and the Staff Manual respectively. Title Pages will be prepared in manuscript.

WAR DIARY
or
~~INTELLIGENCE SUMMARY~~

(Erase heading not required.)

200th Fd Co R.E.

Place	Date	Hour	Summary of Events and Information	Remarks and references to Appendices
			Casualties for January continued	
			- TRANSFERS -	
IVERGNY	22.1.17		80132 Drvr. Rampton W. Transferred to Base Depot ROUEN on 22-1-17. and struck off the strength of the Coy. from that date. AUTHORITY: A.D.M.S. 30 Division. A566/3 dated 15-1-17.	
			- HOSPITAL -	
	11.12.16.		81369 Cpl Southern W. Hospital in England since 11.12.16. Struck off the strength. AUTHORITY. R.E. Base Records R.E./C/59757 17/1/17 + R.E. Records R26/44185 13-1-17.	
			[signature] Clavering Major RE O.C. 201st Fd Co R.E.	

2449 Wt. W14957/M90 750,000 1/16 J.B.C. & A. Forms/C.2118/12.

SECRET

Vol 14

WAR DIARY

OF THE

200th Field Company, Royal Engineers

FOR THE MONTH OF

February 1917.

(VOLUME XIV).

APPENDIX A.

Direct Hit on Dugout by Heavy Minenwerfer Bomb.

22nd Feb 1917. G Subsector M 15 a 5.5.

Map $\frac{1}{10000}$ NEUVILLEVITASSE. 51B.S.W. 1.

The dugout had 12' cover of which about 6' was chalk. As the result of the explosion of the bomb a crater 6' deep was formed, and the roof of the dugout fell in forming a domed cavity 4' in height.

The dugout was timbered with good material but the construction was faulty in that:-

a. The joists rested on the posts without any form of fastening whatever; they were not halfed, nor shouldered nor tenoned nor spiked.

b. There were no distance pieces between the joists.

c. The posts were not strutted longitudinally.

The force of the explosion knocked the joists off the posts and the roof fell in. Though the dugout had been constructed a long while, the timber was quite sound.

M W Draper Clavering
Maj RE.

27. Feb 1917

O.C. 200th Field Co RE.

Army Form C. 2118.

Instructions regarding War Diaries and Intelligence Summaries are contained in F. S. Regs., Part II. and the Staff Manual respectively. Title pages will be prepared in manuscript.

WAR DIARY
or
~~INTELLIGENCE SUMMARY.~~
(Erase heading not required.)

VOL XIV.

200th Field Company R.E.

Place	Date	Hour	Summary of Events and Information — Map. 1/10000 NEUVILLE VITASSE 51 B.S.W.1. Ed 3A	Remarks and references to Appendices
ACHICOURT SIMENCOURT	1.2.17		No 1 Sec. Lt HILL employed on Grenade Store at M9a 3.7. and on dugouts in CHEMIN CREUX at M14a 4.8. No 2 Sec. Lt CHUGGEY employed on Brig. HQ. Dugout at M14a 50.95. in conjunction with 201st Fld Co. RE. No 3 Sec workshops Lt LESLIE. No 4 Sec Lt BARKER, employed ~~(1 Sec. 202nd Co.)~~ at Trench mortar emplacements in 30th Divisional area. Severe frost continues, ground frozen to a considerable depth and covered with a few inches of snow. Digging very difficult. Camouflage of work difficult owing to snow	
	2.2.17. 3.2.17.		Work continued.	
	4.2.17.		Work on Brigade HQ dugouts at M14a 50.95. taken over from 201st Fld Co RE.	
	5.2.17. 6.2.17. 7.2.17.		Work continued.	
AGNY	8.2.17.		62nd Fld Co RE moved out of AGNY. Dump at M8b 7.3 taken over. Transport & horse lines still at SIMENCOURT.	
	9.2.17		Four sections moved from ACHICOURT to AGNY. Nos 1, 2, 4 Sections to billets in or near AGNY CHATEAU, No 3 to the dump. The Section of 202nd Fld Co remained at ACHICOURT and were joined by remainder of Company this day.	
	10.2.17.		1 Platoon 11th S Lancs Pioneers Lt STRUTHERS attached. used for work on Heavy Trench Mortar Emplacements. Work in 21st Brigade area handed over to 202nd Fld Co. RE. leaving this company to work on 27 Medium T.M. Emplacements and bomb stores between M14c 4.2 and M15a 8.7 and 9 Heavy T.M. Emplacements, dugouts etc. between M14b 1.3 and M9c 1.1. No 4 Section continued work on Medium T.M.	
	11.2.17 12.2.17 13.2.17		Work continued. Weather still fine and cold with frost: slight thaw at midday.	
DAINVILLE	14.2.17		Company HQ. moved from AGNY to DAINVILLE. GOAT ST prepared for widening & deepening but progress slow on account of frost.	
	15.2.17		Work continued.	
	16.2.17.		Work continued. Thaw set in and traffic restrictions imposed as from 17.2.17. No materials can therefore be brought up.	
	17.2.17.		Brigade Grenade Dump dugout at M9a 3.7. finished. No 3 Sec. working on Div. Grenade Store at M2c 75.15.	
	18.2.17. 19.2.17.		Work continued.	
	20.2.17.		2Lt BARKER moved to HALLOY to set out trenches for practice attack. Platoon of 11th S Lancs attached moved to LAHERLIERE for work in Divisional workshops. Widening of GOAT ST in hand under Lt HILL RE.	
	21.2.17.		Work continued.	
	22.2.17.		Work continued. A dugout in Support Line at M15a 6.6. was hit by a heavy Minenwerfer Bomb and the roof fell in resulting in the death of one officer. A separate report as to causes of failure attached.	APPENDIX A.

Army Form C. 2118.

WAR DIARY
or
~~INTELLIGENCE SUMMARY.~~
(Erase heading not required.)

Instructions regarding War Diaries and Intelligence Summaries are contained in F. S. Regs., Part II. and the Staff Manual respectively. Title pages will be prepared in manuscript.

Vol. XIV (cont)

200th Field Company R.E.

Place	Date	Hour	Summary of Events and Information Map 1/10000 NEUVILLEVITASSE 51 B. S.W. 1. Ed. 3A.	Remarks and references to Appendices
DAINVILLE AGNY SIMENCOURT	23.2.17		Work continued. Dn. Grenade Store at M 2 c 75.15 completed. Of the six dugout entrances constructed at M 14 a 4.8, two have been allotted as Brig. Bomb Store for 89th Brigade. These two entrances have been joined up by a passage and three chambers 8' x 12'6" have been started.	
MONCHIET			Transport and horse lines moved from SIMENCOURT to MONCHIET.	
	24.2.17		Work continued	
	25.2.17		Work continued. News received of important advance on ANCRE. Vigorous patrolling ordered. 12 Bangalore torpedoes 12' long with Guncotton charges prepared by midnight.	
	26.2.17 27.2.17		Work continued but much delayed by lack of material. Thaw restrictions of traffic still in force	
	28.2.17		Work continued.	

Arw Hayes-Clarsing [signature]
Maj RE.
O.C. 200th Field Co RE.
1. March 1917.

Instructions regarding War Diaries and Intelligence Summaries are contained in F. S. Regs., Part II. and the Staff Manual respectively. Title pages will be prepared in manuscript.

WAR DIARY

~~or~~

~~INTELLIGENCE SUMMARY.~~

(Erase heading not required.)

Army Form C. 2118.

200th Field Coy R.E.

Place	Date	Hour	Summary of Events and Information	Remarks and references to Appendices
			Casualties for the month of February 1917	
			– HOSPITAL –	
ACHICOURT SIMENCOURT AGNY DAINVILLE MONCHIET	1-2-17	-	1 O.R. to Hospital (Sickness) 1-2-17	
	17.2.17	-	2 O.R. do do 17-2.17	
	20.2.17	-	1 O.R. do do 20-2.17	
	21.2.17	-	1 O.R. do do 21. 2.17	
	27.2.17	-	1 O.R. do do 27-2.17	
	7.2.17	-	1 O.R. do do 7-2.17	
	5-2.17	-	1 O.R. Rejoined from Hospital 5-2.17	
	23-2.17	-	1 O.R. do do 23-2.17	
	7-2.17	-	1 O.R. To Hospital (Sickness) 7-2.17 To C.C.S. Struck off the strength of the Company.	
			– REINFORCEMENTS –	
	11.2.17	-	1 O.R. Arrived from R.E. Base Depot 11-2-17 Taken on the strength of Coy.	
			– EXCHANGES –	
	27.1.17	-	43355 Cpl. Ingledew E. From R.E. Training Centre NEWARK to 200th Fd Co R.E. in exchange with 83434 Cpl. McLean E. 200th Fd Co R.E. to ENGLAND. AUTHORITY: War Office letter No 121/Drafts/2934 (AG7) dtd 17.10.16 & A.G. Base OR. 586/2	
			– TRANSFERS –	
	23.2.17	-	83454 Spr. Sheehan J. Transferred to Base 23-2.17. AUTHORITY: A.D.M.S. 20 Division No 441/4 dated 20-2-17	

Instructions regarding War Diaries and Intelligence Summaries are contained in F. S. Regs., Part II. and the Staff Manual respectively. Title pages will be prepared in manuscript.

WAR DIARY
or
~~INTELLIGENCE SUMMARY~~.
(Erase heading not required.)

Army Form C. 2118.

201st Field Coy R.E.

Place	Date	Hour	Summary of Events and Information	Remarks and references to Appendices
			Casualties for February contd	
			2nd Lieut. J. H. Gledhill R.E. (T) This officer was unable to return overseas from his leave of absence owing to being found medically unfit and was struck off the strength of this Company from the 17th December 1916.	
			W.O. letter No. 9/Engineers/7231 dated 29th Jany. 1917. and R.E. Base Records letter dated 5-2-17.	
			M.W. Harper Clarring Major R.E.	
			O.C. 201st Field Coy. R.E.	

SECRET

Vol 15

WAR DIARY

OF THE

200th Field Company, Royal Engineers.

FOR THE MONTH OF

March 1917

(VOLUME. XV)

1/4/17

Instructions regarding War Diaries and Intelligence Summaries are contained in F. S. Regs., Part II. and the Staff Manual respectively. Title pages will be prepared in manuscript.

WAR DIARY
or
~~INTELLIGENCE SUMMARY.~~
(Erase heading not required.)

Army Form C. 2118.

VOL XV. 200th Field Co. R.E.

Place	Date	Hour	Summary of Events and Information Map 1/10000 NEUVILLE VITASSE. 51 B.S.W. 1. Ed. 3A.	Remarks and references to Appendices
DAINVILLE AGNY MONCHIET	1.3.17		Co. HQ. at DAINVILLE. Transport and Horse Lines at MONCHIET. 4 Sections at AGNY CHATEAU and AGNY. No 1 Section employed on Heavy T.M. Emplacements (seven) in G1 Subsector, Brigade Grenade Store at M14a 4.8. Dugout at M14a 5.9. and repair of dugout at R11a 65.36. No 2 Section on Brigade H.Q. Dugouts at M14a 50.95. No 3 Section on Workshops, Dump, and on felling trees for R.A. No 4 Section on Medium T.M. Emplacements (27) in G1 Subsector.	
	2.3.17		Work continued. Stores supply better owing to removal of tram restrictions on traffic.	
	3.3.17		Work continued, repair of three bridges for field guns over R. CRINCHON taken in hand.	
	4.3.17		Work continued. "A" Emplacement H.T.M. completed. Gas alarm at 8 p.m. no gas in this neighbourhood. Work in hand on dugout for Brigade Runners etc at M14a 47.87.	
	5.3.17		Work continued.	
	6.3.17		Work continued. Repair of dugout at R11a 65.36 completed. The enemy bombarded the right of G1 subsector with T.M. bombs doing considerable damage to trenches & blowing in two dugout entrances.	
	7.3.17		Brigade grenade store at M14a 4.8. completed. Work started on repair of entrance & strengthening of dugout at M14d. 3.6.	
	8.3.17		Repair of bridges over R. CRINCHON completed.	
	9.3.17		Work begun on strengthening dugout at M14d 21.55 for use as Trench Dump Dugout.	
	10.3.17 11.3.17		Work continued.	
	12.3.17		Trench Dump dugout at M14d 25.55 completed.	
	13.3.17		Work started on provision of extra dugout accommodation at M14c 93 45. in LITTLE GEM ST for use as Bn. HQ.	
	14.3.17		No infantry working parties. Work in morning clearing up details. Lt HILL to hospital with sickness.	
	15.3.17 16.3.17 17.3.17		No work. whole company resting.	
	18.3.17	7 a.m.	Enemy front line trenches occupied by our troops. Enemy in retreat.	
		11 a.m.	1 NCO & 3 men sent to report to each of the three Battalions in the line with wirecutters to deal with mines etc.	
		Noon	Co. HQ moved to AGNY.	
		1.30 pm	Orders received to take in hand construction of strong points at approx M15d 4.1 and M30a 9.6. 2Lt LESLIE sent with NCO's from Nos 3 & 4 Sections to reconnoitre.	
		4.30 pm	Nos 3 & 4 Section started for work. Strong points sited at M21a 40.95 and M20b 0 4. Work finished about midnight.	
		6.30 pm	Started with Nos 1 & 2 sections to form dump of RE material at M8d 0.0. Work completed at 11.15 pm.	
	19.3.17	4.0 pm	Nos 1 & 2 Sections sent out to clear a road for pack transport from M26b 1.3 to M28d 4.6. Completed 7.15 pm.	
			No 3 section completing wiring of strong point at M20b 0.4.	

2353 Wt. W2544/1454 700,000 5/15 D. D. & L. A.D.S.S./Forms/C. 2118.

Army Form C. 2118.

WAR DIARY
or
~~INTELLIGENCE SUMMARY.~~
(Erase heading not required.)

Instructions regarding War Diaries and Intelligence Summaries are contained in F. S. Regs., Part II. and the Staff Manual respectively. Title pages will be prepared in manuscript.

Vol XV (cont) 200th Field Company RE

Place	Date	Hour	Summary of Events and Information	Remarks and references to Appendices
AGNY	20.3.17		No 2 Section worked on the improvement of the road from AGNY to the ARRAS-BUCQUOY road. Nos 3 & 4 Sections worked with two platoons of 11th S Lancs Pioneers on the removal of concrete barrier and earth barricade at M15 b 6.2.	Maps FRANCE 51 B. S.W. Edition 4a - 1/20000
MONCHIET	21.3.17		Work continued on barricade — 8 ft track cleared to original road level by 7 pm. to enable 6" How. ~~guns~~ to get forward. Reconnaissance of Railway cutting in S3 for accommodation for Reserve Bn.	
	22.3.17		Reconnaissance of BLAIREVILLE for billets. Lt HILL rejoined from hospital	FICHEUX Ed. 3 b 1/10,000
BLAIREVILLE	23.3.17	8.30 am.	Advanced party left under 2/Lt BARKER for BLAIREVILLE. Company marched out at 11 am and rear party at 5 pm. Transport left MONCHIET at 1.30 pm and bivouaced for night in no man's land at M 34 a 0.3. Company billeted at about X 4 a 9.6	
	24.3.17		All sections to railway cutting in S2 to collect material from German works nearby. Transport and horse lines established at M 27 c 9.1.	
	25.3.17		Work begun with working party of 200 infantry on the construction of splinterproof shelters in railway cutting. Twelve shelters started - 2/Lt BARKER detached for construction of fresh picture ground	
	26.3.17		Work continued. 2/Lt HOFFMAN joined as supernumerary officer.	
	27.3.17 28.3.17		} Work continued.	
	29.3.17		Work continued. 21st Brigade HQ moved into shelters erected. 22 shelters now in hand.	
	30.3.17 31.3.17		} Work continued. No infantry party on 31st	

M. Napier Clavering
Major RE
O.C. 200th Fld Co RE.

Instructions regarding War Diaries and Intelligence Summaries are contained in F. S. Regs., Part II. and the Staff Manual respectively. Title pages will be prepared in manuscript.

WAR DIARY
or
~~INTELLIGENCE SUMMARY.~~ 200th Field Coy. R.E.

(Erase heading not required.)

Army Form C. 2118.

Place	Date	Hour	Summary of Events and Information	Remarks and references to Appendices
DAINVILLE AGNY MONCHIET BLAIREVILLE			Casualties for the month of March 1917	
			= HOSPITAL =	
	2.3.17	–	1 O.R. to Hospital (Sickness) 2-3-17	
	6.3.17	–	1 O.R. do do 6.3.17	
	11.3.17	–	2 O.R. do do 11.3.17	
	17.3.17	–	3 O.R. do do 17.3.17	
	14.3.17	–	Lieut L. A. Hill R.E. Admitted to Hospital (Sickness) 14-3-17	
	22.3.17	–	Lieut L. A. Hill R.E. Rejoined from Hospital 22-3-17	
	1.3.17	–	1 O.R. Rejoined from Hospital 1-3-17	
	2.3.17	–	2 O.R. do 2-3-17	
	5.3.17	–	1 O.R. do 5-3-17	
	20.3.17	–	2 O.R. do 20-3-17	
	6.3.17	–	1 O.R. to Hospital 6-3-17 } To C.C.S. Struck of the strength of the Company.	
	2.3.17	–	1 O.R. do 2-3-17 }	
	11.3.17	–	1 O.R. do 11-3-17 }	
	17.3.17	–	2 O.R. do 17-3-17 }	
			= REINFORCEMENTS =	
	5.3.17	–	3 O.R. Arrived from R.E. Base Depot 5-3-17 } These men having joined the unit on dates shown are taken on the strength of the unit.	
	11.3.17	–	1 O.R. do do 11.3.17 }	
	25.3.17	–	2 O.R. do do 25.3.17 }	
	25.3.17	–	II Lieut. C. C. Hoffman R.E. Joined from R.E. Base Depot 25-3-17 Supernumerary Officer	

Instructions regarding War Diaries and Intelligence Summaries are contained in F. S. Regs., Part II. and the Staff Manual respectively. Title pages will be prepared in manuscript.

WAR DIARY
or
~~INTELLIGENCE SUMMARY.~~ 200th Field Coy. R.E.

(Erase heading not required.)

Army Form C. 2118.

Place	Date	Hour	Summary of Events and Information	Remarks and references to Appendices
DAINVILLE			= ATTACHMENT =	
AGNY				
MONCHIET	4.3.17		61496 Dvr. Howells S.J. From H.Qrs. C.R.E. 3rd Division to 200th Fd Co R.E. 4.3.17	
BLAIREVILLE	"		83446 " Roberts H.J. From 200th Fd Co R.E. to H.Qrs. C.R.E. 3rd Division 4.3.17	
			= DETACHED =	
	28.3.17		81866 A/Cpl Reeves J.H. To R.E. Base Depot 28.3.17. Instructional duties at R.E. Base Dept.	

W. Draper Clavering
Major

O.C. 200TH FIELD CO., R.E.

1.4.17.

2353 Wt. W2544/1454 700,000 5/15 D. D. & L. A.D.S.S./Forms/C. 2118.

WAR DIARY
or
INTELLIGENCE SUMMARY.
(Erase heading not required.)

Army Form C. 2118.

Instructions regarding War Diaries and Intelligence Summaries are contained in F. S. Regs., Part II. and the Staff Manual respectively. Title pages will be prepared in manuscript.

VOL XVI (cont) 200th FIELD COMPANY R.E.

Place	Date	Hour	Summary of Events and Information	Remarks and references to Appendices
BEAURAINS	24.4.17.	12.45 pm	Received orders from CRE. to place Nos 1 & 4 Sections at disposal of 21st Bde for consolidation of enemy front line system.	Maps. FRANCE 1/20000 51B.S.W. Ed 4A.
		7.0 pm.	Message received from Lt HILL stating that 21st Brigade had referred him to 89th Bde for work. at 5.30 pm. No1 Section went up to assist 17th Kings. No4 to 20th Kings Liverpool Regt. No1 Section dug a strong point at N 30 c 9.5. No4 assisted in digging support line with 5 MG. and 4 Lewis Gun emplacements from N 30 c 7.1 to N 35 b 9.0.	Casualties nil.
	25.4.17.	2.0 am.	Received orders from CRE. to use one Section from 10 am on construction of Advanced Dressing Station at N 28 c 2.2.	
		7.50 am	OC. 97th Field Ambulance came to explain requirement of ADS.	
		9.0 am.	No2 Section 2Lt CHIDGEY marched out to work on ADS. returned at 7.0 pm.	Casualties nil.
		4.30 pm	No3 Section 2Lt HOFFMAN marched out to construct splinter proof shelter at Adv. Bde HQ at N 22 d 45.15. Work completed by 2.30 am.	
	26.4.17.	7.30 am	No2 Section marched out to continue work on ADS. completed at 6.0 pm. with help from 1 Section of 202nd Fld Co. RE	Casualties nil.
		9.0 am.	No1 Section, & No4 Section marched out to work on clearing of wells in HENINEL. 28 wells cleared & repaired	
	27.4.17.	9.0 am.	Nos 1, 3, 4 Sections worked on clearing HENINEL - WANCOURT road and improving the same to N 23 c.6.3.	
GOUY EN ARTOIS	28.4.17.	11.0 am.	Transport and cyclists marched out moving by ACHICOURT & SIMENCOURT to GOUY-EN-ARTOIS where they bivouaced for the night.	FRANCE 1/10000
SIBIVILLE		12 noon.	Remainder of Company marched to ARRAS STATION for entrainment.	LENS 11 Casualties 2 wounded
		2 pm.	Entrained	
		9.0 pm	Arrived PETIT HOUVIN STATION marched to SIBIVILLE and went into billets there.	
	29.4.17.	4.0 pm	Transport marched in from GOUY.	
	30.4.17.		Training. Route march - 9.30 am - 1 pm.	

Mc Raper Claverin[?] Major RE.
OC. 200th Field Co RE.
1 May 1917.

2353 Wt. W2544/1454 700,000 5/15 D. D. & L. A.D.S.S./Forms/C. 2118.

Instructions regarding War Diaries and Intelligence Summaries are contained in F. S. Regs., Part II. and the Staff Manual respectively. Title pages will be prepared in manuscript.

WAR DIARY
~~or~~
INTELLIGENCE ~~SUMMARY.~~
(Erase heading not required.)

Army Form C. 2118.

200th Field Company R.E.

Place	Date	Hour	Summary of Events and Information	Remarks and references to Appendices
Blairville			Casualties for the month of April 1917	
BEAURAINS			– HOSPITAL –	
SIBIVILLE.	31.3.17		1 O.R. to Hospital (Sickness) 31.3.17 To C.C.S. Struck off the strength.	
	23.4.17		1 O.R. to (do) 23.4.17	
	2.4.17		2nd Lieut T.O. LESLIE R.E. to Hospital (Sickness) 2.4.17	
	7.4.17		1 O.R. WOUNDED (Shellfire) to Hospital 7.4.17 To C.C.S. 8/4/17 Struck off the strength.	
	28.4.17		2 O.R. WOUNDED (do) " 28.4.17 (1 O.R. died from wounds at Fd. Amb. 28/4/17)	
			– REINFORCEMENTS –	
	2.4.17		1 O.R. Arrived from No 2 (Reinforcement Coy R.E. 2.4.17	
	15.4.17		1 O.R. do do do 15.4.17	
	17.4.17		2 O.R. do do do 17.4.17	
	22.4.17		3 O.R. do do do 22.4.17	
			– TRANSFERS –	
	23.11.16		236942 Spr. Payne G. from 1st Bedford Regt. to 200th Fd. Coy. R.E. (Transferred to R.E. under A.O. 204/16. AUTHORITY A.G. 38706/118 Y1488/p618 dated 28.3.17.	
	1.4.17		83446 Dvr. Roberts A.F. from 200th Fd. Co. R.E. to H.Qrs. 30th Divl. Engrs. 1.4.17.	
	"		61496 " Howells S.T. from 30th Divl. Engrs. H.Qrs. to 200th Field Company R.E. 1.4.17. (AUTHORITY R.E. Base Records E1/24/296 dated 5.4.17	
	26.4.17		81904 Spr. Scragg E. Transferred to Base for DENTAL TREATMENT (AUTHORITY A.D.M.S. 30th Division No. M995/5 dated 17.4.17.	

W. Draper Clavering Major

O.C. 200TH FIELD CO., R.E.

2353 Wt. W2544/1454 700,000 5/15 D. D. & L. A.D.S.S./Forms/C. 2118.

SECRET

Vol 17

WAR DIARY.

of the

200th Field Company, Royal Engineers.

for the month of

MAY 1917.

(VOLUME: XVII).

Instructions regarding War Diaries and Intelligence Summaries are contained in F. S. Regs., Part II. and the Staff Manual respectively. Title pages will be prepared in manuscript.

WAR DIARY

or

~~INTELLIGENCE SUMMARY.~~

(Erase heading not required.)

Army Form C. 2118.

VOL XVII.

200th FIELD COMPANY R.E.

MAPS. FRANCE 1/100,000 LENS 11 HAZEBROUCK 5A.

Place	Date	Hour	Summary of Events and Information	No 1 Sec.	No 2 Sec.	No 3 Sec.	No 4 Sec.	Remarks and references to Appendices
SIBIVILLE	1.5.17.		Company in billets in SIBIVILLE resting and training. Squad Drill & Rifle Exercises.					Weather. V Fine
	2.5.17.							"
BOFFLES	3.5.17.	12.30pm	Marched under orders of 89th Bde. by FREVENT and VACQUERIE-LE-BOUCQ. to BOFFLES arriving about 4 pm.					"
	4.5.17.		Training, improving billets, making rifle range.					"
	5.5.17.		Training.	Completed range.	Training in laying out Strong Points.			"
	6.5.17.		Church parade at BOFFLES	–	–	–	Work on Dw. Baths at CONCHY-SUR-CANCHE.	"
	7.5.17.		Training	Laying out Strong Points	Rapid wiring	Farm work		"
	8.5.17		" Bridging carried out at MONCHEL	Musketry	Pontoon & trestle bridging	Rapid wiring	"	Rain then fine.
	9.5.17.		" Labour provided daily to assist farmers	Rapid wiring	Musketry	Pontoon & trestle bridging	"	V. Fine
	10.5.17.		" in carrying and spreading manure.	Pontoon & Trestle bridging	Inf. Tr.	Musketry	"	"
	11.5.17.		"	Inf. Tr. & night work.	Laying out S.P. at night. Pontoon & Trestle bridging	Night work	Musketry & night work	"
	12.5.17.		"	Inter section shooting competition			–	"
	13.5.17.		Church parade at FORTEL	–	–	–	–	Thunderstorms.
	14.5.17.		Training	Inf. Tr. and laying out S.P.		Farm work etc.	Rapid wiring.	Fair.
	15.5.17.		"	Use of spars in BACHIMONT wood		Musketry.	Inf. Tr. & night wiring	Dull.
	16.5.17.		"	Inf. Tr. & night wiring	Musketry.	Use of spars	Use of spars.	"
	17.5.17.		"	Musketry	Rapid wiring	Inf Training	Use of spars.	Dull some rain
	18.5.17.		"	Use of spars	Use of spars	Inf Training	Musketry.	Cloudy
	19.5.17.		General fatigues preparatory to move.					Dull
SERICOURT	20.5.17.	9.15am	Marched by VACQUERIE-LE-BOUCQ and LIGNY to SERICOURT. arriving at 12.30 pm.					Fine warm
BELVAL	21.5.17.	8.40am	Marched by ST. POL and TROISVAUX to BELVAL arriving at 2.15pm.					Dull some rain
ECQUEDECQUES	22.5.17.	7.0am	Marched by PERNES, FLORINGHEM and FERFAY ECQUEDECQUES arriving at 1.0 pm.					Rain.
	23.5.17.		Rest.					Fine.
TANNY	24.5.17.	7.30am	Marched by LAPESSES, ST HILAIRE, NORRET, FONTES, LAMBRES, AIRE, NEUFPRE and THIENNES to TANNY					Fine
CAESTRE	25.5.17.	6.30am	Marched by THIENNES, MORBECQUE, HAZEBROUCK and LE BREARDE to CAESTRE arriving 12.30 pm.					Fine warm
	26.5.17	7.45am	Marched by EECKE and STEENVOORDE to area South of WATOU. arriving in billets at 10.45 am.					Fine hot.

Instructions regarding War Diaries and Intelligence Summaries are contained in F. S. Regs., Part II. and the Staff Manual respectively. Title pages will be prepared in manuscript.

WAR DIARY
or
~~INTELLIGENCE SUMMARY.~~
(Erase heading not required.)

Army Form C. 2118.

VOL XVII (cont)

200th Fld Co. R.E.

Place	Date	Hour	Summary of Events and Information MAPS. FRANCE HAZEBROUCK 5A. BELGIUM 1/20000 28. N.W. 1Ed. 5A. ZILLEBEKE 1/10000 Ed. 5A.	Remarks and references to Appendices
BRANDHOEK	27.5.17	8.45am.	Marched by POPERINGHE to camp near BRANDHOEK in G11c arriving at 11.30 am. Lt HILL and 2 NCOs proceeded to YPRES to take over billets and work from 129th Field Co. RE.	Fine
	28.5.17		In camp. resting.	Dull
YPRES.	29.5.17	8.0pm.	Marched by VLAMERTINGHE to YPRES arriving at 9.30 pm. Transport arrived at 3 am. Lines remained as before	Dull to fair.
	30.5.17	10.0pm	Reconnaissance made by O.C. 200, 201, 202 Fld Cos & subalterns. Lt HILL of this Coy. for new front line trench I 18 a 6.5. to I 24 b 3.7. Reconnaissance of present front line by Lts BARKER and HOFFMAN No4 Section working on revetting of MAPLE TRENCH I 24 a 00.75. Transport lines moved to G 12 b. 3.6.	V. Fine & warm.
	31.5.17		No1 repairing tramway. No2 dump duties & stores. No3 & 4 work on strengthening and rebuilding front line trench in Gap A I 24 b. 2.9. No4 also working on MAPLE TRENCH.	Fine warm.

[signature]
Major RE.
O.C. 200th Fld Co RE.

2353 Wt. W2544/1454 700,000 5/15 D. D. & L. A.D.S.S./Forms/C. 2118.

Army Form C. 2118.

WAR DIARY
or
INTELLIGENCE SUMMARY.
(Erase heading not required.)

200th Field Company R.E.

Instructions regarding War Diaries and Intelligence Summaries are contained in F. S. Regs., Part II. and the Staff Manual respectively. Title pages will be prepared in manuscript.

Place	Date	Hour	Summary of Events and Information	Remarks and references to Appendices
			Casualties for the month of May 1917	
			— HOSPITAL —	
BOFFLES	6.5.17		1 O.R. to Hospital (Sickness) 6.5.17.	
	15.5.17		1 O.R. to Hospital (do) 15.5.17.	
	19.5.17		2 O.R. to Hospital (do) 19.5.17	
ACQUEDECQUES	23.5.17		1 O.R. to Hospital (do) 23.5.17	
BRANDHOEK	28.5.17		1 O.R. to Hospital (do) 28.5.17	
	18.5.17		1 O.R. Rejoined from Hospital 18.5.17.	
	19.5.17		2 O.R. to Hospital 19.5.17 To C.C.S 19.5.17 } These men have been struck off the strength of the Company.	
	18.5.17		1 O.R. do 15.5.17 do 18.5.17	
	30.5.17		1 O.R. do 28.5.17 do 30.5.17	
	23.4.17		1 O.R. do 23.4.17 do	
	28.4.17		1 O.R. do 28.4.17 do	
			— REINFORCEMENTS —	
	6.5.17		4 O.R. Joined from No 2 Reinforcement Coy R.E. 6.5.17 } These men have been taken on the strength of the Company.	
	6.5.17		1 O.R. " from R.E. Base Depot 6.5.17	
	10.5.17		1 O.R. " from No 5 Reinforcement Coy R.E. 10.5.17	
			— COMMISSIONS —	
	22.5.17		81321 Sergt BOYES R. To England 22.5.17.	
	24.5.17		81306 IICpl. RAINFORD J. -do- 24.5.17	
			AUTHY: D.A.A.G. 30 Division No A6317 dated 16.5.17.	

2353 Wt. W2544/1454 700,000 5/15 D. D. & L. A.D.S.S./Forms/C. 2118.

Instructions regarding War Diaries and Intelligence Summaries are contained in F. S. Regs., Part II. and the Staff Manual respectively. Title pages will be prepared in manuscript.

WAR DIARY
or
INTELLIGENCE SUMMARY.
(Erase heading not required.)

200th Field Company R.E.

Army Form C. 2118.

Place	Date	Hour	Summary of Events and Information	Remarks and references to Appendices
			Casualties for month of May cont.d	
			– TRANSFERS –	
	25.5.17		81496 Spr. DOOLEY O. from 201st Field Company R.E. to 200th Field Company R.E. on the 25.5.17.	
			AUTHY: R.E. Base Records, A.G's Office, R.E. Section No F1/24/439 dated 13.5.17	

M. Stapes-Dawson [?]
Major R.E.
O.C. 200TH FIELD CO. R.E.

SECRET

Vol 18

War Diary

of the

200th Field Company Royal Engineers.

for the month of June 1917

Volume XVIII

Instructions regarding War Diaries and Intelligence Summaries are contained in F. S. Regs., Part II. and the Staff Manual respectively. Title pages will be prepared in manuscript.

WAR DIARY
or
~~INTELLIGENCE SUMMARY.~~
(Erase heading not required.)

Army Form C. 2118.

VOL. XVIII

200th Field Company R.E.

Place	Date	Hour	Summary of Events and Information 1/10000 ZILLEBEKE 28 NW4 & NE3 parts of. Ed 5A; 1/20000 BELGIUM 28 N.W. Ed 5A	Remarks and references to Appendices
				Weather
YPRES. } BRANDHOEK }	1.6.17		Company in billets in YPRES transport lines at G12b 3.6. No1 employed on repairs to Tramline East of YPRES. No2 on dump and store duties and repairs to VINCE ST. at I22b 90.15. No3 on reconstruction of front line trench at I24b.2.9. No4 on revetting of MAPLE TR. at I24a 00.75 and on BORDER LANE. Transport lines shelled during night of 31st-1st	V. Fine.
	2.6.17		Transport lines moved to G16a 0.4. Repairs to Tramway and store duties continued: remainder of company practised wiring. Lt HILL and 2Lt HOFFMAN and NCO's reconnoitred line for wire from I18a 95.00. to I18d 5.5.	V. Fine.
	3.6.17.		New trench dug in no man's land by 11th S. Lancs Regt Pioneers. Whole company employed in erecting 400 yds of wire entanglement from I18d 95.00. to I18d 5.5.: line traced by Lt HILL. YPRES and area to east was heavily shelled with gas shell during the early morning of 4th	V. Fine. Appendix A.
	4.6.17		No1 Section began to relay the cable to the CULVERT mines in I.18 a. also to erect new shelter at Reg. Aid Post at HALFWAY HOUSE I17c3.6. No2 Section on dumps & stores: Nos 3 & 4 sections with large infantry parties on the improvement of front line Trenches I24.9., I18.1., I18.2. No4 also revetting MAPLE TR.	V. Fine
	5.6.17.		No1 completed Reg. Aid Post & made knife rests. No2 dumps, stores & making knife rests. No3 2Lt HOFFMAN laid out and supervised new trench from I18c 5.7. to I17b 95.65. working party 280 infantry. No4 2Lt BARNER laid out and supervised work on new trench from I18c 95.20. to I24b 0.7. working party 100 infantry.	V. Fine
	6.6.17.		No1, No3, part of No2 making knife rests. 100 yards of wire put out by infantry from I24 a 5.9. southwards. Rem. No2 repaired VINCE ST & No4 erected 50 yds of screen along parados of I24 9. & continued work on MAPLE TR.	V. Fine

2353 Wt. W2544/1454 700,000 5/15 D. D. & L. A.D.S.S./Forms/C. 2118.

Instructions regarding War Diaries and Intelligence Summaries are contained in F. S. Regs., Part II. and the Staff Manual respectively. Title pages will be prepared in manuscript.

WAR DIARY
or
INTELLIGENCE SUMMARY.
(Erase heading not required.)

Army Form C. 2118.

Vol XVIII (cont^d)

200th Field Company R.E.

1/10000 ZILLEBEKE 28 NW 4 + NE 3 parts of. Ed. 5A.
1/20000 BELGIUM 28 NW Ed 5A.

Place	Date	Hour	Summary of Events and Information	Remarks and references to Appendices
				Weather -
YPRES	7.6.17		Zero hour 3.15 am. Xth Corps on our right flank attacked successfully. Company held in readiness in case 85th Bde should	V Fine
BRANDHOEK			become involved. Wiring stores carried to BORDER LANE I 24 b 00.25.	
	8.6.17		Nos 1 & 4 formed dump of battle stores at I 17 d 30.65. No 2 dump duties etc. No 3 took timbers etc to BORDER LANE	V. Fine
	9.6.17	6 pm	Handed over to 201st and 202nd Field Cos. Company marched out to hutments at G 12 b 3.7.	Dull to fine
	10.6.17		Rest. 2/Lt BARKER detailed for work on model picture ground for II Corps.	
	11.6.17		Nos 1 & 3 Sections worked on erection of huts for Corps HQ at G 16 c 0.6. No 2 Section on corduroy track from KRUISTRAAT	Dull showery
			eastwards. No 4 Section on dump etc	
	12.6.17		Work continued. No 4 Section employed on picture ground.	V Fine & Thunder
	13.6.17		Work continued.	
DICKEBUSH HUT	14.6.17		Work continued. Company with HQ and Transport moved into camp at H 26 b 55.75	Fine warm
CAMP	15.6.17		Work continued. Work on forward road by No 2 Section handed over to 190th Field Co. RE	"
	16.6.17		Work continued	"
	17.6.17		Work continued.	Rain
	18.6.17		Work continued. Corps HQ huts finished.	Fair
	19.6.17		Work continued on picture ground. Remainder of company resting.	Thundery
	20.6.17			"

2353 Wt. W2544/1454 700,000 5/15 D. D. & L. A.D.S.S./Forms/C. 2118.

Instructions regarding War Diaries and Intelligence Summaries are contained in F. S. Regs., Part II and the Staff Manual respectively. Title pages will be prepared in manuscript.

WAR DIARY
or
~~INTELLIGENCE SUMMARY.~~
(Erase heading not required.)

Army Form C. 2118.

Vol XVIII (Contd)

200th Field Company R.E.

Sheet ZILLEBEKE 28 N.W. 4 & N.E. 3 parts of. Ed 5 A.
1/20000 BELGIUM 28 N.W. Ed 5 A.

Place	Date	Hour	Summary of Events and Information	Remarks and references to Appendices
DICKEBUSH HUTS	21.6.17.		Rest. No 4 Section continued work on picture ground.	Fair, Showers
CAMP.	22.6.17	2.15 am.	Nos 1, 2, 3 Sections marched to dugouts at I 15 d 0.0. relieving 202nd Field Co RE. Work taken over from 201st Fld Co RE.	Fine
ZILLEBEKE			All work done at night. No 1 Section on 2 Heavy TM Emplacements at I 24 c 8.2. No 2 Section on [illegible] Bn HQ in MAPLE	
BUND			ST at I 24 a 0.6. No 3 Section on stores and improvement of ZILLEBEKE dugouts.	
	23.6.17.	5 am.	No 4 Section marched in from DICKEBUSH HUTS CAMP. Lt BARBER and 20 OR remained to work on picture ground.	Fine
			Work continued and No 4 on PETER ST. Lt HOFFMAN traced assembly trenches from I 17 c 7.3 to I 17 c 7.0. and I 17 c 8.3 to	
			I 17 c 8.0. with two C.T.s between them and one to [illegible] ST. Working party 440 men. ZILLEBEKE BUND heavily	
			shelled during night with HE and gas shells.	
	24.6.17.		Gasworks Dump I 18 a 9.2 heavily shelled 2 NCOs killed. Work continued. Lt HILL RE traced assembly trench	Fine
			from I 24 d 6.9 to I 24 b 2.4. Work was started on it. Work continued on assembly trench begun on 23.6.17	
	25.6.17.		No 1 and No 4 Sections on HTM Emplacements. Work continued as before.	Fine [illegible]
	26.6.17.		Heavy hostile shelling of area west of ZILLEBEKE BUND. Working parties delayed. Work continued. No 3 Sec	Fair.
			constructed splinter-proof shelter for visual signalling point at I 28 a 5.8.	
	27.6.17		Work continued. No infantry parties owing to relief of 21st Bde by 89th Bde. Lt CORDINER joined company	
	28.6.17		Work interfered with by very heavy thunder storm at 10 pm.	Fair. heavy [illegible]
	29.6.17.		Hostile artillery very active. Work continued but much delayed by enemy barrage which lasted	

2353 Wt. W2544/1454 700,000 5/15 D. D. & L. A.D.S.S./Forms/C. 2118.

Army Form C. 2118.

WAR DIARY
or
~~INTELLIGENCE SUMMARY~~.
(Erase heading not required.)

Instructions regarding War Diaries and Intelligence Summaries are contained in F. S. Regs., Part II. and the Staff Manual respectively. Title pages will be prepared in manuscript.

VOL XVIII (cont) 200th Field Company, RE.

Place	Date	Hour	Summary of Events and Information	Remarks and references to Appendices
ZILLEBEKE			from 11.10pm – 12.10 am approx	
BUND	30.6.17		Work continued. Lt HILL traced and supervised work on new trench from I 18c 8.5. to I 24d 0.3.	Rain Dull.
DICKEBUSH HUTS			Work started on the conversion of old gunpits and shelters in MAPLE COPSE, I [illegible] into Bn. HQ.	
CAMP.			A party also worked on the clearing of BORDER LANE	

[illegible] Major RE.
O.C. 200th Field Co. RE

2353 Wt. W2544/1454 700,000 5/15 D. D. & L. A.D.S.S./Forms/C. 2118.

Army Form C. 2118.

Instructions regarding War Diaries and Intelligence Summaries are contained in F. S. Regs., Part II. and the Staff Manual respectively. Title Pages will be prepared in manuscript.

WAR DIARY
~~or~~
~~INTELLIGENCE SUMMARY~~
(Erase heading not required.)

VOL XVIII — 200th Field Company R.E.

Place	Date	Hour	Summary of Events and Information	Remarks and references to Appendices
			Casualties for the month of June 1917	
			– HOSPITAL –	
YPRES				
BRANDHOEK	3.6.17		2 O.R. to Hospital (Sickness) 3.6.17.	
DICKEBUSH HUT CAMP.	5.6.17		2 O.R. -do- (Gas Poisoning) 5.6.17.	
ZILLEBEKE BUND.	6.6.17		2 O.R. -do- (Sickness) 6.6.17.	
	11.6.17		1 O.R. -do- (do) 11.6.17.	
	12.6.17		1 O.R. -do- (do) 12.6.17.	
	19.6.17		1 O.R. -do- (do) 19.6.17.	
	18.6.17		1 O.R. -do- (do) 18.6.17.	
	7.6.17		1 O.R. -do- (do) 7.6.17.	
	26.6.17		2 O.R. -do- (do) 26.6.17.	
	24.6.17		1 O.R. -do- (do) 24.6.17.	
	27.6.17		1 O.R. -do- (do) 27.6.17	
	9.6.17		1 O.R. Rejoined from Hospital 9.6.17.	
	18.6.17		1 O.R. -do- 18.6.17.	
	21.6.17		1 O.R. -do- 21.6.17.	
	28.6.17		1 O.R. -do- 28.6.17.	

2449 Wt. W14957/M90 750,000 1/16 J.B.C. & A. Forms/C.2118/12.

Instructions regarding War Diaries and Intelligence Summaries are contained in F. S. Regs., Part II. and the Staff Manual respectively. Title Pages will be prepared in manuscript.

WAR DIARY
or
~~INTELLIGENCE SUMMARY~~

(Erase heading not required.)

200th Field Company R.E.

Army Form C. 2118.

Place	Date	Hour	Summary of Events and Information	Remarks and references to Appendices
			Casualties for June 1917 contd	
	6.6.17		4 O.R. At Hospital 5.6.17 To C.C.S. 6.6.17.	
	8.6.17		1 O.R. do 8.6.17 -do- 8.6.17.	
	13.6.17		1 O.R. do 11.6.17 -do- 13.6.17.	
	23.5.17		1 O.R. do 23.5.17 -do-	
	26.6.17		1 O.R. do 26.6.17 -do- 26.6.17.	
	24.6.17		1 O.R. do 24.6.17 -do- 24.6.17.	
	18.6.17		1 O.R. do 18.6.17 -do- 18.6.17.	
	25.6.17		1 O.R. do 25.6.17 -do- 26.6.17. } These men have been struck off the strength of the Company.	
	1.6.17		1 O.R. Killed in action (shellfire) 1.6.17.	
	6.6.17		1 O.R. -do- (do) 6.6.17.	
	24.6.17		1 O.R. -do- (do) 24.6.17.	
	2.6.17		3 O.R. Wounded (do) 2.6.17. To C.C.S. 3.6.17	
	24.6.17		1 O.R. -do- (do) 24.6.17 " 24.6.17 } Struck off the strength of the Coy.	
	26.6.17		1 O.R. Slightly wounded (shellfire) 26.6.17 Remains at duty.	
			– REINFORCEMENTS –	
	18.6.17		2 O.R. from R.E. Base Depot 18.6.17.	
	21.6.17		1 O.R. do do 21.6.17.	
	25.6.17		7 O.R. from No 4 Reinforcement Coy R.E. 25.6.17. } These men have been taken on the strength of the Company	
			– TRANSFERS –	
	27.6.17		Lieut. F.E.R. DIXON from 155th Fd.Co.R.E. to 200th Fd.Co.R.E. 27.6.17	
			AUTHY: A.G.s No A/22358/724 dated 19.6.17. Hdqrs 50 Div. No A/1322 dated 21.6.17	

2449 Wt. W14957/M90 750,000 1/16 J.B.C. & A. Forms/C.2118/12.

Vol 19

WAR DIARY

of

200th FIELD COMPANY, ROYAL ENGINEERS

for the

month of

JULY 1917.

(VOLUME XIX)

Instructions regarding War Diaries and Intelligence Summaries are contained in F. S. Regs., Part II. and the Staff Manual respectively. Title pages will be prepared in manuscript.

WAR DIARY
or
~~INTELLIGENCE SUMMARY.~~
(Erase heading not required.)

Army Form C. 2118.

VOL XIX

200th Field Company R.E.

Place	Date	Hour	Summary of Events and Information 1/10000 ZILLEBEKE 28 NW4 & NE3 parts of. Ed 5A. 1/20000 BELGIUM 28 NW. Ed 5A.	Remarks and references to Appendices
				Weather.
ZILLEBEKE BUND.	1.7.17		Enemy exploded dump of 6" shell at GAS WORKS R.E. DUMP at about 2.0 pm destroying dump & dugout. NCO i/c killed and two	Dull.
DICKEBUSH HUTS CAMP.			assistants injured shellshock. 2Lt HOFFMAN slightly wounded while searching for NCO. Work continued by Nos 1 & 4 Section	
			on H.T.M. Emplacements, No 2 on MAPLE TR. Bn HQ's, No 3 on MAPLE COPSE Bn HQ & STRAND.	
	2.7.17.		Work continued. Great difficulty in getting stores forward owing to constant damage to tramline by shelling.	V. Fine.
	3.7.17.		Work continued. Reconnaissances made by Lt DIXON and 2Lt CHIDGEY for routes for 6" Howitzers from [illegible] road to ZILLEBEKE and for field guns from ZILLEBEKE to SANCTUARY WOOD respectively.	V. Fine.
	4.7.17.		Work continued. MAPLE COPSE Bn HQ completed. Hostile artillery very active.	Dull.
	5.7.17		Work continued. BUND heavily shelled from 9-11 am. Many shelters destroyed. Artillery also active against YPRES	Dull & Fine
	6.7.17		Work on Heavy TM Emplacements handed over to 80th Fld Co. RE. The remainder to 79th Fld Co RE.	Fine.
	7.7.17	2.50 am	Transport arrived at BUND loaded up and left for Transport lines.	Fine.
		3.45 am	Company marched out from ZILLEBEKE BUND to DICKEBUSH HUTS CAMP.	
	8.7.17.		Rest.	Rain. Dull.
	9.7.17.		Nos 1 & 2 sections working on camouflaging of the PROMENADE 121 b [illegible] to 122 a ~~[illegible]~~ 25.95. [illegible] sent to No 5 Mobile Workshops for work under [illegible]. 13 OR working under Lt BARRETT on Corps Model Picture Ground.	Dull. Drizzle
	10.7.17		Work on PROMENADE taken on by 80 Fld Co RE. Stores sent up by us. Other work carried on. [illegible]	Cloudy
	11.7.17.		Work & training continued.	Cloudy.

2353 Wt. W2544/1454 700,000 5/15 D. D. & L. A.D.S.S./Forms/C. 2118.

Instructions regarding War Diaries and Intelligence Summaries are contained in F. S. Regs., Part II. and the Staff Manual respectively. Title pages will be prepared in manuscript.

WAR DIARY
or
~~INTELLIGENCE SUMMARY.~~
(Erase heading not required.)

Army Form C. 2118.

VOL XIX (cont)

200th Field Company R.E.

SECRET $\frac{1}{10000}$ ZILLEBEKE 28 NW4 & NE3 parts of 5A; $\frac{1}{20000}$ BELGIUM 28 NW. Ed 5A.

Place	Date	Hour	Summary of Events and Information	Remarks and references to Appendices
DICKEBUSCH HUTS	12.7.17.		Infantry training. Work on picture ground continued	V.Fine
CAMP.	13.7.17.		Rapid wiring practice. "	V.Fine
	14.7.17.		Laying out strong points. Nos 1 & 4 inoculated. "	Thunder. cloudy
	15.7.17.		Work continued. "	Rain to fine.
	16.7.17.		Reconnaissance made of Track No1. from LILLE ROAD to STAFFORD TRENCH. Nos 2 & 3 inoculated.	Fine
	17.7.17.		Nos 1 & 4 Sections worked on Track No1 under Lt CAMERON. Work on picture ground as usual.	Fine
	18.7.17.		Work continued with working party of 30 infantry on track.	Dull to Fair.
	19.7.17.		No1 Section on track. No3 with infantry parties making auxiliary water points at G 24 c 15.40., H 26 a 4.8., H 25 b 6.3.	Cloudy to fine.
	20.7.17.		No2 Section on track. No3 as before. Attempt made to get battle stores to VALLEY COTTAGE DUMP near I 23 c 8.5. owing to a block in the road the stores had to be dumped on the road in I 21 central.	V.Fine
	21.7.17.		Work continued. No1 Section succeeded in getting the greater part of the stores required up to VALLEY COTTAGES.	V.Fine.
	22.7.17.		Work continued. Nos 3 & 4 working as well on accessories for Adv. Div. HQ. H 27 b 6.7. Camp shelled at 6 pm.	
	23.7.17.		Work continued. Track No11 (formerly No1) completed. 500 of R [illegible] & remainder of battle stores [illegible] 400 short. Some pickets dumped at VALLEY COTTAGES. [illegible] 2nd [illegible] Capt [illegible] evacuated to England sick.	Cloudy [illegible]
	24.7.17.		Nos 1 & 2 Sections resting & refitting. Nos 3 & 4 Sections working on Advanced Div. HQ.	Fair. Dull.

2353 Wt. W2544/1454 700,000 5/15 D. D. & L. A.D.S.S./Forms/C. 2118.

Army Form C. 2118.

Instructions regarding War Diaries and Intelligence Summaries are contained in F. S. Regs., Part II. and the Staff Manual respectively. Title pages will be prepared in manuscript.

WAR DIARY
or
~~INTELLIGENCE SUMMARY.~~
(Erase heading not required.)

Vol XIX (cont)

200th Field Company R.E.

Maps: 1/10000 ZILLEBEKE 28 N.W. 4 + NE 3. parts of Ed 5A; 1/20000 BELGIUM 28 N.W. Ed 5A.

Place	Date	Hour	Summary of Events and Information	Remarks and references to Appendices
DICKEBUSCH HUTS	25.7.17.		Work as for 24.7.17	Rain to Fair.
CAMP	26.7.17.		No4 Section sent up to clear RITZ ST and WELLINGTON CRESCENT. No1 Section working on tracks 10 & 11 and track H east of CHATEAU SEGARD. No3 Section working on Adv Div. HQ.	
	27.7.17		No1 on tracks. No4 practicing loading of pack transport.	Fine
	28.7.17		Company held in readiness in case the retirement of the enemy from his front line North of YPRES should lead to developments on Div front. Party from No4 Section sent to bury cables on track H from DICKEBUSCH to CHATEAU SEGARD.	V Fine.
	29.7.17		No1 Section working on tracks 11 & 12. No2 Section clearing RITZ ST, No3 clearing VINCE ST, WELLINGTON CRESCENT and MAPLE TR. No4 making concertina barbed wire. 2Lt LANNON arrived from 155th Fd Co in exchange for 2Lt DIXON M.C.	Rain thunder.
		9.0pm.	Four sections + OC moved into bivouacs in assembly area at H 29 a 7.6.	
	30.7.17.	6.0pm	Convoy of 44 mules for carriage of RE stores taken over at H 26 a 8.8 and moved up to assembly area. 2Lt SANVILLE joined as supernumerary.	Fair.
	31.7.17.	3.50 am	ZERO. Division attacked with 21st + 30th Bdes in the line.	Dull. ... very ...
		7.30 am.	No1 Section 2Lt CAMERON, No2 Section 2Lt CHIDGEY, No3 Section 2Lt BARKER, with three platoons of 11th S Lancs Regt paraded at H 29 a 7.6 for work. also mule convoy loaded with stores for wiring three two platoon strong points in support of the GREEN LINE	
		9.15am	Whole party arrived at VALLEY COTTAGES and took cover to await orders to advance. O.C. reported to	

2353 Wt. W2544/1454 700,000 5/15 D. D. & L. A.D.S.S./Forms/C. 2118.

Army Form C. 2118.

WAR DIARY
or
INTELLIGENCE SUMMARY

(Erase heading not required.)

Instructions regarding War Diaries and Intelligence Summaries are contained in F. S. Regs., Part II. and the Staff Manual respectively. Title Pages will be prepared in manuscript.

Vol. XIX (cont). 200th Field Company R.E.

Place	Date	Hour	Summary of Events and Information	Remarks and references to Appendices
	31.7.17		HQ. 89th Bde in I 17d there learning that the advance was held up in the neighbourhood of the Blue Line on the STIRLING CASTLE ridge	
		5.0pm	Received orders to employ the party on the consolidation of BLUE LINE and arranged with Brigade to construct three strong points for one platoon and one MG at approx J.19b.3.8, J 13 d 4 6, and J. 13b 6.3.	
		7.0pm	Started oading the mule convoy. four mules out of action so far.	
		8.0pm	Parties started from VALLEY COTTAGES.	
			In spite of darkness, rain, and considerable hostile shellfire, all sections succeeded in reaching their destinations. No 1 Section constructed a point at J 19b 25.80. Lt CAMERON was wounded, two sappers killed, four sappers wounded and five pioneers wounded. No 2 Section dug a point at J 13 d 45.65 and No 3 section, after consultation with O.C. 17th Bn K.L.R., at J13 d 6.8. The mule convoy had great difficulty in crossing the difficult ground in I. 18 c and d and only 18 mules reached the MENIN road where the stores they carried were dumped at approx J. 13b.1.1. Owing to the extreme darkness of the night it was not possible to inform the sections of this and consequently no one of the strong points dug was wired.	

M.W. Napier Clavering
Major RE.
O.C. 200th Field Co R.E.

2449 Wt W14957/M90 750,000 1/16 J.B.C. & A. Forms/C.2118/12.

Army Form C. 2118.

WAR DIARY
or
~~INTELLIGENCE~~ SUMMARY
(Erase heading not required.)

200th Field Coy. R.E.

Instructions regarding War Diaries and Intelligence Summaries are contained in F. S. Regs., Part II. and the Staff Manual respectively. Title Pages will be prepared in manuscript.

Place	Date	Hour	Summary of Events and Information	Remarks and references to Appendices
			Casualties for the month of July 1917.	
ZILLEBEKE				
DICKEBUSCH	30.6.17		1 (OR) to Hospital (Sickness) 30.6.17	
	2.7.17		1 (OR) " " 2.7.17	
	3.7.17		1 (OR) " " 3.7.17	
	2.7.17		1 (OR) " " 2.7.17	
	6.7.17		1 (OR) " " 6.7.17	
	11.7.17		1 (OR) " " 11.7.17	
	12.7.17		1 (OR) " " 12.7.17	
	15.7.17		1 (OR) " " 15.7.17	
	17.7.17		1 (OR) " " 17.7.17	
	24.7.17		1 (OR) " " 24.7.17	
	26.7.17		1 (OR) " " 26.7.17	
	6.7.17		1 (OR) Rejoined from Hospital 6.7.17	
	14.7.17		1 (OR) " " " 14.7.17	
	19.7.17		1 (OR) " " " 19.7.17	
	2.7.17		1 (OR) To Hospital 2.7.17 To C.C.S. 2.7.17	
	27.6.17		1 (OR) " 27.6.17 " 27.6.17	
	21.6.17		1 (OR) " 29.6.17 " 21.6.17	
	30.6.17		1 (OR) " 30.6.17 " 5.7.17	
	12.7.17		1 (OR) " 12.7.17 " 18.7.17	
	3.7.17		1 (OR) " 3.7.17 " 8.7.17	
	18.7.17		1 (OR) " 17.7.17 " 18.7.17	
	11.7.17		1 (OR) " 11.7.17 " 12.7.17	

2449 Wt. W14957/M90 750,000 1/16 J.B.C. & A. Forms/C.2118/12.

Instructions regarding War Diaries and Intelligence Summaries are contained in F. S. Regs., Part II. and the Staff Manual respectively. Title Pages will be prepared in manuscript.

Army Form C. 2118.

WAR DIARY
or
~~INTELLIGENCE SUMMARY~~
(Erase heading not required.)

200th Field Coy. RE

Place	Date	Hour	Summary of Events and Information	Remarks and references to Appendices
			Casualties for month of July contd	
ZILLEBEKE	1.7.17		2nd Lt Hoffman C.C. Slightly wounded (shellfire) to CCS	
	4.7.17		1 (OR) Slightly wounded – Remains at duty	
	1.7.17		1 (OR) Killed by shellfire 1.7.17	
	31.7.17		2nd Lt Cameron A.M. Slightly wounded (shellfire) to CCS	
	"		2 (OR) Killed by shellfire 31.7.17	
	"		7 (OR) Wounded " 31.7.17	
			Reinforcements	
	3.7.17		1 (OR) Rejoined from RE Base Depot 3.7.17	
	9.7.17		2nd Lt Cameron A.M. Joined from RE Base Depot 9.7.17	
	11.7.17		8 (OR) Joined from No 6 Reinforcement Coy RE 11.7.17	
	7.7.17		1 (OR) Rejoined from No 4 Staty Hosptl. 7.7.17	
	17.7.17		2 (OR) Joined from No 6 Reinforcement Coy RE 17.7.17	
	18.7.17		5 (OR) " " No 11 -do- 18.7.17	
	21.7.17		6 (OR) " " No 1 -do- 21.7.17	
	23.7.17		1 (OR) Rejoined from No 1 Wing RE Base Depot 23.7.17	
	24.7.17		1 (OR) " " " " 24.7.17	

[illegible]
Major RE
O.C. 200th Fld Coy RE

2449 Wt. W14957/M90 750,000 1/16 J.B.C. & A. Forms/C.2118/12.

Secret

Vol 20

WAR DIARY.

of the

200th Field Company Royal Engineers.

for the month of.

August 1917.

(Volume XX.

Instructions regarding War Diaries and Intelligence Summaries are contained in F. S. Regs., Par: II. and the Staff Manual respectively. Title Pages will be prepared in manuscript.

WAR DIARY
or
~~INTELLIGENCE SUMMARY~~
(Erase heading not required.)

Army Form C. 2118.

Vol XX

200th Field Company R.E.

Place	Date	Hour	Summary of Events and Information 1/10000 ZILLEBEKE 28 NW 4 & NE 3 Ed 6A. 1/10000 BELGIUM 28 NW Ed 6.A. 1/20000 BELGIUM & FRANCE 27 SE Ed 2. 1/40000 FRANCE 36A Ed 6.	Remarks and references to Appendices
H 29a 7.6. and DICKEBUSCH HUTS CAMP.	1.8.17		Rest in assembly area.	Rain.
	2.8.17.		Orders received to employ the whole company on the wiring of the front line in J 13. b and d	Rain.
		3.45pm	Mule convoy of 24 mules for carriage of wiring stores arrived at H 29a 7.6.	
		4.30 pm	Four sections. No1 Lt SANVILLE, No2 Lt CHIDGEY each with 25 men from 11th S. Lancs. Regt., No3 Lt LANNON, No4 Lt BARKER paraded and marched with mule convoy to VALLEY COTTAGE dump.	Dull misty
		6.30 pm	Arrived at VALLEY COTTAGES and started to load mules. Two sections of 201st Fd Co under Lt BROOMHALL reported.	
		7.45pm.	Started for line moving by DORMY HOUSE, on track No4 north of ZOUAVE WOOD to HOOGE arriving at Bn HQ at approx J 13 b 1.1. at 9.30 pm. All the convoy got through successfully and stores were offloaded.	
		10.30pm.	Working parties started out. No1 Section and 1 platoon pioneers erected 200 yds of single wire fence from J 20 a 1.9. to J 13 d 90.25. No2 Section and 1 platoon pioneers erected 250 yds of fence from J 13 d 90.25 to J 13 d 97.75. Nos 3 & 4 sections erected 250 yds of fence from J 13 d 85.85 to J 13 b 6.4. The two sections of 201st Fd Co RE wired 250 yds from J 13 b 6.4 to J 13 b 8.9. Two men slightly wounded.	
	3.8.17.	2.0pm.	Sections moved from assembly area to DICKEBUSCH HUTS CAMP.	Dull. Some rain
	4.8.17	9.30am	Transport moved out marching by RENINGHELST and GODEWAERSVELDE to EECKE.	Fair showers
		2.45pm	Dismounted men moved out to embark in buses at DICKEBUSCH	
		6 opm	Arrived at EECKE and moved into billets in BUTTERBAEGIGADE Farm at Q 13 c 0.0.	
EECKE	5.8.17. 6.8.17.		} Rest, cleaning and refitting.	Fine
	7.8.17	7.00am	Company moved out marching with 89th Bde group by EECKE, road fork S.W of GODEWAERSVELDE, LE COQ DE TAILLE, FONTAINE HOUCK, METEREN & OUTTERSTEENE to billets in the farm at F 9 b 0.3.	Fair

2449 Wt. W14957/M90 750,000 1/16 J.B.C. & A. Forms/C.2118/12.

Instructions regarding War Diaries and Intelligence Summaries are contained in F. S. Regs., Part II. and the Staff Manual respectively. Title Pages will be prepared in manuscript.

WAR DIARY
or
~~INTELLIGENCE SUMMARY~~
(Erase heading not required.)

Army Form C. 2118.

VOL XX

200th Field Co. R.E.

Place	Date	Hour	Summary of Events and Information 1/40000 FRANCE 36A. Ed 6. 1/20000 BELGIUM & FRANCE 27 SE. 2nd Ed. 1/20000 FRANCE 28 SW. Ed 5A	Remarks and references to Appendices
OUTTERSTEENE	8.8.17.		Overhauled transport etc.	Fine. Thunderstorm
	9.8.17.		Y/BARKER with billeting party sent to ST. JANS CAPPEL in advance.	Fine
Cx. DE POPERINGUE	10.8.17.	6.45 pm.	Marched out of camp moving by METEREN and ST JANS CAPPEL to camp at M 32 d 8.5. arriving at 9.30 pm.	Fine.
	11.8.17		Camp arrangements.	Showery.
	12.8.17.		Church parade with 2nd Bedfordshire Regt.	Fine Thunderstorm
	13.8.17		Training.	Showery
	14.8.17.		Training continued. No 3 Section loaded stores in afternoon at BAILLEUL Dump and unloaded at TRENT ammunition Dump at S 27 a preparatory to work on the roofing of the dump.	Showery
	15.8.17.		Nos 2, 3, 4, sections worked at TRENT dump until noon. Work stopped owing to orders for move to VIERSTRAAT area for work on RIDGE DEFENCES. 5 NCOs & 3 men attached to 89th Bde for training.	Showery
KEMMEL	16.8.17.	10 am.	Marched by LOCRE and KEMMEL to camp at N 16 d 3.3 Captain BEAL 2 officers and 100 men of 2nd Bn BEDFORDSHIRE Regt attached as working party	Fine.
	17.8.17.		Camp arrangements. Reconnaissance of Corps Line in sector allotted to company, that is approx O 20 c 7.6 to O 20 a 7.6. A Co. 11th S. Lancs Regt attached for work	V Fine
	18.8.17.		Nos 1 & 2 Sections and 40 inf. worked on front line of RIDGE defences in O 20 c. No 3 Section and 20 inf on Support line in O 20 d. No 4 Section on support line in O 20 a. Pioneers worked on digging of drain forward from O 20 a 7.5 to drain flooded trenches.	V Fine
	19.8.17.		Church Parade with 201st and 202nd Field Cos at N 17 c 0.0.	V. Fine
	20.8.17.		Work continued as on 18.8.17. Orders received to stop work in evening preparatory to move	V. Fine
	21.8.17.		Awaiting orders	V. Fine
	22.8.17.		Reconnaissance of communication trenches DORSET ST and BOB ST in O 21 & 27 1/10000 Special Sheet 8150/4	V Fine
LINDENHOEK	23.8.17.		Moved camp to N 28 b 3.7. 2nd Bn Royal Scots Fusiliers placed at disposal for working parties. Nos 2 & 4 Sections with 75 R.S.F. each worked from 8.30 pm – 1.30 am on deviations in C.T.s near ANZAC FARM and GUN FARM respectively.	Dull & Fine

2449 Wt. W14957/M90 750,000 1/16 J.B.C. & A. Forms/C.2118/12.

Instructions regarding War Diaries and Intelligence Summaries are contained in F. S. Regs., Part II. and the Staff Manual respectively. Title Pages will be prepared in manuscript.

Army Form C. 2118.

WAR DIARY
or
~~INTELLIGENCE SUMMARY~~
(Erase heading not required.)

Vol XX (cont)

200th Field Co. R.E.

1/10000 Special Sheet 28SW/4

Place	Date	Hour	Summary of Events and Information	Remarks and references to Appendices
LINDENHOEK	24.8.17		Work continued on same part of line	
	25.8.17			
	26.8.17			
	27.8.17			
	28.8.17			
	29.8.17			
	30.8.17	–	Major N.W. NAPIER CLAVERING admitted to hospital (sick)	
	31.8.17	–	Attached Infantry relieved by party of 25 men from each battn of 89th Bde	

2449 Wt. W14957/M90 750,000 1/16 J.B.C. & A. Forms/C.2118/12.

Instructions regarding War Diaries and Intelligence Summaries are contained in F. S. Regs., Part II. and the Staff Manual respectively. Title pages will be prepared in manuscript.

WAR DIARY
~~or~~
~~INTELLIGENCE SUMMARY.~~
(Erase heading not required.)

Army Form C. 2118.

20th Field Company R.E.

Place	Date	Hour	Summary of Events and Information	Remarks and references to Appendices
			Casualties for the month of August 1917.	
	2.8.17		3 O.R. To Hospital (Sickness) 2.8.17.	
	4.8.17		1 O.R. " " 4.8.17.	
	8.8.17		2 O.R. " " 8.8.17	
	9.8.17		1 O.R. " " 9.8.17.	
	15.8.17		1 O.R. " " 15.8.17.	
	22.8.17		1 O.R. " " 22.8.17.	
	26.8.17		1 O.R. " " 26.8.17	
	27.8.17		1 O.R. " " 27.8.17.	
	29.8.17		1 O.R. " " 29.8.17.	
	28.8.17		1 O.R. " " 28.8.17	
	11.8.17		1 O.R. Rejoined from Hospital. 11.8.17.	
	25.8.17		1 O.R. " " " 25.8.17.	
	31.8.17		1 O.R. " " " 31.8.17.	
	3.8.17		1 O.R. To Hospital 2.8.17 To C.C.S. 3.8.17.	
	4.8.17		1 O.R. " 4.8.17 " 4.8.17.	
	9.8.17		1 O.R. " 8.8.17 " 9.8.17. } These men have been struck off the strength of the Company from dates shown.	
	16.8.17		1 O.R. " 15.8.17 " 16.8.17.	
	18.8.17		1 O.R. " 18.8.17 " 18.8.17.	
			-REINFORCEMENTS-	
	30.7.17		2nd Lieut G. Danville R.E. Joined from R.E. Base Depot 30.7.17	
	8.8.17		2nd Lieut C. Evans R.E. " " " " 8.8.17.	

Instructions regarding War Diaries and Intelligence Summaries are contained in F. S. Regs., Part II. and the Staff Manual respectively. Title pages will be prepared in manuscript.

WAR DIARY
~~or~~
~~INTELLIGENCE SUMMARY.~~
(Erase heading not required.)

Army Form C. 2118.

200th Field Company R.E.

Place	Date	Hour	Summary of Events and Information	Remarks and references to Appendices
			Casualties for August contd.	
	8.8.17		1 O.R. Rejoined from R.E. Base Depot 8.8.17	These men have been taken on the strength of the Coy. from dates shown.
	24.8.17		1 O.R. " " " " 24.8.17	
	28.8.17		1 O.R. " " " " 28.8.17	
	21.8.17		8 O.R. Joined from No 11 Reinforcement Coy R.E. 21.8.17	
			— TRANSFERS. —	
	29.7.17		Lieut. F. E. R. Dixon from 200th Fd. C. R.E. to 155th Fd Coy R.E. 29.7.17	
	"		II Lieut. R. J. Lannon " 155th Fd Coy R.E. to 200th Fd Coy R.E. 29.7.17	
			Authy: 5th Army A/666/2387 dtd 25/7/17. 30 Div. A/718 dtd 27.7.17.	
			— COMMISSIONS —	
	25.8.17		81587 Sgt. Firth A. To England 25.8.17	
			Authy. W. O. Letter 100/ Engineers/1144 (S.D.3.D.) dtd 9.8.17	

L. Hill Capt. R.E.
O.C. 200th FIELD CO., R.E.

Instructions regarding War Diaries and Intelligence Summaries are contained in F. S. Regs., Part II, and the Staff Manual respectively. Title pages will be prepared in manuscript.

Army Form C. 2118.

WAR DIARY
or
~~INTELLIGENCE SUMMARY.~~
(Erase heading not required.)

200th Field Coy R.E.

Place	Date	Hour	Summary of Events and Information	Remarks and references to Appendices
			— Casualties for the month of September 1917. —	
	1.9.17		1 O.R. Admitted to Hospital (Sickness) 1.9.17.	
	4.9.17		1 O.R. " " " 4.9.17.	
	5.9.17		1 O.R. " " " 5.9.17.	
	8.9.17		1 O.R. " " " 8.9.17.	
	11.9.17		2 O.R. " " " 11.9.17.	
	12.9.17		2 O.R. " " " 12.9.17.	
	14.9.17		3 O.R. " " " 14.9.17.	
	15.9.17		1 O.R. " " " 15.9.17.	
	18.9.17		1 O.R. " " " 18.9.17.	
	19.9.17		1 O.R. " " " 19.9.17.	
	21.9.17		2 O.R. " " " 2?.9.17.	
	26.9.17		1 O.R. " " " 26.9.17	
	27.9.17		1 O.R. " " " 27.9.17	
	29.9.17		2 O.R. " " " 29.9.17.	
	3.9.17		1 O.R. Rejoined from Hospital 3.9.17	
	15.9.17		1 O.R. " " 15.9.17	
	13.9.17		1 O.R. " " 13.9.17.	
	16.9.17		3 O.R. " " 16.9.17.	

D. D. & L., London, E.C.
(A:883) Wt. W807/M672 350,000 4/17 Sch. 52a. Forms/C/2118/14

Instructions regarding War Diaries and Intelligence Summaries are contained in F. S. Regs., Part II. and the Staff Manual respectively. Title pages will be prepared in manuscript.

WAR DIARY
or
~~INTELLIGENCE~~ SUMMARY.
(*Erase heading not required.*)

Army Form C. 2118.

200th Field Coy. R.E.

Place	Date	Hour	Summary of Events and Information	Remarks and references to Appendices
			Casualties for September Contd	
	20.9.17		1 OR. Rejoined from Hospital 20.9.17	
	24.9.17		1 OR. " " " 24.9.17.	
	22.9.17		1 OR. " " " 22.9.17	
	26.9.17		1 OR. " " " 26.9.17.	
	27.9.17		1 OR. " " " 27.9.17.	
	1.9.17		1 OR. To Hospital 29/8/17 To C.C.S. 1.9.17. } These men have been struck off the strength of the unit from dates shown.	
	4.9.17		1 OR. " 4/9/17 " 4.9.17.	
	11.9.17		3 OR. " 1/5/9/17 " 11.9.17.	
	6.9.17		1 OR. " 5/9/17 " 6.9.17.	
	9.9.17		1 OR. " 9/9/17 " 9.9.17.	
	13.9.17		1 OR. " 13/9/17 " 13.9.17	
	12.9.17		1 OR. " 12/9/17 " 14.9.17.	
	14.9.17		1 OR. " 14/9/17 " 17.9.17.	
			— Reinforcements —	
	2.9.17		2 OR. Joined from 11 Reinforcement Coy. R.E. 2.9.17. } These men have been taken on the strength.	
	4.9.17		1 OR. Rejoined from R.E. Base Depot 4.9.17.	

D. D. & L., London, E.C. (A7383) Wt. W2073/M1672 350,000 4/17 Sch. 52a Forms/C/2118/14

Instructions regarding War Diaries and Intelligence Summaries are contained in F. S. Regs., Part II, and the Staff Manual respectively. Title pages will be prepared in manuscript.

WAR DIARY
or
~~INTELLIGENCE~~ SUMMARY.
(Erase heading not required.)

Army Form C. 2118.

200th Field Coy. R.E.

Place	Date	Hour	Summary of Events and Information	Remarks and references to Appendices
			Casualties for Sept. Cont'd.	
	5.9.17		1(OR) Joined from 6 Reinforcement Coy. R.E. 5.9.17 } These men have been	
	9.9.17		1(OR) Rejoined from 1st Aust. C.C.S. 9.9.17 } taken on the strength	
	16.9.17		2(OR) Joined from R.E. Base Depot 16.9.17	
			– Transfers. –	
	11.9.17		56426 Spr. Langton M. From 200th Field Coy. R.E. to No 1 Army Tramway Coy.	
			THIRD ARMY 11.9.17. Auth: 3rd Echelon Telegram d/9/9/17 No C.W. 9348.	
			– Promotions –	
	11.9.17		83211 2nd Cpl. Burgess H. Promoted A/Corporal (Paid) 11.9.17.	
	"		81686 L/Cpl. Simson W. " A/2nd Corporal (Paid) 11.9.17.	
	22.9.17		2/Lt. C. J. Barker authorised to wear badges of rank of Lieutenant by G.O.C. Division	

A. Hill Capt.
O.C. 200TH FIELD CO., R.E

D. D. & L., London, E.C.
(A7853) Wt. W501/M1672 350,000 4/17 Sch. 52a Forms/C2118/14

SECRET

Vol 21

War Diary

of the

200th Field Company, Royal Engineers.

for the month of

September 1917.

(Volume XXI).

Instructions regarding War Diaries and Intelligence Summaries are contained in F. S. Regs., Part II, and the Staff Manual respectively. Title pages will be prepared in manuscript.

WAR DIARY
or
INTELLIGENCE SUMMARY.
(Erase heading not required.)

Army Form C. 2118.

Vol XXI

200th FIELD COY RE

Place	Date	Hour	Summary of Events and Information	Remarks and references to Appendices
LINDENHOEK	1.9.17		Work on dimensions of CTs near ANZAC FARM & GUN FARM.	FINE
	2.9.17		2 Sections No 2 "Lt CHIDGEY No 1 "Lt SANVILLE & 50 attached Infantry (19th & 20th KLR) moved to advanced billets GRAND BOIS O.13.a.3.3. 89th Brigade took over new sector. Nos 1 & 2 Sections working in front line under GOC 89th Brigade. Nos 3 & 4 Sections & working party from 17th Manchesters working on PIONEER LANE & OLIVE TRENCH.	FINE
	3.9.17 4.9.17		Work continued.	
	5.9.17		Do CAPT HENRY (17th KLR) relieved by CAPT PIERCE (17th KLR) - attached Infantry.	
	6.9.17		Work continued - 8 men proceeded on leave to U.K.	
	7.9.17		Work continued - Sapper DELANEY interviewed by GOC 89th Brigade & passed for Commission.	Dull & threatening
	8.9.17 9.9.17		Work continued.	
	10.9.17		Work continued - Following received :- Please accept my thanks for the kindness of 2Lt LANNON & your men in conveying Pte RIGBY (wounded) to the Dressing Station where he unfortunately died of wounds. Had it not been for Mr LANNON'S action Pte RIGBY might not have been missed, as the night was very dark, until the party returned to camp. E FEARNSIDE Major Commanding 17th Batt MANCHESTER Regt.	
	11.9.17		Work continued 89th Brigade took over new sector from VERNE ROAD to YPRES COMINES CANAL	

D. D. & L., London, E.C.
(A7834) Wt. W603/M1672 350,000 4/17 Sch. 52a Forms C/2118/14

Instructions regarding War Diaries and Intelligence Summaries are contained in F. S. Regs., Part II, and the Staff Manual respectively. Title pages will be prepared in manuscript.

WAR DIARY
or
INTELLIGENCE SUMMARY.
(Erase heading not required.)

Army Form C. 2118.

VOL XXI (Contd).

Place	Date	Hour	Summary of Events and Information	Remarks and references to Appendices
LINDENHOEK	12.9.17		Work Continued – No 3 Section working on OAK AVENUE.	Fine
	13.9.17		Work Continued –	"
	14.9.17		2/Lt BARKER returned from leave. Work Continued.	"
	15.9.17 16.9.17		Work Continued.	Fine
	17.9.17		Work Continued – No 3 Section "Lt LANNON commenced work on INFANTRY BRIGADE TRANSPORT LINES	"
			DAYLIGHT CORNER.	"
	19.9.17	6.0pm	Work Continued. Nos 1 & 2 Sections returned to camp from GRAND BOIS	"
	20.9.17		No 1 Section "Lt SANVILLE took over Battery Transport Camp DAYLIGHT CORNER from 202nd Field Coy.	"
			No 2 Section 2/Lt CHIDGEY took over work at DAYLIGHT CORNER from No 3 Section. Nos 3 & 4 Sections	"
			2/Lts LANNON & EVANS working on X & Y Lines. MAJOR NAPIER CLAVERING returned from Hospital	"
	21.9.17		Work continued. MAJOR CLAVERING acting CRE 30th Division 2/Lt LANNON proceeded on leave UK	"
	22.9.17 23.9.17 24.9.17 25.9.17 26.9.17 27.9.17 28.9.17 29.9.17 30.9.17		Work Continued.	"

D. D. & L., London, E.C.
(A7853) Wt. W593/M1672 350,000 4/17 Sch. 52a Forms C/2118/14

SECRET

Vol 22

War Diary

of the

200th Field Company, Royal Engineers,

for the month of

October 1917.

(Volume XXII)

Instructions regarding War Diaries and Intelligence Summaries are contained in F. S. Regs., Part II, and the Staff Manual respectively. Title pages will be prepared in manuscript.

VOL XXII

WAR DIARY

~~or~~

~~INTELLIGENCE SUMMARY.~~

(Erase heading not required.)

Army Form C. 2118.

200 Field Company R.E.

Place	Date	Hour	Summary of Events and Information	Remarks and references to Appendices
N28b2.6	1.10.17		Sections 1 + 4 working on hutting. 2 + 3 in the line	
TAFFIN FARM	2.10.17		ditto	
	3.10.17		" Lt Nannon RE returned from hospital	
	4-10		Sections 1 + 4 working on hutting Daylight Camp Nayabok Camp. 2 + 3 in the line	
	11.10.17		No 3 Section relieved No 1 Section fort GRAND BOIS.	
	12.10.17		No 1 + 4 Sections move to GRAND BOIS at 9.30 AM + take over from 202nd Fd Cy RE	
	17.10.17		No 3 Section relieved No 1 Section at GRAND BOIS.	
	19.10.17		Sections 1 + 2 moved from Camp at N21b3.7 to KEMMEL CAMP N21b1.4 at Noon.	
KEMMEL CAMP N.21b1.4	21.10.17		HQ + transport moved to KEMMEL CAMP. No 2 section relieved No 4 Section	
	22.10.17		" Lt Nannon RE to hospital slightly wounded.	
	26.10.17		No 1 Section relieved No 3 Section at GRAND BOIS at 2.30 pm	
	28.10.17		" Lt Nannon RE returned from hospital	
	29.10.17		Major Napier Clavering RE rejoined from A/CRE 30 Division	
	31.10.17		" " " " proceeded on 14 days leave	
	31.10.17		No 4 Section relieved No 2 Section at GRAND BOIS at 2.30 pm	

J. Hill Capt RE
A/OC 200 Field Company RE

D. D. & L., London, E.C.
(A7883) Wt. W593/M1672 350,000 1/17 Sch. 52a Forms C/2118/14

Instructions regarding War Diaries and Intelligence Summaries are contained in F. S. Regs., Part II. and the Staff Manual respectively. Title pages will be prepared in manuscript.

WAR DIARY
or
~~INTELLIGENCE~~ SUMMARY.
(Erase heading not required.)

200th Field Company R.E.

Army Form C. 2118.

Place	Date	Hour	Summary of Events and Information	Remarks and references to Appendices
			Casualties for the month of October 1917.	
	4.10.17		1 (OR) To Hospital (Sickness) 4.10.17	
	5.10.17		1 (OR) " " 5.10.17	
	2.10.17		1 (OR) " " 2.10.17	
	7.10.17		1 (OR) " " 7.10.17	
	8.10.17		1 (OR) " " 8.10.17	
	10.10.17		1 (OR) " " 10.10.17	
	12.10.17		1 (OR) " " 12.10.17	
	14.10.17		1 (OR) " " 14.10.17	
	15.10.17		1 (OR) " " 15.10.17	
	16.10.17		2 (OR) " " 16.10.17	
	20.10.17		1 (OR) " " 20.10.17	
	24.10.17		1 (OR) " " 24.10.17	
	29.10.17		1 (OR) " " 29.10.17	
	31.10.17		1 (OR) " " 31.10.17	
	22.10.17		II Lieut R. J. LANNON R.E. Admitted to Hospital 22.10.17 (Slightly wounded)	
	28.10.17		II Lieut R. J. LANNON R.E. Rejoined Company from Hospital 28/10/17	
	5.10.17		1 (OR) To Hospital 2/10/17 To Duty 5.10.17	

D. D. & L., London, E.C. (A:883) Wt. W503/M1672 350,000 4/17 Sch. 52a Forms/C/2118/14

Instructions regarding War Diaries and Intelligence Summaries are contained in F. S. Regs., Part II, and the Staff Manual respectively. Title pages will be prepared in manuscript.

WAR DIARY

or

~~INTELLIGENCE SUMMARY.~~ 200th Field Coy R.E.

(Erase heading not required.)

Army Form C. 2118.

Place	Date	Hour	Summary of Events and Information	Remarks and references to Appendices
			Casualties for October continued	
	10.10.17		1 (OR) Rejoined from Hospital 10.10.17	
	8.10.17		1 (OR) " " " 8.10.17	
	5.10.17		1 (OR) " " " 5.10.17	
	13.10.17		1 (OR) " " " 13.10.17	
	14.10.17		1 (OR) " " " 14.10.17	
	18.10.17		2 (OR) " " " 18.10.17	
	22.10.17		1 (OR) " " " 22.10.17	
	25.10.17		1 (OR) " " " 25.10.17	
	24.10.17		1 (OR) " " " 24.10.17	
	26.10.17		1 (OR) " " " 26.10.17	
	28.10.17		1 (OR) " " " 28.10.17	
	30.10.17		1 (OR) " " " 30.10.17	
			— CASUALTIES —	
	21.10.17		2 (OR) Wounded on 21.10.17 To C.C.S. 21.10.17. } These men have been	
	6.10.17		1 (OR) To Hospital (Sickness) 4.10.17 To C.C.S. 6.10.17. } struck off the strength of	
	15.10.17		1 (OR) " " 8.10.17 " " 15.10.17 }	
	11.10.17		1 (OR) " " 10.10.17 " " 11.10.17 } the Company.	

Instructions regarding War Diaries and Intelligence Summaries are contained in F. S. Regs., Part II, and the Staff Manual respectively. Title pages will be prepared in manuscript.

WAR DIARY

or

~~INTELLIGENCE~~ SUMMARY. 200th Field Company R.E.

(*Erase heading not required.*)

Army Form C. 2118.

Place	Date	Hour	Summary of Events and Information	Remarks and references to Appendices
			Casualties for October contd.	
			— REINFORCEMENTS —	
	5.10.17		3 (OR) Joined from RE Base Depot 5.10.17 } These men have been	
	9.10.17		2 (OR) " " " " 9.10.17 } taken on the strength	
	12.10.17		1 (OR) " " " " 12.10.17 } of the Company.	

D. D. & L., London, E.C. (A7883) Wt. W1091/M1672 350,000 1/17 Sch. 52a Forms/C/2118/14

SECRET

Vol 23

WAR DIARY.

of the.

200th Field Company, Royal Engineers.

for the month of

NOVEMBER 1917.

(VOLUME. XXIII)

Instructions regarding War Diaries and Intelligence Summaries are contained in F. S. Regs., Part II. and the Staff Manual respectively. Title pages will be prepared in manuscript.

WAR DIARY
or
INTELLIGENCE SUMMARY.
(Erase heading not required.)

Army Form C. 2118.

VOL. XXIII.

200th Field Co. R.E.

Place	Date	Hour	Summary of Events and Information — BELGIUM 28 S.W. 28 N.W. 9d 6A.	Remarks and references to Appendices
KEMMEL CAMP	1.11.17		Two sections working on hut camps, two in the line.	
N21b.1.4.	2.11.17		Work continued.	
	3.11.17		" "	
	4.11.17		" "	
	5.11.17		" "	
	6.11.17		" " DAYLIGHT and LAYNEBOK camps occupied.	
	7.11.17		" "	
	8.11.17		" " Detachment of 19th K.L.Regt. returned to Bn.	
	9.11.17		" "	
	10.11.17		" " Two sections returned from forward billets in GRAND BOIS. Remaining inf. rejoined Bns.	
YPRES	11.11.17		Company moved by motor 'bus to YPRES. Transport to VLAMERTINGHE.	
	12.11.17		Reconnaissance of WIELTJE – KANSAS CROSS road with 4th Canadian Fd Co.	
	13.11.17		Sections worked in conjunction with 4th Can. Fd Co.	
KAAIE + VLAMERTINGHE	14.11.17		Work on road continued. Billets at KAAIE taken over from 4th Can. Fd Co. at I 2 c 1.7. Transport lines at VLAMERTINGHE at H 3 c 1.1.	
	15.11.17		Work continued with working party of 100 pioneers of 14th Div.	

D. D. & L., London, E.C. (A7883) Wt. W10/M1672 350,000 5/17 Sch. 52a Forms C/2118/14

Instructions regarding War Diaries and Intelligence Summaries are contained in F. S. Regs., Part II. and the Staff Manual respectively. Title pages will be prepared in manuscript.

Army Form C. 2118.

WAR DIARY
or
~~INTELLIGENCE SUMMARY.~~
(Erase heading not required.)

VOL XXII cont.

200th Fld Co. RE

Place	Date	Hour	Summary of Events and Information BELGIUM 28 N.W. & 28 N.E. Ed 6A. ZILLEBEKE 28 I.W 4 and I.E 3 (parts of) Ed 6A	Remarks and references to Appendices
				Weather.
KAMIE & VLAMERTINGHE	16.11.17		Work continued Major NAPIER-CLAVERING returned from leave.	Foggy
	17.11.17		Work continued. Spr DAVIES wounded and died of wounds. Co. warned to be ready to move to rest at STEENVOORDE.	Dull
	18.11.17			
	19.11.17		Capt HILL sent to STEENVOORDE to take over billets.	Dull
	20.11.17		Awaiting orders.	Fair
	21.11.17		Lt BARKER sent to VIII Corps HQ. to construct picture ground. 2/Lt CHIDGEY to horselines.	Rain & Dull
	22.11.17		No 3 Sec. worked on tramline north of KANSAS CROSS under 201st Fld Co. 2am–7am.	Dull drizzle
	23.11.17		No 1 Sec on tramline. Orders to move on 24th to relieve 227th Fld Co at MOUNT SORREL.	Fine.
CANADA ST Dugouts	24.11.17		Transport moved to camp at N 10 c 9.8. HQ and 4 Sections moved to CANADA ST dugouts. I 30 a 5.0.	Fine.
a VERSTRAAT.	25.11.17		No 2 Section worked on duckboard tracks Nos 3 & 4 on increasing accessory accommodation. 90 RB No 3 to R.A.	Fine showery
	26.11.17		Work continued No 1 clearing dugout and carrying stores with 50 inf to SUSSEX AVENUE J 19 d 2.0.	Fine
	27.11.17		Work continued No 1 began revetment of SUSSEX AVENUE.	Rain & fair
	28.11.17		" " No 2 clearing & reclaiming concrete dugouts.	Fine
	29.11.17		" " Reconnaissance of proposed Reserve line in J 20 b and d.	Fair.
	30.11.17		" " Nos 2 & 4 Secs with 1 Co 11th S Lancs dug borrow pit for Reserve line from J 20 d 8.2 to J 20 b 9.8.	Showers
				~~Dull~~

M Napier Clavering
Major RE.
O.C. 200th Fld Co RE.

D. D. & L., London, E.C. (A7853) Wt. W1093/M1672 350,000 4/17 Sch. 52a Forms/C/2118/14

Instructions regarding War Diaries and Intelligence Summaries are contained in F. S. Regs., Part II. and the Staff Manual respectively. Title pages will be prepared in manuscript.

WAR DIARY
or
~~INTELLIGENCE SUMMARY.~~
(Erase heading not required.)

Army Form C. 2118.

200th Field Coy. R.E.

Place	Date	Hour	Summary of Events and Information	Remarks and references to Appendices
			Casualties for the month of November 1917.	
	8.11.17		1 (OR) To Hospital (Sickness) 8.11.17.	
	9.11.17		1 (OR) " " 9.11.17.	
	11.11.17		1 (OR) " " 11.11.17.	
	17.11.17		1 (OR) " " 17.11.17.	
	20.11.17		1 (OR) " " 20.11.17	
	26.11.17		1 (OR) " " 26.11.17.	
	27.11.17		2 (OR) " " 27.11.17.	
	28.11.17		1 (OR) " " 28.11.17.	
	4.11.17		1 (OR) Rejoined from Hospital 4.11.17.	
	11.11.17		1 (OR) " " 11.11.17.	
	20.11.17		2 (OR) " " 20.11.17.	
	25.11.17		1 (OR) " " 25.11.17.	
	13.11.17		1 (OR) To Hospital (Sickness) 11/11/17 To C.C.S. 13.11.17. } These men have been	
	18.11.17		1 (OR) " " 17/11/17 To C.C.S. 18.11.17. } struck off the strength	
	28.11.17		1 (OR) " " 27/11/17 To C.C.S. 28.11.17. } of the Company.	

D. D. & L., London, E.C.
(A7SS.) Wt. W593/M1672 350,000 4/17 Sch. 52a Forms/C/2118/14

Instructions regarding War Diaries and Intelligence Summaries are contained in F. S. Regs., Part II. and the Staff Manual respectively. Title pages will be prepared in manuscript.

WAR DIARY
or
~~INTELLIGENCE SUMMARY.~~
(Erase heading not required.)

Army Form C. 2118.

Place	Date	Hour	Summary of Events and Information	Remarks and references to Appendices
			— Casualties for November contd. —	
			— CASUALTIES —	
	17.11.17		1 (OR) Wounded 17.11.17. Died from wounds at 3 Can. C.C.S. 18.11.17.	
			— REINFORCEMENTS —	
	8.11.17		2 (OR) Joined from R.E. Base Depot 8.11.17. } These men have been	
	30.11.17		1 (OR) " " " " 30.11.17. } taken on the strength.	
			— APPOINTMENTS —	
	4.11.17		155327 Sapr WEST G.W. Appointed Lce. Corporal (Paid) from 4.11.17.	
			— COMMISSIONS —	
	19.11.17		81641 L/Cpl Manning W.G. To England for Commission 19.11.17	
	"		83106 Sapr. Delaney J. do do 19.11.17	
			Authy: C.R.E. 30th Division 4695/1 dated 14.11.17.	
			— MISCELLANEOUS —	
	16.11.17		Major N.W. NAPIER CLAVERING R.E. rejoined from leave.	

N.W. Napier Clavering
Major R.E.

O.C. 200TH FIELD CO., R.E.

D. D. & L., London, E.C. (A7883) Wt. W703/M1672 350,000 4/17 Sch. 52a Forms C/2118/14

SECRET

Vol 24

War Diary

of the

200th Field Company, Royal Engineers

for the month of

December 1917.

(Volume XXIV)

Instructions regarding War Diaries and Intelligence Summaries are contained in F. S. Regs., Part II, and the Staff Manual respectively. Title pages will be prepared in manuscript.

WAR DIARY
or
~~INTELLIGENCE SUMMARY.~~
(Erase heading not required.)

Army Form C. 2118.

Vol XXIV — 200th Fd Co. R.E. — Ref Sheet 28.

ZILLEBEKE 28 NW 4 & NE 3 parts of Ed 6A. BELGIUM 28 NW.

Place	Date	Hour	Summary of Events and Information	Remarks and references to Appendices
CANADA ST dugouts	1.12.17		Work continued. No 1 Sect on SUSSEX AVENUE, Nos 2 & 4 on RESERVE LINE. No 3 on RFA Bty positions and	
& VERSTRAAT			on reclaiming concrete dugouts. Work started on supporting points at I 20 d 9.9 and I 20 b 9.5.	
	2.12.17.		Work continued Borrow pit of reserve line completed up to MENIN ROAD	
	3.12.17.		Work continued	
	4.12.17		Work continued. Lt CHOGEY to transport lines to do duties of O/c Transport during absence of Capt HILL on leave	
	5.12.17		Work continued	
	6.12.17		Work continued. Capt G D ATKINSON MC arrived to take over command of company	
	7.12.17		Major N.W. NAPIER CLAVERING DSO RE left for RE School of Instruction GHQ.	
	8.12.17		Work as usual.	
	9.12.17		Work as usual. No 3 section started work on providing gas doors for TORR TOP Tunnels as well	
	10.12.17		Lt EVANS reconnoitred reserve line North of MENIN Road. Wiring of the Reserve Line was	
			started, the material being taken up by Pack mule. Lt G.H. SCOTT joined the company	
	11.12.17		Work as usual	
	12.12.17		Nos 1 and 3 sections relieved at 7 am by 2 sections 201st Field Company RE and marched	
			to 201st Fd Coy's billet at 131 a 05. Remaining Sections worked on Reserve Line as usual.	
	13.12.17		Remaining 2 sections and Hd Qrs relieved by remaining sections and HdQrs 201st Fd Coy. Nos 1 and	

D. D. & L., London, E.C. (A7883) Wt. W593/M1672 350,000 4/17 Sch. 52a Forms/C.2118/14

Army Form C. 2118.

Instructions regarding War Diaries and Intelligence Summaries are contained in F. S. Regs., Part II. and the Staff Manual respectively. Title pages will be prepared in manuscript.

WAR DIARY
or
INTELLIGENCE SUMMARY.
(Erase heading not required.)

Place	Date	Hour	Summary of Events and Information	Remarks and references to Appendices
	13.12.17		3 worked on hutting. No 1 Section moved to camp at N2a37 near HALLEBAST Corner	
	14.12.17		Works as follows. No 1 section working on horse lines for two RFA Batteries at N2a37	
			Nos 2, and 4. working on horse lines for one field Company at H30c36. Completion	
			of 202nd field Company horse lines at the same place, and completion of horse	
			Standings for Pur Battalion also at the same place.	
			No 3 Section worked on Divl Bombt Store at I19c70 ; gumboot drying room	
			at H36b 6.8. ; YMCA hut at I26a66	
	15.12.17		2Lt EVANS admitted to hospital. Work as usual	
	16.12.17		Work continued.	
	17.12.17		Work continued	
	18.12.17		Work Started on horse lines for one Infantry battalion at I30c64 Lt SCOTT	
			left the company temporarily to be employed as Division Officer RE	
	19.12.17		Work as usual 2Lt EVANS Struck off strength	
	20.12.17		Work continued	
	21.12.17		4 half sections relieved 4 half sections 202nd field Company at I19a99, JACK	
			DAW TUNNELS. All the work in hand in the back area is nearing completion	

D. D. & L., London, E.C. (A7889) Wt. W80/M1672 350,000 4/17 Sch. 52a Forms C2118/14

3.

Army Form C. 2118.

Instructions regarding War Diaries and Intelligence Summaries are contained in F. S. Regs., Part II. and the Staff Manual respectively. Title pages will be prepared in manuscript.

WAR DIARY
or
INTELLIGENCE SUMMARY.
(Erase heading not required.)

Place	Date	Hour	Summary of Events and Information	Remarks and references to Appendices
	21.12		Except for the horse lines for an infantry battalion	
	22.12		Remaining half sections, and Company Hd Qrs, relieved remainder of 202nd Field Coy RE. Lt J.P. MALLALIEU temporarily attached from 11th Bn South Lancs. Work taken over is as follows:– No 1 Section reclaiming pillboxes. No 2 Section constructing Gumboot Stores at J.19.a.99 and J.30.a.5.0. No 3 Section working outfront in early morning for 4 hours, and then working on barbed wire entanglements on returning to billets. No 4 Section on Pillboxes	
	23.12		Work as usual	
	24.12		Work as usual except that No 3 Section did not work during day. At 10.30 pm No 3 Section, accompanied by a carrying party of 35 Infantry, left billets to wire the front from JERICHO J.22.a.60.100 to the SCHERRIABEEK J.22.a.35.65. This was accomplished successfully the party returning about 3.30 am	
	25.12		Being Christmas day, no work was done	
	26.12		No 3 Section started to put Elephant Shelters in reserve line, starting a Strong Point J.15.c.21. No 2 took on the following additional work; repair of HQ test box 1.18.b.3.4. R.A.P. J.13.a.2.3 (repairs). Reclaiming Pillboxes at AMBROSE Farm J.21.c.2.2 for a	

D. D. & L., London, E.C.
(A.8.5.) Wt. W5093/M1672 350,000 4/17 Sch. 52a Forms/C.2118/14

Army Form C. 2118.

Instructions regarding War Diaries and Intelligence Summaries are contained in F. S. Regs., Part II, and the Staff Manual respectively. Title pages will be prepared in manuscript.

WAR DIARY
or
INTELLIGENCE SUMMARY.
(Erase heading not required.)

Place	Date	Hour	Summary of Events and Information	Remarks and references to Appendices
	26.12		for a Company Hd.Qrs	
	27.12		Work as usual	
	28.12		Work as usual. 2Lt F. THURLBY joined the company	
	29.12		No 1 Section started working at night on F track, instead of by day.	
	30.12		No 3 Section put in 2 Shelters in Reserve Line; up to date they had only been able to put in one a night	
	31.12		No 1 Section took over work from No 3. No 4 Section took over work from No 1. No 2 Section took over work from No 4 in addition to its own work. No 3 Section started work on converting a group of Pill boxes at J 19 b 6.4 into a Strong Point.	

[illegible] Major R.E.
O.C. 500th Field Company R.E.

D. D. & L., London, E.C. (A7839) Wt. W6o/M1672 350,000 1/17 Sch. 52a Forms/C/2118/14

Army Form C. 2118.

WAR DIARY

~~INTELLIGENCE SUMMARY.~~

(*Erase heading not required.*)

200th Field Co. R.E.

Instructions regarding War Diaries and Intelligence Summaries are contained in F. S. Regs., Part II, and the Staff Manual respectively. Title pages will be prepared in manuscript.

Place	Date	Hour	Summary of Events and Information	Remarks and references to Appendices
			Casualties for the month of December. 1917	
	2.12.17		2 (OR) To Hospital (Sickness) 2.12.17	
	4.12.17		1 (OR) " " 4.12.17	
	5.12.17		1 (OR) " " 5.12.17	
	9.12.17		3 (OR) " " 9.12.17	
	10.12.17		3 (OR) " " 10.12.17	
	21.12.17		1 (OR) " " 21.12.17	
	24.12.17		1 (OR) " " 24.12.17	
	26.12.17		1 (OR) " " 26.12.17	
	3.12.17		1 (OR) Rejoined from Hospital 3.12.17	
	1.12.17		1 (OR) " " " 1.12.17	
	12.12.17		2 (OR) " " " 12.12.17	
	14.12.17		1 (OR) " " " 14.12.17	
	10.12.17		1 (OR) " " " 10.12.17	
	11.12.17		1 (OR) " " " 11.12.17	
	10.12.17		1 (OR) " " " 10.12.17	
	16.12.17		1 (OR) " " " 16.12.17	
	21.12.17		1 (OR) " " " 21.12.17	

D. D. & L., London, E.C. (A7883) Wt. W605/M1672 350,000 1/17 Sch. 52a Forms/C/2118/14

Instructions regarding War Diaries and Intelligence Summaries are contained in F. S. Regs., Part II, and the Staff Manual respectively. Title pages will be prepared in manuscript.

WAR DIARY
or
~~INTELLIGENCE SUMMARY.~~
(Erase heading not required.)

200th Field Coy. R.E.

Army Form C. 2118.

Place	Date	Hour	Summary of Events and Information	Remarks and references to Appendices
			Casualties for December contd.	
	23.12.17		1 (OR) Rejoined from hospital 23.12.17	
	13.12.17		1 (OR) To Hospital (Sickness) 5.12.17. To Base 13.12.17. } These men have been struck off the strength of the Company.	
	23.12.17		1 (OR) " " 9.12.17 To 53 C.C.S. 23.12.17 }	
			— CASUALTIES —	
	3.12.17		1 (OR) Wounded by shellfire 3.12.17. To C.C.S. 3.12.17. } These men have been struck off the strength of the Company.	
	5.12.17		1 (OR) " " 5.12.17 To C.C.S. 5.12.17 }	
			— REINFORCEMENTS —	
	11.12.17		4 (OR) Joined from R.E. Base Depot 11.12.17. } These men have been taken on the strength of the Company.	
	17.12.17		1 (OR) " " " 17.12.17 }	
	28.12.17		9 (OR) " " " 28.12.17 }	
	10.12.17		Lieut. G.V. SCOTT R.E. " 10.12.17	
	28.12.17		II Lieut. F. THURLBY R.E. " 28.12.17	
			— APPOINTMENTS —	
	18.12.17		83070 Sapr. SOUTHERN F.G. Appointed L/Cpl. (paid) from 18.12.17	
	"		83304 " PRESTON J. " " " " 18.12.17.	

D. D. & L., London, E.C. (A7883) Wt. W703/M672 350,000 4/17 Sch. 52a Forms/C2118/14

Instructions regarding War Diaries and Intelligence Summaries are contained in F. S. Regs., Part II. and the Staff Manual respectively. Title pages will be prepared in manuscript.

WAR DIARY
or
~~INTELLIGENCE SUMMARY.~~
(Erase heading not required.)

Army Form C. 2118.

200th Field Co. R.E.

Place	Date	Hour	Summary of Events and Information	Remarks and references to Appendices
			Casualties for December 1917. contd.	
			- TRANSFERS -	
	6.12.17		Capt. O.D. ATKINSON R.E. from 30th Divisional Engineers to 200th Field Co. R.E.	
	7.12.17		Major N.W. NAPIER CLAVERING R.E. from 200th Fd. Co. R.E. to R.E. School of Instruction BLENDECQUES.	
AUTHY.			Second Army wire A307/243 d/4/12/17 and 30 Division wire A/340.	
	21.12.17		Lieut. C.J. BARKER R.E. from 200th Field Co. R.E. to be Adjt. 30th Divl. Engineers.	
AUTHY.			Fourth Army No A/307/289. IX Corps No A/6058. 30 Division No A442.	
	6.12.17		83468 Dvr. CLAYTON G. from 30th Divl. Engrs to 200th Field Co. R.E.	
	7.12.17		38358 " King J. from 200th Field Co. R.E. to R.E. School of Instruction BLENDECQUES	
AUTHY.			Second Army wire A/307/243 d/4/12/17 and 30 Division wire A/340.	
	21.12.17.		146291 Sapr. Hollington G. from 200th Fd. Co. R.E. to R.E. Base Depot. 21.12.17.	
AUTHY.			A.D.M.S. 30 Division. M 7813 dated 18/12/17.	
			- HOSPITAL -	
	19.12.17		II Lieut. EVANS E. R.E. Admitted to hospital. (Sick) 18.12.17. Evacuated to Base from 53 C.C.S. 19.12.17. Struck off the Strength of Coy.	

D. D. & L., London, E.C. (A7883) Wt. W807/M1672 350,000 4/17 Sch. 52a Forms C/2118/14

SECRET.

Vol 25

War Diary
of the
200th Field Company Royal Engineers.
for the month of
January 1918.

(Volume. XXV.)

Army Form C. 2118.

WAR DIARY
or
~~INTELLIGENCE SUMMARY.~~
(Erase heading not required.)

Instructions regarding War Diaries and Intelligence Summaries are contained in F. S. Regs., Part II, and the Staff Manual respectively. Title pages will be prepared in manuscript.

Vol XXV

200th Field Company RE

REFERENCE SHEET 1/100,000 HAZEBROUCK 5A, AMIENS 17, ST. QUENTIN 18.

Place	Date	Hour	Summary of Events and Information	Remarks and references to Appendices
YPRES	1.1.18.		Work continued.	
	2.1.18		Work continued	
	3.1.		Work on putting Shelters in Reserve Line Completed. No new work started owing to coming relief.	
	5.1.18		Remaining work carried on as usual.	
	6.1		Relieved by 83rd Field Company RE. 20th Division. Mounted Section marched to BERTHEN. Dismounted Sections marched to DICKEBUSH.	
	7.1.		Mounted Section marched to HEURINGHEM. Dismounted Sections marched to LA CLYTTE and entrained. Disentrained at EBBLINGHEM and marched to HEURINGHEM arriving at	
	8.1. ~~[illegible]~~		1.30 am 8th	
	9.1.		Training Started, and continued on 10th.	
	11.1.		Company marched to STEENBECQUE entraining with transport and wagons at 1.30 am	
	12.1.		12th. Disentrained at 1PM at LONGEAU near AMIENS and ~~[illegible]~~ marched to THEZY.	
	13.1.		Company marched to BAYONVILLERS (14 miles).	
	14.1.		marched to PROYART (6 miles).	
	15.1.		marched to HERLY (14 miles)	

D. D. & L., London, E.C. (A7882) Wt. W593/M1672 350,000 1/17 Sch. 52a Forms/C/2118/14

Instructions regarding War Diaries and Intelligence Summaries are contained in F. S. Regs., Part II. and the Staff Manual respectively. Title pages will be prepared in manuscript.

WAR DIARY
or
INTELLIGENCE SUMMARY.
(Erase heading not required.)

Army Form C. 2118.

Place	Date	Hour	Summary of Events and Information	Remarks and references to Appendices
	16.1.		Marched to OFFOY (8 miles). Officer attended a Corps C.E. conference at 3.0pm. at XVIII Corps Hd. Qrs. on the subject of the Battle Zone on which the company is to be employed	
	17.1		Officers proceeded to ATTILLY to reconnoitre billets.	
	18.1.		Company marched to ATTILLY; dismounted portion billetted in dugouts near the village. Horse lines at VAUX.	
	19.1.		Sections working on billets. Officers reconnoitring work on Battle Zone	
			The Battle Zone is a zone of defence which runs from the Northern Corps boundary E of MAISSEMY, E. of ST QUENTIN and HOLNON woods, W of SAVY to the neighbourhood of ROUPY at the Southern 61st Divisional front.	
			Work on the Battle Zone on the 61st Divisional front is under the charge of Major G.D. ATKINSON RE. who has at his disposal the following:–	
			200th Field Company RE.	
			A Company 11th Bn South Lancs Regt Pioneers	
			The Reserve Bde 61st Division working 5 days out of 8.	
			It is divided into 4 battalion Subsectors, on each of which is employed	

D. D. & L., London, E.C. (A7839) Wt. W593/M1672 350,000 4/17 Sch. 52a. Forms C/2118/14

Instructions regarding War Diaries and Intelligence Summaries are contained in F. S. Regs., Part II. and the Staff Manual respectively. Title pages will be prepared in manuscript.

WAR DIARY
or
INTELLIGENCE SUMMARY.
(Erase heading not required.)

Army Form C. 2118.

Place	Date	Hour	Summary of Events and Information	Remarks and references to Appendices
	19.1.		1 Section 200th Field Coy.	
			1 Platoon A Coy [illegible] S Lancs	
			1 Battalion Reserve Bde 55 Div working 5 days out of 8.	
	21.1		The sites for the actual Infantry fire positions were chosen by the Corps Staff and approved by the Corps Commander. The detail joining up of fire positions and the plan of the wiring was done by the Officers of the company, the principles being laid down by the Corps Staff. The CE XVIII Corps laid down the sections and trace of trenches. All digging was to be done by task work, the task being 50 cubic feet per man per day.	
	22.1		Infantry working parties started for the Northern two Battalion Sectors.	
	23.1		Infantry working parties started for the Southern two Battalion Sectors	
	24.1		Work progressed satisfactorily. It was found that most units completed	
	25.1.		their task in about 2 hours.	
	26.1.		Owing of Bde relief Sappers working without Infantry	
	27.1.		Company had day off.	
	28.1.		New Bde Started work.	

D. D. & L., London, E.C. (A7884) Wt. W2o7/M1672 350,000 4/17 Sch. 52a Forms C/2118/14

Army Form C. 2118.

Instructions regarding War Diaries and Intelligence Summaries are contained in F. S. Regs., Part II. and the Staff Manual respectively. Title pages will be prepared in manuscript.

WAR DIARY
or
INTELLIGENCE SUMMARY.
(Erase heading not required.)

Place	Date	Hour	Summary of Events and Information	Remarks and references to Appendices
	29.1		Work as usual.	
	30.1		Work as usual. The RE. Sections are employed in supervising the Infantry digging, in taping out work, and in cleaning out the trenches and sloping the sides after the Infantry have finished their task. The Pioneer Company is employed exclusively on wiring.	
	31.1.		Work Continued.	

H. A. [illegible] Major RE.
O.C. 200th Field Company RE.

SECRET

War Diary

Vol 26

200th Field Company Royal Engineers.

for the month of

February 1918.

(Volume. XXVI)

Instructions regarding War Diaries and Intelligence Summaries are contained in F. S. Regs., Part II. and the Staff Manual respectively. Title pages will be prepared in manuscript.

Army Form C. 2118.

WAR DIARY
or
~~INTELLIGENCE~~ SUMMARY.
(*Erase heading not required.*)

Vol. XXVI

200 Field Co RE

Place	Date	Hour	Summary of Events and Information Reference SHEET 1/100000 S QUENTIN 18	Remarks and references to Appendices
ATTILLY	1-2-18	—	Work on Battle Zone continued.	
	2		2/Lt BENNET attached for work from 201st Field Company.	
	6		Capt HILL proceeded to R.E School of Instruction BLENDEQUES	
	8		2/Lt CHIDGEY proceeded on leave to U.K.	
	8-23		Work continued on Battle Zone.	
	23		30th Division took over the line. Southern boundary S.30 c 3.0 along S. QUENTIN CANAL to A.10 c.4.0 – F 23 central – BRAY S CHRISTOPHE – A 13 d.0.8 Northern boundary S.11 d 6.2 – S.10 d 5.8 – S 9 c 8.4 – S 8 d 7.0 – X 23 b 0.2 X.15.c central thence to VAUX + GERMAINE	
	25		30th Division RE + 11th Bn S Lancs Regt come under orders of G.O.C 30 Division.	
	24.		Work continued as above. 2/Lt Bennet rejoined his Company.	
DOUCHY	25.		No 1 Section moved to DALLON. No 2 Section to DOUCHY " 3 " " " HAMEL " 4 " " DALLON Horse Lines + H.Q moved to DOUCHY.	
	26.		The following work is being carried out by Sections in the new	

D. D. & L., London, E.C. (A.5834) Wt. W2071/M1672 350,000 4/17 Sch. 52a Forms/C/2118/14

Army Form C. 2118.

Instructions regarding War Diaries and Intelligence Summaries are contained in F. S. Regs., Part II. and the Staff Manual respectively. Title pages will be prepared in manuscript.

WAR DIARY
or
~~INTELLIGENCE~~ SUMMARY.
(Erase heading not required.)

Place	Date	Hour	Summary of Events and Information	Remarks and references to Appendices
DOUCHY	26		Nos 1 + 4 Work on DALLON Redoubt + Defences	
			2 Work on billets etc at DOUCHY.	
			3 Attached 148 Bde RFA for work on gun positions	
	27		Lt Vernon R.E proceeded on leave to U.K	
	28		Work continued.	
Weather	for		the month – Fine, cold, small rainfall.	

[signature] R.E.

O.C. 200TH FIELD CO. R.E.

D. D. & L., London, E.C.
(A7833) Wt. W10/M1672 350,000 4/17 Sch. 52a Forms C/2118/14

Instructions regarding War Diaries and Intelligence Summaries are contained in F. S. Regs., Part II. and the Staff Manual respectively. Title pages will be prepared in manuscript.

WAR DIARY
or
~~INTELLIGENCE SUMMARY.~~
(*Erase heading not required.*)

Army Form C. 2118.

200th Field Co. R.E.

Place	Date	Hour	Summary of Events and Information	Remarks and references to Appendices
			Casualties for the month of February	
ATTILLY			REINFORCEMENTS	
ARLICHY	11.2.18		II Lieut Evans E. from RE Base Depot 11.2.18	
	9.2.18		2 (OR) Joined from RE Base Depot 9.2.18	
	17.2.18		6 (OR) " " 17.2.18	
	19.2.18		2 (OR) " from 61st C.C.S 19.2.18	
	23.2.18		1 (OR) " " " 23.2.18	
			TRANSFERS	
	17.2.18		83436 Sergt. Summers A. from 200th Field Co RE to P.M. 5th Army	
			Authy. DAG. GHQ 3rd Echelon Ct. No 870/+/3007/A d/17.2.18	
			PROMOTIONS	
			83208 Cpl. Hargreaves J.E. Promoted to A/Sergeant (paid) from 17.2.18	
			51385 II Cpl. Hampton J. " " A/Corporal (paid) " 17.2.18	
			99718 L/Cpl. Cassin H " " A/II Corporal (paid) " 17.2.18	

D. D. & L., London, E.C. (A7883) Wt W807/M1672 350,000 4/17 Sch. 52a Forms C/2118/14

Vol 28

WAR DIARY

of the

200th Field Company Royal Engineers,

for the month of.

APRIL 1918

(Volume. XXVIII)

30th Div.

WAR DIARY

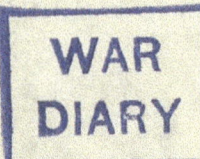

200th FIELD COMPANY, R.E.

M A R C H

1 9 1 8

Attached:-

Appendix "A".

SECRET

30

VR 27

WAR DIARY.

200th Field Company Royal Engineers.

for the month of

MARCH 1918.

(Volume. XXVII)

Instructions regarding War Diaries and Intelligence Summaries are contained in F. S. Regs., Part II, and the Staff Manual respectively. Title pages will be prepared in manuscript.

WAR DIARY
or
INTELLIGENCE SUMMARY.
(Erase heading not required.)

Army Form C. 2118.

VOL XXVII

200 Field Company RE

Reference Sheet 1/100,000 S. QUENTIN 18, AMIENS 17, ABBEVILLE 14

Place	Date	Hour	Summary of Events and Information	Remarks and references to Appendices
DOUCHY	1		Section 1 + 4 at DALLON No 2 at DOUCHY No 3 attached 148 Bde RFA near HAMEL.	
	2		Section 2 moved to MANCHESTER HILL. No 1 attached to 149 Bde RFA at VAUX. No 3 as above	
			No 4 to EPINE DE DALLON	
	3		Capt. HILL rejoined from RE School of Instruction BLENDEQUES.	
	4-13		As above, weather fine + dry.	
	14		Section 3 relieved No 4 at DALLON + No 4 moved to FLUQUIERES + HAPPENCOURT	
			No 1 moved to EPINE DE DALLON to assist No 3 + No 2 to assist No 4.	
	16		Lt LANNON returned from leave.	
	17		Lt LANNON took over command of No 3 Section from Lt EVANS RE.	
	18		Lt THURLOY rejoined from XVIII Corps Gas School.	
	21		Enemy opened offensive at 4.30 AM. The order Man Battle Stations was received	
			from DHQ Transport proceeded to DURY + other personnel to FLUQUIERES	
			No 2 Section who were located in Gunpits in Aviation Wood arrived at the	
			assembly position first + without casualties at 7 AM.	
			No 4 Section arrived at 8 AM less 4 men. 3 of these eventually rejoined the Coy.	
			Nos 1 + 3 Sections had great difficulty in reaching the rendez-vous. The former	

D. D. & L., London, E.C. (A7833) Wt. W593/M1672 350,000 4/17 Sch. 52a Forms C2118/14

Instructions regarding War Diaries and Intelligence Summaries are contained in F. S. Regs., Part II. and the Staff Manual respectively. Title pages will be prepared in manuscript.

WAR DIARY
or
INTELLIGENCE SUMMARY.
(Erase heading not required.)

Army Form C. 2118.

(2)

Place	Date	Hour	Summary of Events and Information	Remarks and references to Appendices
			arrived at 11·30 AM with the loss of 7 men & the latter about noon with the loss of 10 men.	
			At 3 pm the Coy: moved to AVIATION WOOD & at 10·30 pm to AUBIGNY.	
AUBIGNY	22nd	12·30 AM	The Company arrived at AUBIGNY & at 11·30 AM marched to HAM to work on the HAM Defences which were started on at 2·30 pm. At 5·30 pm the Coy knocked off work & held the defences until relieved by the 89th Inf: Bde.	
	23rd	12·30 AM	The Company was relieved by the 89th Inf: Bde Details & returned to billets in HAM at 1·30 AM. ~~[illegible]~~	
			At 5·30 pm the Company moved to NOHILLE VILETTE & thence to ESMERY HALLON.	
			Lt LANNON RE successfully demolished the Eastern Bridge of the S. QUENTIN Canal at HAM.	
ESMERY HALLON	23rd	6·30 AM	The Company arrived & eventually took up a defensive position in front of the village which was to be held at all costs. This was held till mid-night when the Company was relieved by the 17th Battn Manchester Regt	

(3)

Instructions regarding War Diaries and Intelligence Summaries are contained in F. S. Regs., Part II, and the Staff Manual respectively. Title pages will be prepared in manuscript.

WAR DIARY
or
INTELLIGENCE SUMMARY.
(Erase heading not required.)

Army Form C. 2118.

Place	Date	Hour	Summary of Events and Information	Remarks and references to Appendices
ESMERY HALLON	24	1.30 AM	~~[illegible]~~ The Company ~~the~~ moved out to dig a new selected line at 1.30 AM & again returned to billets at 4 AM.	
			At 12.30 pm the Company moved to RAMIECOURT & commenced work on a line east of ERCHEU till 3.30 pm.	
			The Company arrived at SOLENTE at 6 pm where it billetted for the night	
SOLENTE	25	5.30 AM	At 5.30 AM the Company marched out to work in the locality of SOLENTE - OMENCOURT & worked till 2 pm. The Company then moved to SOLENTE & formed up with all available troops for the defence of SOLENTE. The whole force was later ordered to march to ROIGLISE where it arrived at 5.30 pm.	
		11.20 pm	The Company moved to PLESSIER	
PLESSIER	26	8.30 AM	The Company arrived & at 9 AM moved off to BOUCHOIR according to orders & came under orders of G.O.C. 89th Inf. Bde.	
			At 10.30 pm the Company proceeded to dig a trench through all roads on the Brigade front with a view to stopping armoured cars.	

D. D. & L., London, E.C. (A;853) Wt. W1031/M1672 350,000 5/17 Sch. 52a Forms/C/2118/14

(5)

Army Form C. 2118.

Instructions regarding War Diaries and Intelligence Summaries are contained in F. S. Regs., Part II. and the Staff Manual respectively. Title pages will be prepared in manuscript.

WAR DIARY
or
INTELLIGENCE SUMMARY.
(Erase heading not required.)

Place	Date	Hour	Summary of Events and Information	Remarks and references to Appendices
BOUCHOIR	27	10 AM	The Company under orders occupied the position in front of PLESSIER which was handed over to the French at 10.30 pm + the Company marched to MOREUIL	
MOREUIL	28	9.30 AM	The Company marched to ROUVREL	
ROUVREL	29	Noon	The Company started work on a defensive position to cover the Crossing of the AVRE astride the MOREUIL AILLY Road. The men worked till 5.30 pm + returned to ROUVREL	
	30		The Company entrained at SALEUX for VALERIE sur SOMME	
	31		arrived at VAUDRICOURT.	
		Note:	A more detailed report of the operations was made to the CRE 35 Division on April 3 1918. See Appendix A.	

H.H. Newman Major RE
OC 200 Fd Coy RE

D. D. & L., London, E.C. (A7883) Wt. W5o7/M1672 350,000 4/17 Sch. 52a Forms/C/2118/14

A P P E N D I X "A".

Appendix "A"

C.R.E.,
30th Division.

In accordance with your instructions, I forward herewith a narrative of the work of the 200th Field Coy. R.E. during the period 21st/31st March, 1918.

On the 20th March the Company was located as follows:-
Two sections were working on the defences of the EPINE de DALLON, one of whom (No. 3) lived in dugouts on the right of the main St. QUENTIN Road about ¼ of a mile short of the EPINE de DALLON; the other (No. 1) was billetted in some old gun positions on the left of the road about ½ a mile short of the EPINE.
Nos. 2 and 4 Sections were working on gun positions in the fron t and Battle Zones for 148th Brigade R.F.A. Of these the whole of No. 2 Section was located at AVIATION WOOD. The majority of No. 4 Section was billetted in HAPPENCOURT, but had 1 sapper working and living with each of the Batteries in the forward zone.

The instructions I received from you were that in the event of an enemy attack, the Company should assemble at FLUQUIERES.
On the evening of the 20th I heard ~~xxxxxxxx~~ that an enemy attack was expected the following morning. I therefore rang you up to find out whether there was sufficient grounds for withdrawing the
20th. two forward sections near the EPINE de DALLON. On receiving a negative answer from you, I telephoned Lieut. LANNON, the senior officer at DALLON, to be ready to move at very short notice, and in case I could not get orders through to him, to move the sections at his own discretion.
At 4-30 a.m. 21st March, the enemy barrage came down, and at the same time the enemy started to shell DOUCHY, waking up all the Coy. H eadquarters personnel.
21st. Steps were immediately taken to man Battle Stations.
The Company assembled behind a small bank 200 yards West of Brigade Headquarters in FLUQUIERES.
No. 2 Section, who were all located together in gunpits in AVIATION WOOD, arrived at the assembly position first, and without casualties, at about 7-a.m.
O.C. No. 4 Section had some difficulty in finding his section, owing to the fact that he was making his way across country in the dark, but eventually arrived at the assembly position, short only of the 4 men who had been attached to forward batteries, at about 8-a.m. 3 of these 4 men eventually found the Company, though some of them did not for a few days.
Nos. 1 and 3 Sections had great difficulty in reaching the rendez-vous. The barrage on the entrance of both their billets was intense, and the gas lay heavy on the ground. Added to the dark, this made the operation of withdrawing the forward sections very difficult. Lieuts. LANNON and SANVILLE formed their Sections and sent them off in small bodies under N.C.O's. No. 1 Section eventually arrived at FLUQUIERES at 11-30 a.m, with the loss of 7 men, and No. 3 Section arrived at about noon, with the loss of 10 men, of whom 5 were known to be wounded, and one of whom was badly gassed. Of the remaining men, some were working in the EPINE de DALLON redoubt at the time the Battle started, and remained there to fight.
Throughout the day, FLUQUIERES was subjected to harassing fire, but no casualties were suffered.

At 3-p.m. I received your orders to move the Company to the quarry behind AVIATION WOOD. On arrival at this spot I received instructions from O.C., 11th South Lancs. that the three Field Coys. and 11th South Lancs. might be required to hold a line running North and South in front of MILL WOOD, with the left on DOUCHY, and that I would be responsible for the safety of the left flank.
Accompanied by the **Officers** I reconnoitred the position , and took preliminary measures to occupy it should it become necessary to do so, but for the time being left the sections in the quarry. The quarry was subjected to slight shelling during the day, but no

casualties were suffered.

When Battle Stations were manned the Transport moved to DURY, Headquarters remaining at DOUCHY. In the course of the afternoon, I obtained your permission to move Headquarters to DURY also.

At about 10-30 p.m. I was informed by O.C. 11th S. Lancs. that the situation in front had become serious and was instructed by him, acting under the Divl. Commanders orders, to occupy the position that had been selected, to dig in, and to hold the position at all costs. Whilst making the necessary arrangements I received your orders to move at once to AUBIGNY, and to billet the night there.

A conference was then held between O.C. 11th S. Lancs. and the three Field Coy. Commanders in order to decide with which order to comply, as there was some doubt as to which order was the
22nd latest. It was then decided to act on your order, and the Coy. marched to AUBIGNY, arriving there at 12-30 a.m. 22nd March. Picquets were posted and the Coy. billetted in a barn. Early in the morning the Company was moved to a better billet.

At 9-a.m. I found that there was a Bde. H.Q. of the 20th Division in the village, and reported the presence of the Company in the village to the B.G.C. as the senior Officer present.

Under his instructions, in Company with the O.C. 20th M.G. Battn. and an officer of the Brigade Staff, I selected a line of defence to the East and South East of AUBIGNY. On returning to Brigade H.Q. to report, I met G.O.C. 30th Div. and O.C., 202nd Field Coy. R.E.

General Williams informed O.C. 202nd Field Coy. R.E. and myself that his policy was that the Field Companies should not, if possible, become involved in fighting, but that they should remain well forward in order to do any work that might be of value. He further added that it would not always be possible to get orders to Field Coy. Commanders, but that the latter should use their own discretion to a very large measure in what work they should do and when they should move.

At 11-30 a.m. the Company was formed up in order to start work on the line that had been selected for the defence of AUBIGNY when I received your orders to move ~~the~~ to HAM at once for work on the HAM Bridgehead Defences. The Coy. marched to HAM at once and arrived in billets at 1-p.m. In the meantime I reported at your H.Q., and received from you information as to the situation and your instructions to work on the North Eastern sector of the defences.

The Company marched away from the billet at 1-30 p.m. and started work at 2-30 p.m. Later in the day I reported to you and was instructed that when work was finished I should hold the trenches until relieved by elements of the 89th Inf. Bde. Accordingly, in order not to tire the men excessively, I knocked off work at 5-30 p.m., and occupied the position.

At 12-30 a.m. on the 23rd the Company was relieved by 89th Bde. details, and marched back to their billets at HAM, arriving
23rd there at 1-30 a.m. I then received instructions from you to wire the front line along the canal bank to the East of HAM on the morning of the 23rd.

On reporting to G.O.C. 89th Inf. Bde., I was informed by him that he would rather I wired a line running East and West about ¼ of a mile South of HAM, which he considered his main line of resistance. I then obtained permission from you by telephone to do this.

At 5-p.m. heavy machine gun fire broke out in the outskirts of the town, and a few minutes later a picquet that I had posted came in to report that the firing appeared to be coming closer. I consequently fell in the Company and prepared to move off. I sent 2nd Lieut. THURLBY to the 89th Bde. Signal Office to find out what he could about the situation. He returned a few minutes later with information that the enemy had already penetrated the

Northern outskirts of the town. I consequently moved the Company off by the road South of the St. QUENTIN canal and marched to NOUILLE VILETTE.

During the afternoon of the 22nd I had been ordered by you to detail an Officer to demolish the Eastern bridge over the St. QUENTIN CANAL when it should become necessary. Lieut. LANNON was detailed for this duty and successfully accomplished it at 7-a.m.

My intention in marching to NOUILLE VILLETTE was to halt there till daylight and to work from that spot on the line which G.O.C. 89th Inf. Bde. wished me to wire. On arrival at the village however, I was informed by the artillery billetted there that HAM was by this time completely in the hands of the enemy. As all the available stores of wiring material were in HAM I gave up all prospect of wiring the line, and withdrew the Company to ESMERY HALLON.

On arrival at ESMERY HALLON at 6-30 a.m. the Company breakfasted, and I then endeavoured to get into touch with any of the Bde. Headquarters in order to find out the situation and to decide on what was to be done next. I eventually met General STANLEY on the road at 9-a.m., and was informed by him that the situation in front was critical. I was instructed by him to take up a rearguard position behind the village on the left of the 202nd Field Coy. R.E., and to look out for my left flank, which would be in the air.

His idea was that the Infantry in front should, if necessary retire through the three Field Companies who were holding this position, and should reorganize in rear of them. This position was taken up at 10-a.m.

The Infantry in front, who were holding a line through VERIAINES maintained their position, and consequently at 12-30 p.m. I received orders to leave the present position and to take up a position in front of the village, which was to be held at all costs. I agreed with O.C. 202nd Field Coy. R.E., who was commanding all the three Field Companies, to be responsible for the safety of the left flank.

The position taken up crossed at right angles a valley which ~~ran North and South. The left flank was again in the air.~~

Occasional shelling was experienced throughout the day, one man being wounded.

This position was held till midnight 23rd/24th when it was handed over to the 17th Battn. Manchester Regt.

24th. The Company marched back to a billet in the middle of the village, and had a hot meal which had been prepared. I had intended when the men had had their meal to dig trenches in the position just vacated for the 17th Manchesters but in the meantime I received a message from O.C. 202nd Field Coy. R.E. that the enemy had taken GOLANCOURT. He informed me that he was forming a defensive flank to the line in front of the village.

The village line ran through the O of HALLON at right angles to the ESMERY HALLON - HAM Road and turned at right angles to the ESMERY HALLON - GOLANCOURT Road. The flank taken up by O.C. 202nd Field Coy. R.E. ran parallel to the l'ALLEMAGNE river.

24th. I accordingly brought the 200th Field Coy. into line in prolongation of his right and started to dig in at 1-30 a.m. Later I found G.O.C. 21st Inf. Bde., who was going round the line. He informed O.C. 202nd Field Coy. R.E. and myself that the situation on the right flank was now more satisfactory, and that he had made other arrangements for the defence of the right flank. The 200th and 202nd Field Companies accordingly marched back to billets in ESMERY HALLON arriving there at 4-a.m.

At 5-a.m. the enemy started to shell the village, and at 6-a.m. the shelling grew heavier, a good many shells falling in the vicinity of the billets. As all the men were concentrated in a single ADRIAN hut, I decided to evacuate the village and marched out to a quarry on the left hand side of the road a quarter of a mile short of

ESMERY HALLON. One man had been wounded during the shelling of the village.

At the quarry the Company halted and had breakfast.

At 8-30 a.m. a French Cavalry patrol came through the village and reported that the enemy had broken through in front. The three Field Companies immediately took up the rearguard position that they had held during the previous day.

Whilst deploying to take up this position the Company was attacked by a low flying aeroplane, but no casualties were suffered.

Considerable numbers, I should estimate about 200, of stragglers coming back from the front line were stopped and formed up in prolongation of the left flank.

At 11-a.m. I received your orders to withdraw to the West bank of the Canal, to assemble at RAMIECOURT, and to assist the French Infantry, who were holding the line of the canal, to dig a reserve line.

The Company accordingly marched to RAMIECOURT arriving at 12-30 p.m., and then I received your further instructions to dig a line of trenches 200 yards to the East of ERCHEU for the 129th Regt. of French Infantry. The Coy. commenced to dig at 1-p.m. each shovel being double-manned by a sapper and a French Infantryman, as the latter had no tools. Work was carrier on till 3-30 p.m. by which time a continuous trench 3' 6" deep had been dug for the garrison along their whole front.

The Company then marched to SOLENTE, where they arrived at 6-p.m. and billetted the night. On arrival at SOLENTE I received your verbal instructions to reconnoitre that night the village of OMENCOURT with a view to forming SOLENTE and OMENCOURT into a defended locality, the other two Field Companies working on the SOLENTE FRONT and the junction of the two villages.

Your orders were that work was to start early the following morning, the 25th. This was accordingly done and the the Company marched out of SOLENTE at 5-30 a.m. , work being started immediately on arrival at OMENCOURT.

A working party 200 strong arrived about 9-a.m. Work was carried on till 2-p.m., a line of posts being dug round the village, and a keep being constructed to cover the CRESSY Road near its rear. At 2-p.m. I received orders from G.O.C. 21st Inf. Bde. to march to SOLENTE. The Company formed up there together with all the available troops in the neighbourhood.

After waiting some time for orders the whole force marched to ROIGLISE arriving there at 5-30 p.m.

At ROIGLISE I received your instructions to move early the following morning to HANGEST en SANTERRE. This destination was afterwards changed to PLESSIER-ROZANVILLERS, and arrangements were made to move off at 5-a.m. 26th March.

At 11-20 p.m. I received a message from O.C. 202nd Field Coy. R.E. informing me that as far as he could find out, the situation in front had become critical, enemy batteries being in action to the West of SOLENTE, and that the enemy was advancing. I accordingly made arrangements to move off at midnight.

26th. The traffic between ROIGLISE and ROYE was very congested, and the 3 kilometres between these places took 2½ hours to cover. From that point onwards the route was uninterrupted to PLESSIER. A halt was made at BUCHOIR for breakfast, and the Coy. arrived at PLESSIER at 8-30 a.m.

At 9-a.m. I received very urgent orders from you to get into touch at once with G.O.C. 89th Inf. Bde., under whose orders I would act, and to move the Company to BOUCHOIR without delay. I was informed by the 89th Brigade that the Division was taking up a line from ROUVROY to Le QUESNOY, the 89th Bde. being on the left. The French Division in front was retiring in a South Westerly direction and would come into line on the right.

I was instructed to place the Company in support of the 18th K.L.R. at a point to be selected near the <u>R</u> in BOUCHO<u>IR</u>, at which place I would meet the Brigade Major as early as possible.

The Company moved off at 9-30 a.m. and the Officers went ahead to reconnoitre.

The Bde. Major 89th Bde. failed to arrive at the rendezvous

and as I was informed by G.O.C. 90th Inf. Bde. that the plan had now been changed, and that it was intended that the line ROUVROY-BOUCHOIR and not the line ROUVROY-LE QUESNOY should be held, I halted the Company at the East end of BOUCHOIR.

I then placed the Company at the disposal of the 90th Inf. Bde., and instructed Lieut. SCOTT to conform to the action taken by the 201st Field Coy. R.E. until such time as I could find the H.Q. of the 89th Inf. Bde. and obtain further orders from them.

I found General STANLEY at LA FOLIE at about 5-30 p.m. and was ordered by him to withdraw to a position in reserve which I should select in an area West of LA FOLIE and East of the MONTDIDIER-ROSIERES railway. The Coy. therefore moved at 7-p.m. from BOUCHOIR to dugouts 100 yards North of the main ROYE-AMIENS road, and 100 yards East of the railway.

At 10-30 p.m. I received orders from G.O.C. 89th Brigade to block against armoured cars all the three roads leading through the Brigade front.

No. 3 Section moved off at midnight and dug trenches 3' 6" wide and 2' 6" deep across these roads, arriving back at the dugouts at 5-a.m. 27th.

27th. At 10-a.m. 27th I was informed by G.O.C. 89th Bde. that the situation on the right flank was uncertain and that the Division would shortly retire to a line in front of PLESSIER.

I was to proceed at once to take up a position 200 yards East of PLESSIER and astride the PLESSIER HANGEST Road: the 89th Bde. would fall back and take up a position on my left, the 90th on my right. The Company moved off from the dugouts at 10-a.m., arriving in front of PLESSIER AT 11-30 p.m.

On arrival at PLESSIER I found that the position was already occupied by three Battalions of the 133rd French Division.

I occupied a trench in the front line of the system and asked for further orders.

At 10-15 p.m. I received your instructions to move at once to MOREUIL, to spend the night there, and to march the next morning to ROUVREL. The line was handed over to the French at 10-30 p.m., the Company arriving at MOREUIL at 12 midnight.

28th. Leaving MOREUIL at 9-30 a.m., ROUVREL was reached at 11-a.m. Throughout the day the Company stood by at ROUVREL ready to entrain

29th. On the morning of the 29th I received orders from you to construct a defensive position to cover the crossing of the AURE astride the MOREUIL AILLY Road. Work was started at 12 noon, and carried on till 5-30 p.m., when the Company marched back to ROUVREL. By this time a series of posts to cover the crossing had been dug to a fightable depth.

On the following day the Company marched to SALEUX in accordance with your instructions and entrained for VALERIE-sur-SOMME.

x x x

The work undertaken by the Company throughout the period in question consisted almost entirely in the digging of rearguard positions and in holding them until relieved by the Infantry, or else in digging positions with the intention of holding them while the Infantry passed through to reorganize.

As regards the selecting of the positions the main difficulty encountered was to get into touch with the unit on the outer flank, but this seems scarcely avoidable under the circumstances.

Had the situation at any time been clearer, a considerable amount of useful work could have been done, such as destroying buildings and cratering roads. I was unwilling to undertake this work on my own responsibility, however, as I was not aware whether such roads or buildings would be required in the event of a general counter attack.

As regards the work itself, it would seem that men cannot be called upon to dig more than 8 ft. run~~ning~~ of fire trench a day if they are also marching an average of ten to fifteen miles a day, without detriment to their efficiency.

I would suggest that to meet the contingencies of open warfare, Field Companies should be given more opportunities of training as Infantry, as their capacity for open order work at present is limited.

The equipment carried was:-

Leather jerkins.
Battle Order, the haversack containing the Iron Rations and the days rations.
1 shovel.
1 rolled blanket.
Each man carried 150 rounds of ammunition.

I found that the only way to avoid losing rations and tools was for each man to carry his own.

Greatcoats were not carried, and the general concensus of opinion was that leather jerkins and a rolled blanket were of greater value.

By far the greatest difficulty was that of providing hot food for the men.

The men were undergoing unaccustomed exertions and had very little sleep. In addition to this, for five days out of the first six, the men had no food from breakfast till late evening, except scraps of biscuits and a very short ration of bully, and their efficiency consequently suffered considerably.

I would strongly urge that a Travelling Kitchen should be put on the Mobilization Store Equipment of a Field Company in lieu of the mess cart as the only way of meeting this difficulty in open warfare.

The men stood the strain remarkably well, for in spite of the fact that during the period in question the Company marched a total of about 100 miles, dug for a total of 25 hours, and occupied trenches for considerable lengths of time, not one man went sick and not one man fell out of the line of march.

H. A. Dinnen [signature]

Major, R.E.

3rd April, 1918. O.C., 200th Field Coy. R.E.

REFERENCE MAPS

[illegible]

200TH FIELD COMPANY R.E. ORDER

10.3.18

1. No. 4 Section, 200th Field Coy R.E. now located at A.[illegible] c.9.5. will relieve No. 3 Section 200th Field Coy. R.E. now located at F.23.d.8.1 on the night 14/15 March 1918.

2. No. 3 Section will continue its present work up to the evening of 15th March 1918.
The Section will be bathed on the 14th inst. and will be marched by O.C. No. 3 Section to 89th Brigade Baths at FLUQUIERES, to start bathing at 9.0 a.m.
It will march across country to new billets, leaving its present billets at 6 p.m.
O.C. No. 3 Section will arrange to start work on the Forward Zone mined dugouts at the 6.0 a.m. – 12 Noon shift on the 15th inst.

3. No. 4 Section will continue its present work, up to and including the 6.0 a.m. – 12 Noon shift on the 14th inst.
The section will parade at 6.0 pm. and will march across country to its new billets.
The section will be bathed at the 89th Brigade Baths, FLUQUIERES at 9.0 a.m. 15th inst., and will reconnoitre work on the 15th inst.
Work will be started on the Battery positions on the morning of the 16th inst.

4. O.C. Transport will arrange transport to transfer Cooks gear, blankets and Officers Kit, to report to No. 3 Section billet at 6.30 pm. 14th inst. and to No. 4 Section billet at 7.30 pm. on 14th inst.

5. Section Officers will arrange to send an advance party on the afternoon of the 14th to take over the new billets, and each Section will leave behind 2 Senior N.C.O.'s for 2 days to hand over the work.

6. Great care is to be taken that all work in hand or projected is handed over.

[illegible]

Copy No. 1. O.C. No. 3 Section
2. " 4 "
3. O.C. Transport
4. C.R.E. 30 D[illegible]
5. 14[illegible] Brigade R.F.A.
6. [illegible]

SECRET

30

Vol 16

WAR DIARY

200th Field Company, Royal Engineers,

for the month of

April 1917

(VOLUME XVI

Instructions regarding War Diaries and Intelligence Summaries are contained in F. S. Regs., Part II. and the Staff Manual respectively. Title pages will be prepared in manuscript.

WAR DIARY
or
INTELLIGENCE SUMMARY.
(Erase heading not required.)

Army Form C. 2118.

VOL XVI 200th FIELD COMPANY R.E.

Place	Date	Hour	Summary of Events and Information	Remarks and references to Appendices
BLAIREVILLE	1.4.17.		HQ and 4 Sections billeted at BLAIREVILLE. Transport + horse lines at R.27 c.9.1. Work continued on construction of 22 Splinter-proof shelters in Railway Cutting in S3, for accommodation of 3 Bde HQ, and 4 Artillery Group HQ.	France 51B. S.W. 1/20000 Ed. 4a. Ficheux Ed 3b 1/10,000
	2.4.17.		Work continued. No infantry parties on 1st or 2nd on account of attack on HENIN SUR COJEUL. 2/Lt LESLIE to Hospital.	
	3.4.17.		Work continued. Working parties of 1 Co 11th S. Lancs Pioneers and 200 infantry from 90th Bde. Work begun on Bn. HQ at S4c 8.2. for reserve Bn of 89th Bde.	
	4.4.17.		Work continued. Working party 250 infantry. 2Lt BARKER rejoined. Transport of stores to battle dumps at S11b 95.60. begun. Instructions received from CRE. that the company will be employed during forthcoming operations on the following work. 1 Section bridging COJEUL RIVER at HENINEL and above WANCOURT. 1 Section on strong points about N24c 5.4. and N29b 4.6. 1 Section on defences of HENINEL. 1 Section in reserve.	
	5.4.17.		Section Officers and NCO's reconnoitred HENIN SUR COJEUL with a view to selection of rendezvous and site for leaving trestle wagon with stores for bridge. Work on shelters continued.	
	6.4.17.		22 shelters in Railway Cutting and 2 shelters at S4c 8.2 completed.	
	7.4.17.		Sections practised laying out trenches and rapid wiring. Trestle wagon with one trestle and 30' of roadway taken up after dark to rendezvous at T1c 8.2.	
	8.4.17.		Further practice owing to postponement of zero for 24 hours.	
	9.4.17.		Zero hour 5.30 am.	Weather. Wet early, clearing later. Snow in evening
		2.0 pm	1 NCO + 6 men from reserve section – No 3 – sent to repair trench bridge in S11. for R.A.	
		3.0 pm	Nos 1, 2, 4 Sections paraded for work + marched out 3.25 pm. Team for trestle wagon marched with No 1. One platoon of 17th Manchester Regt attached to No 2. 2 platoons to No 4. Pack mules sent up to carry forward French wire. Tool carts sent with party to rendezvous.	
		5.0 pm	Information received from CRE. that situation is not clear. Sections ordered to remain at rendezvous.	
		10.30 pm	O.C. proceeded under orders from CRE. to Bde HQ in Railway Cutting in S.3. to find out situation and to arrange for the employment of R.E. and infantry working parties.	
		11.30 pm	Found that both 21st and 89th Brigades had been held up by uncut wire in front of HINDENBURG LINE. Arranged with G.O.C. 90th Bde to put parties to work on trenches from N26 central to N27 c1.5.	
	10.4.17.	1.30 am	Parties left rendezvous. Tool carts returned to horse lines.	Weather. Dull, cold. Snow in evening.
		4.0 am	Work stopped. Infantry parties returned to Bn. Sections returned to HQ. at 7.30 am.	
		3.0 pm	Orders received from CRE. to send 1 Section to construct strong point at about N29c 6.6. One platoon to meet Section at S12a 0.5.	
		4.15 pm	No 3 Section marched out. The attack was unsuccessful and no work was possible. Section returned to HQ at 2.45 am.	
	11.4.17.	5.0 pm	Nos 1, 2, 4. Sections marched out to work on the clearing of road from BOIRY BECQUERELLE to ST MARTIN SUR COJEUL. Road cleared from T1c 8.2 through T2a 9.8. N32d 3.1. N33a 3.0. to N33a 1.4.	Weather. Fine early, dull later, snow.
		2.30 am	Sections returned to HQ.	

Army Form C. 2118.

Instructions regarding War Diaries and Intelligence Summaries are contained in F. S. Regs., Part II. and the Staff Manual respectively. Title pages will be prepared in manuscript.

WAR DIARY
or
INTELLIGENCE SUMMARY.
(Erase heading not required.)

VOL XVI (cont). 200th FIELD COMPANY R.E.

Place	Date	Hour	Summary of Events and Information	Remarks and references to Appendices
BLAIREVILLE	12.4.17.	9.15am	Ordered by CRE to send two sections with two platoons of 11th S. Lancs. Pioneers to consolidate HINDENBURG LINE at about N27b.8.6, N28c7.8, N28d 2.6, N28d 3.3.	FRANCE 51B.SW. 1/20000 Ed 4.A.
		10.0am	One section only to go. No3.	
		11.45am	Party marched out.	
		2.0pm	Work begun on strong points at N27b 95.45, N28c45.65 and N28d 25.40. Work completed 7.0pm.	
		11.15pm	Section returned to HQ.	
BAILLEULMONT	13.4.17.	7.50am	Company left BLAIREVILLE marching by BELLACOURT & BASSEUX to BAILLEULMONT arriving at 11.0 am.	FRANCE, LENS 11. 1/100,000
FAMECHON	14.4.17.	4.30pm	Company left BAILLEULMONT marching by LA CAUCHIE, GAUDIEMPRÉ, PAS, to FAMECHON	
	15.4.17.		Rest.	
	16.4.17.		Training Squad Drill etc.	
	17.4.17.		Training. No4 Sect. pontoon & trestle bridging	
	18.4.17.		Training. No1 Sect pontoon & trestle bridging	
	19.4.17.		Orders to move to POMMIER. Orders cancelled at 10.30am.	
	20.4.17.	6.15am	Company less transport and cyclists marched out to COUIN, embussed there at 8.0 am.	
ACHICOURT		9.0am	Transport marched out moving by PAS, MONDICOURT - BEAUMETZ - DAINVILLE to ACHICOURT bivouacked 1 mile N.W. of ACHICOURT.	
BEAURAINS		6.0pm	Company arrived at BEAURAINS.	
	21.4.17.	5.0pm	Transport lines moved to BEAURAINS.	
	22.4.17.		Ordered by CRE to place two sections at disposal of O.C. 201st Fd Co for work on crossings over R. COJEUL at HENINEL.	
		2.30pm	Lt HILL & 2Lt CHIDGEY reported to O.C. 201st Fd Co.	
		5.30pm	Nos 1 & 2 Sections marched out. No1 made a crossing over river at N29a 5.8. No2 at N28d 80.95. returned 5.0 am.	Casualties nil.
		6.0pm	Nos 3 & 4 Sections with trestle wagon, GS wagon, & three forage carts moved out to work on road between N28b 8.8. and HENINEL. A track fit for field artillery was completed into HENINEL. Sections returned 5.0 am.	
	23.4.17.	4.45am	Zero. Attack at first successful but Divisions on both flanks were forced to fall back by heavy counter attacks, and 30th Div had also to withdraw. 200th Fd Co. in Divisional reserve.	
		2.30pm	No2 Section 2Lt CHIDGEY sent to work from 3-6pm to assist 202nd Fd Co in construction of Adv. Div. HQ.	
		4.30pm	Orders received to send up two sections to relieve two Sections of 202nd Fd Co. waiting at N28b 7.7 to consolidate enemy front line system.	Casualties nil
		5.30pm	No3 Section 2Lt HOFFMAN sent to continue work done by 201st Fd Co on Adv. Brigade H.Q. at N29c 6.3.	
		6.0pm	No1 Section Lt HILL and No4 Section 2Lt BARKER moved out. O.C. went to Adv Brigade HQ at N22d 45.15. and arranged for employment of sections if situation should permit it, on consolidation of enemy support line at approx. N30c 9.0 and N30b 5.1. A second attack was launched at 6.0pm but did not make much progress owing to heavy counter attacks.	
	24.4.17.	2.45am	Nos 1 & 4 Sections ordered by G.O.C. Div. to return to 201st Fd Co's billets near NEUVILLE VITASSE	
		5.0am	No3 Section returned to HQ. having completed Bde HQ. in spite of heavy hostile shellfire	
		7.30am	No2 Section proceeded to work to assist 202nd Fd Co. on Adv. Div. HQ. Work completed at 7.0pm.	

Instructions regarding War Diaries and Intelligence Summaries are contained in F. S. Regs., Part II, and the Staff Manual respectively. Title pages will be prepared in manuscript.

VOL XXVIII

WAR DIARY
or
INTELLIGENCE SUMMARY.
(Erase heading not required.)

Army Form C. 2118.

200 Field Company RE

Reference Sheet 1/100,000 ABBEVILLE 14 HAZEBROOK 5A
" 1/40,000 No 28

Place	Date	Hour	Summary of Events and Information	Remarks and references to Appendices
	April			
VAUDRICOURT	1	–	The transport left MAREUIL at 9 AM + joined the Company at VAUDRICOURT.	
	2.3		" Company remained at VAUDRICOURT	
	4		" " marched to FRESSENVILLE + entrained leaving 8.40 pm.	
ELVERDINGHE	5		" " arrived at ROUSBRUGGE at 11.30 AM + proceeded to ELVERDINGHE	
	6		" transport moved to SOLFERINO CAMP	
	7		" Company less Transport moved to CALEDONIA AVENUE C.9.C.4.5 + took over work from	
			26th + 23rd Field Companies RE. Sector south of YPRES – STADEN Railway	
	7-15		Company engaged on defences + demolition work – preparation of roads etc	
	12		" Lt CHIGGEY RE killed in action at Divisional HQ while attached to C.R.E 30 Division	
	13		" Lt LANNON RE attached to CRE 30th Division as Assistant Adjutant	
	15		Company moved to LOTHIAN Camp.	
	16		Retirement of our forces to STEENBECK line. Demolition of dugouts, pill boxes	
			+ roads carried out by Lt ~~Scott~~ SCOTT RE + " Lt THURLOY RE in evacuated area	
			Transport moved to Camp on POPERINGHE – ELVERDINGHE Road 1 mile W of the ~~Chateau~~	
	17		Company standing by to move.	
BRANDHOEK	18		Company moved to BRANDHOEK + came under XXII Corps.	

(D. D. & L., London, E.C. (A7853) Wt. W593/M1672 350,000 4/17 Sch. 52a Forms/C/2118/14

Army Form C. 2118.

Instructions regarding War Diaries and Intelligence Summaries are contained in F. S. Regs., Part II. and the Staff Manual respectively. Title pages will be prepared in manuscript.

WAR DIARY
or
INTELLIGENCE SUMMARY.
(Erase heading not required.)

Place	Date	Hour	Summary of Events and Information	Remarks and references to Appendices
BRANDHOEK	19th		Company working in old G.H.Q. line	
	20–22		Ditto	
	23rd		Lt C.H. SIMMONDS RE joined the Company	
	25th		The Company moved to St LAWRENCE Camp & were placed under orders of CRE 49th Division, the CRE & staff 30 Division having gone to back areas	
	28th		Transport left BRANDHOEK at 1pm & marched to camp near POPERINGHE	
	29th		Company moved to Camp near HOUTKERQUE E 7 & came under orders of VIII Corps.	
	30th		Work on WATOU line commenced	

[signature]
Major RE.
O.C. 200th Field Coy RE.

Vol 29

WAR DIARY

OF THE

200th Field Company, R. E.

FOR THE MONTH
OF

May 1918

(Volume XXIX)

WAR DIARY
or
INTELLIGENCE SUMMARY.
(*Erase heading not required.*)

Army Form C. 2118.

Instructions regarding War Diaries and Intelligence Summaries are contained in F. S. Regs., Part II. and the Staff Manual respectively. Title pages will be prepared in manuscript.

Vol XXIX

200th Field Coy R.E.

Place	Date	Hour	Summary of Events and Information — Reference BELGIUM & FRANCE SHEET 27 1/40,000.	Remarks and references to Appendices
Near HOUTKERQUE E7 a 6.8	1.5.18.		Work on WATOU LINE continued. 90th INFANTRY BRIGADE details attached for work.	
	2+3.		do do do	
	4.		do do do Nos 1 & 4 Section moved to camp near ABEELE L.19.c and commenced work on ABEELE LINE.	
	5-9.		Work on WATOU & ABEELE LINES continued	
	10		ditto Attached Infantry Brigade left to join Divl H.Q.	
	11		ditto No 1 Section returned to camp from ABEELE.	
	12.		Work on WATOU LINE continued. No 4 Section returned from ABEELE	
	13-17.		ditto by whole Company	
	18		ditto Lieut P.E. HART R.E. joined for duty from XXII Corps.	
	19-21		ditto	
	22		ditto Lieut G.Y. SCOTT admitted to Hospital	
	23-25		ditto Received orders from C.R.E XXII Corps to move on 26th.	
Nr PROVEN E18 b.9.5.	26.		Handed over work on WATOU LINE to 201st FIELD Coy R.E. Company moved to camp near PROVEN E18.b.9.5. Officers reconnoitred site of ADVANCED WATOU LINE. E.5.c.8.5 – E.30.b.8.5.	
	27.		Work commenced on ADVANCED WATOU LINE. Working parties 121 & 129 Labour Companies.	
	28-31		Work continued.	
			Weather during May. — Fine.	

X Hill Capt R.E.
O.C. 200th FIELD CO. R.E.

D. D. & L., London, E.C. (A10266) Wt W5300/P713 750,000 2/18 Sch. 52 Forms/C2118/16.

SECRET

Vol 30

WAR DIARY

of the

200th Field Company, Royal Engineers.

for the month of

JUNE 1918.

(Volume XXX).

Instructions regarding War Diaries and Intelligence Summaries are contained in F. S. Regs., Part II. and the Staff Manual respectively. Title pages will be prepared in manuscript.

WAR DIARY
or
INTELLIGENCE SUMMARY.
(Erase heading not required.)

Army Form C. 2118.

VOL XXX

200 Field Company RE

Reference BELGIUM + FRANCE Sheet 27 1/40,000

Place	Date	Hour	Summary of Events and Information	Remarks and references to Appendices
PROVEN	1		Lt HART RE left the Company to join 557 AT Coy RE. 34th Division.	
			Work on Advanced WATOU Line continued. E5C 8.5 to E30 b 4.5	
"	2		Work continued.	
EECKE.	3		Left PROVEN Area at 7 AM + marched to near EECKE Q28 c 0.5 where Camp was built	
"	4		Major O D ATKINSON proceeded on leave. Captain BUDGE, Field Engineers, arrived.	
			Reconnaissance of Le Peuplier Switch Line. Q 31.32.33 34 35 36 27 28 29 V 2.3 4.5	
"	5		Work started on Le Peuplier Switch Line, with 121 Labour Company to assist, under Major BELLAMY RE as CRE Le Peuplier Switch	
"	6 to end of month		Work Continued with various small changes in frontage + work generally speaking the work consisted in rendering the existing trenches fightable by deepening, draining, clearing foreground + by the addition of wire (three belts), machine gun emplacements etc	
"	12		Lieut G.V Scott obtained 21 days sick leave (12-6-18 to 3-6-18) from Base.	
"	15		The Company to take up battle positions in Le Peuplier Switch by 9 pm + remain there till further orders. The Company being in Reserve rendez-voused at Q32 c 0.4 + stood down at	

D. D. & L., London, E.C.
(A10266) Wt W5300/P713 750,000 2/18 Sch. 52 Forms/C2118/16.

Instructions regarding War Diaries and Intelligence Summaries are contained in F. S. Regs., Part II. and the Staff Manual respectively. Title pages will be prepared in manuscript.

WAR DIARY
or
INTELLIGENCE SUMMARY.
(Erase heading not required.)

Army Form C. 2118.

Place	Date	Hour	Summary of Events and Information	Remarks and references to Appendices
EECKE	16		The Company again stood-to at 9 pm in Reserve Battle positions	
	21		Major O D ATKINSON returned from leave.	
			Weather — fine generally, cold.	
			3.7.18. [illegible] Major R.E. O.C. 206th Fld Coy R.E.	

D. D. & L., London, E.C.
(A10266) Wt W5300/P713 750,000 2/18 Sch. 52 Forms/C2118/16.

SECRET

Vol 31

WAR DIARY

of the

200th Field Company Royal Engineers.

for the month of

JULY 1918.

(Volume XXXI)

Instructions regarding War Diaries and Intelligence Summaries are contained in F. S. Regs., Part II, and the Staff Manual respectively. Title pages will be prepared in manuscript.

Army Form C. 2118.

WAR DIARY
or
~~INTELLIGENCE SUMMARY.~~
(Erase heading not required.)

VOL XXXI

200th Field Company R.E

Reference BELGIUM + FRANCE Sheet 27 1/40,000

Place	Date	Hour	Summary of Events and Information	Remarks and references to Appendices
EECKE 27/ Q28.c.0.5	1.7.18	–	The Company employed on LE PEUPLIER SWITCH. Work consisting in rendering trenches fightable by deepening, draining, clearing foreground, constructing M.G. Emplacements etc. etc.	
	4.7.18		"Lt SANVILLE RE to course of instruction at RE Training School ROUEN	
	10.7.18		Work on LE PEUPLIER SWITCH handed over.	
CASSEL (Mt Recollet)	11.7.18		Company marched to P8d.2.9 + transport to P8c.1.1 where camps were pitched under canvas.	
	12.7.18		Training of Company Commenced.	
	15.7.18		"Lt PEARSON RE joined the Company from the base.	
	16.7.18		Lt SCOTT returned from 21 days sick leave	
	17.7.18		Inter-Company Cricket Match with 201st Field Company which resulted in our favour. Dinner + concert for the men in the evening. Orders to man Battle Stations received about 11 pm which were cancelled later.	
	18.7.18		The four sections moved to Q28c.0.5 for work on Battle trenches.	
	19.7.18		Lt SCOTT RE left the Company to join the 97 Field Company RE as	

D. O. & L., London, E.C. (A7885) Wt. W803/M1672 350,000 4/17 Sch. 52a Forms C/2118/14

Instructions regarding War Diaries and Intelligence Summaries are contained in F. S. Regs., Part II. and the Staff Manual respectively. Title pages will be prepared in manuscript.

WAR DIARY
or
~~INTELLIGENCE~~ SUMMARY.
(Erase heading not required.)

Army Form C. 2118.

Place	Date	Hour	Summary of Events and Information (continued)	Remarks and references to Appendices
CASSEL			second-in-command.	
	20.7.18		No 4 Section returned from Q28 c.0.5 & moved to CASSEL to work on Road demolitions.	
	24.7.18		Divisional Commander inspected Horse Lines at 4 pm.	
	26.7.18		No 2 Section returned to H.Q to train.	
	27.7.18		No 1 Section moved from Q28 c.0.5 to ST. SYLVESTRE CAPPEL to continue Battle Tracks. No 3 Section returned to H.Q for training. Work on Brigade Battle H.Q finished.	
	28.7.18		Lt THURLBY R.E proceeded on leave to U.K	
			Weather – The month had alternate spells of wet & dry weather with four days of very hot. Good on the whole.	

[signature]

Major R.E.
O.C. 200th Field Co. R.E.

Secret 2

Vol 32

WAR DIARY

OF THE

200th Field Company Royal Engineers.

FOR THE MONTH OF

AUGUST 1918.

(Volume XXXII)

Instructions regarding War Diaries and Intelligence Summaries are contained in F. S. Regs., Part II. and the Staff Manual respectively. Title pages will be prepared in manuscript.

WAR DIARY
or
~~INTELLIGENCE SUMMARY.~~
(Erase heading not required.)

Army Form C. 2118.

VOL XXXII

200th Field Coy R.E.

Place	Date	Hour	Summary of Events and Information	Remarks and references to Appendices
CASSEL	1st		As before.	
	2nd		No 1 Section finished work on battle tracks and moved from ST SYLVESTRE CAPPEL to P.8.d.3.9	
	3rd		No 4 Section mining roads in CASSEL. Other Sections training.	
	4th		No 2 Section relieved No 4 Section in CASSEL. 2/Lt BUMPSTEAD went on special leave.	
			2/Lt JASANVILLE returned from RE Course at ROUEN.	
	5th		Training continued	
	6th		" 2/Lt JASANVILLE went on leave	
	7th & 8th		Training continued	
	9th		30th Div took over the line from 35th Div. Company marched from Sh 27 P.8.d.3.9 to Sh 28 M.21.a.2.2	
	11th		Work started as follows: 1 Section working on mined dugout at M.21.a.2.2 - 2 Sections on SP 5 - 1 Section making	
			mule track from M.20.d.75 to M.28.c.77	
	14th		Same work continued till 16th - on night 14/15 a mined dugout at M.22.a.85.30 was started, to act as Adv.	
			Bde HQ for forthcoming attack on DRANOUTRE ridge.	
	16th		Same work continued. On 16th night work was started in screening the mule track from	
			observation, so that after the attack on the DRANOUTRE ridge it could be used for carrying	
			stretchers in daylight.	

D. D. & L., London, E.C.
(A7883) Wt. W803/M1672 350,000 4/17 Sch. 52a Forms C/2118/14

Instructions regarding War Diaries and Intelligence Summaries are contained in F. S. Regs., Part II. and the Staff Manual respectively. Title pages will be prepared in manuscript.

WAR DIARY
or
INTELLIGENCE SUMMARY.
(Erase heading not required.)

Army Form C. 2118.

Place	Date	Hour	Summary of Events and Information	Remarks and references to Appendices
	20.		The same work was continued till the night of 20th. Work on O.P.s handed over to 204 Field Coy RE	
	21st		at 2 a.m. 21st the 8th and 9th Inf Bde attacked the DRANOUTRE ridge. No 2 Section 205th Fld Coy. followed the attack in order to open up tracks. See Appendix A attached.	
			On the night 21/22 No 1 Section carried on this work.	
	22nd.		2 Sections in dugouts M21a22	
			1 Section in new dugout M27c46	
	23rd.		Work on BLUE Line M27c. taken over from 20[illegible] Field Coy in addition to other work.	
	27th.		Same work continued till 27th when the work on O.P.s was taken back from 204 Field Coy RE.	
	29th		Work started on [illegible] RAP at M27a75.	
	30.th		Enemy retired from DRANOUTRE. The Company followed up with the work of clearing the road from M32.25 through KOUDEKOT M33d.12 S4.56.34 S3.b.95 to CRUCIFIX CORNER S18a.62. This road was in good order by 6. p.m 1st September	

3.9.18.

[illegible] Major RE
[illegible] Coy RE

D. D. & L., London, E.C.
(A10266) Wt W5300/P713 750,000 2/18 Sch. 52 Forms/C2118/16.

APPENDIX "A"

C.R.E. A1017

30th British Division

With reference to your 439 of 21.8.18.

No 2 Section, 200th Field Company R.E with one platoon 'D' Coy. 6th Bn. S. Wales Borderers (Pioneers) less one section, was detailed to open up a track from the head of LOCKE CHATEAU drive to PIGOT FARM, M35.a.3.7.

The Platoon of Pioneers, less officers and were very short of ~~officers and~~ N.C.Os, and so it was decided that the 3 sections of Pioneers should be interspersed between the 4 squads of No 2 Section, 200th Field Company R.E.

The location of the ~~route~~ track decided on was forwarded to you yesterday with my Weekly Works Report.

The party got into their working formation, i.e. 1 squad, No. 2 Section, 200th Field Company R.E., 1 section 6th S.W.B. (Pioneers), 1 R.E. squad, 1 Pioneer section etc, at this billet M21.a.2.2. at midnight 20/21st and marched in that formation to their assembly position in the trench at M28.a.7.3. Assembly was complete by 1.0am. 21.8.18.

O.C. 200th Field Company R.E. was at Battn. HQ. 2nd South Lancs. Regt. at M.28.a. 85.00. in order to keep in touch with the situation.

The enemy barrage came down shortly after zero but though the shelling was fairly heavy near PLACID FARM, no casualties were suffered.

Owing to the fog and the fact that wires were cut by the shelling no news was obtained from forward by O.C. 2nd South Lancs. Regt, but as, at about 3.30am. walking wounded stated that MOWBRAY WOOD had been taken I instructed O.C. No 2 Section (II Lieut. F. THURLBY R.E) to move on.

The party moved on by squads, with 1 minute interval between squads. The whole party had started working by 4.15am.

Work was carried on till 5.30am. in the fog, at which time the fog showed signs of lifting and consequently II Lieut. Thurlby R.E. decided to bring the party back to camp.

The party moved back

independently by squads, arriving back about 6.30 am.

Since 3.30 am the enemy's shellfire had been very slight, and no casualties were suffered.

During the 1½ hours work, the track was made fairly passable for men in single file and possible for mules in bright weather in single file; notice boards were erected at prominent places.

[illegible]

Major R.E.,
O.C. 200th Field Coy R.E.

22.8.18

SECRET.

V8 33

WAR DIARY

OF THE

200th Field Company, Royal Engineers.

FOR THE MONTH OF

September 1918.

(Volume XXXIII)

Army Form C. 2118.

WAR DIARY
or
~~INTELLIGENCE SUMMARY.~~
(*Erase heading not required.*)

Instructions regarding War Diaries and Intelligence Summaries are contained in F. S. Regs., Part II. and the Staff Manual respectively. Title pages will be prepared in manuscript.

VOL. XXXIII

200th Field Company R.E.

Place	Date Sept.	Hour	Summary of Events and Information	Remarks and references to Appendices
M21a 2.2	1.		Work on roads continued.	
	2.		Horse lines moved to M3a2.6. 1 Section worked on Div H.Q. [illegible] remaining sections working on roads.	
	3-5		Work continued on roads and D in H.Q.	
N31d1.7.	6		Coy moved from MONT VIDAIGNE to near DONEGAL FARM N31d1.7 and dug in in a Sunken Road.	
	7.		Work as follows. 1 Section on Bde H.Q. ARMOOR FARM. T3b5.8. 1 Section on mined dugout for ADS at N31d1.1. 2 Sections working on tracks and trenches forward area.	
	9.		Transport lines moved to S.5a.	
	10.		Capt L.A. HILL returned from leave.	
	11.		Transport lines moved to M11a, central.	
	15.		Sgt THURLBY to hospital sick.	
	17.		Sgt SANVILLE to hospital sick. Sgt BUMPSTEAD returned from leave.	
	19.		Since 7th. Work has been continued as before. Work taken over nights from 36 Div on NEUVE EGLISE Sector.	
	20.		No 4 Section moved T14c.1.7. from work on NEUVE EGLISE Sector. ADS handed over to 202 nd Fd Coy on same day.	
	24.		Work on NEUVE EGLISE Sector given up. No 4 Section returned to N31d1.7	

D. D. & L., London, E.C. (A10266) Wt W5300/P713 750,000 2/18 Sch. 52 Forms/C2118/16.

Instructions regarding War Diaries and Intelligence Summaries are contained in F. S. Regs., Part II. and the Staff Manual respectively. Title pages will be prepared in manuscript.

WAR DIARY
or
INTELLIGENCE SUMMARY.
(Erase heading not required.)

Army Form C. 2118.

Place	Date	Hour	Summary of Events and Information	Remarks and references to Appendices
N 31 a 1 7.	26th		Work in forward area handed over to 23rd Fld Coy	
			Work in intermediate area taken over from 2nd Fld Coy and started on 27th	
	27th			
	26th		4/Lt THORLBY rejoined from hospital	
	28th.		4/Lt EVANS went on leave.	
			Flanders Offensive Started. Company stood by to work on MESSINES road, but did not work on that day.	
	29th		Work started on main road through MESSINES at 5.0 am and handed over to 23rd Fld Coy at 12 noon. The Road was clear for Lorry traffic by 4.0 pm.	
	30th		Nos 1 and 2 Sections moved to ENFER WOOD at 10 am O.25 d.6.6.	

[signature] Major
B ... Fld Coy R.E.

D. D. & L., London, E.C.
(A10266) Wt W5300/P713 750,000 2/18 Sch. 52 Forms/C2118/16.

SECRET

Nd 34

WAR DIARY

OF THE

200th Field Company, Royal Engineers.

FOR THE

MONTH OF.

October 1918.

(Volume XXIV)

OCTOBER

WAR DIARY
or
INTELLIGENCE SUMMARY.
(Erase heading not required.)

Army Form C. 2118.

Instructions regarding War Diaries and Intelligence Summaries are contained in F. S. Regs., Part II. and the Staff Manual respectively. Title pages will be prepared in manuscript.

VOL XXIV.

200th Field Company R.E.

Place	Date	Hour	Summary of Events and Information (Reference Belgium + France Sheets 28. 29. 37 1/40,000)	Remarks and references to Appendices
N31 d 1 7	1		Company moved from N31 d. 1.7 to HOUTHEM P.19 a + Horse Lines to N 29 a 3.7	
	2		2/Lt G. SANVILLE rejoined from hospital.	
	3 to 8		Company employed on road repairs in the vicinity of HOUTHEM.	
	9		Company relieved by 201st Field Company RE + returned to Horse Lines.	
	10		Sections training + working on Div: HQ at Grand Bois.	
	11 to 13		Ditto. Baths arranged + whole Company bathed.	
	14		2/Lt EDGAR RE joined the Company.	
	15		No 4 Section moved to vicinity of AMERIKA P 12 b.	
P. 12. b			At 5.30 pm orders were received to proceed at once to bridge the River LYS at BOUSBECQUE as the enemy was believed to have retired across it. No 3 Section was sent by motor lorry to pick up No 4 at AMERIKA + the bridging equipment of all three Field Companies under Capt: HILL proceeded at once to the same point. All three parties met as arranged about half an hour after	
	16		mid-night + proceeded to the site of proposed bridge. Considerable obstacles in the shape of barbed wire + bricks were encountered in WERVICQ where there was also much shelling. The Convoy reached the site about 2 AM + proceeded to lay medium pontoon bridge. The enemy was on the other bank, not far distant. The wagons pulled right up to the water's edge. The Bridge, 105', was completed just before daylight + was in use during the day, after the enemy had withdrawn. Company transport moved to N 24 a. 7.7 + Sections 2 joined 3 + 4 at AMERIKA No 1 Section remained at WYTCHAETE for special work. 2/Lt SANVILLE left the Company to join the 559 A.T. Company R.E.	

D. D. & L., London, E.C.
(A10266) Wt W5300/P713 750,000 2/18 Sch. 52 Forms/C2118/16.

Instructions regarding War Diaries and Intelligence Summaries are contained in F. S. Regs., Part II. and the Staff Manual respectively. Title pages will be prepared in manuscript.

WAR DIARY (Continued)
or
INTELLIGENCE SUMMARY.
(Erase heading not required.)

Army Form C. 2118.

Place	Date	Hour	Summary of Events and Information	Remarks and references to Appendices
P. 12. b	17		Weather fine. No 1 Section rejoined.	
Q 27 b. 5. 0	18		Company + transport moved to WERVICQ. Company employed in building a timber trestle bridge at Q 27 b. 5. 0. suitable for three ton motor lorries. This was to replace the medium pontoon bridge already put down + which was in full use. Sections working in shifts + work continuous.	
	19		Bridge completed at NOON. Pontoon Bridge just showing signs of wear.	
ROLLEGHEM.	20		Company took up pontoon bridge. Company transport + bridging convoy moved at 9. AM + main portion later by lorry to ROLLEGHEM.	
DOTTIGNIES	21		Company, transport + bridging convoy moved to T27 b. 1. 4 near DOTTIGNIES. Major O.D. ATKINSON wounded while making reconnaisance for bridge across SCHELTE near HELCHIN. In the evening orders were received to pontoon the SCHELTE the same night. Sections 3 + 4 + the bridging convoy proceeded to HELCHIN + threw a bridge over at C 5 a. 3. 5. The enemy put up considerable machine gun opposition from the opposite bank but no casualties were sustained. The bridge was completed about 4. AM. The sluice at C. 5. a. 1. 4 was blown open by laying a charge of 60 lbs of guncotton + the water from the flooded surrounding country allowed to enter the canal. No 2 Section attached to 21st Inf Bde	
	22		No 1 Section relieved No 2 Section.	

D. D. & L., London, E.C.
(A10266) Wt W5300/P713 750,000 2/18 Sch. 52 Forms/C2118/15.

Instructions regarding War Diaries and Intelligence Summaries are contained in F. S. Regs., Part II. and the Staff Manual respectively. Title pages will be prepared in manuscript.

WAR DIARY (Continued) or INTELLIGENCE SUMMARY.

(Erase heading not required.)

Army Form C. 2118.

Place	Date	Hour	Summary of Events and Information	Remarks and references to Appendices
DOTTIGNIES	23		Fine. Section 4 threw two light Infantry Bridges across the SCHELTE at C.4.a.9.3 + C.5.a.2.5 in face of the enemy. No 1 Section sustained five casualties at S. GENOIS.	
	24		Company relieved by 201st + 202nd Field Companies in the right + left sectors.	
	25		Fine. Company doing barrel piering drill. Lt THURLBY to hospital.	
	26		Major E.O. ALABASTER joined the Company from XXII Corps	
	27		" O.D. ATKINSON died of wounds received on 21st	
	28		2/Lt LANNON rejoined the Company. Lt EDGAR transferred to 201 Field Coy.	
	30		Company moved from DOTTIGNIES to billets at W.2.b.9.4 + employed on bridge for 3 ton lorry transport at MOEN.	
	31		Work continued as above.	
			Weather for the month. Soft + warm, a good deal of overcast + some wet days. Good on the whole.	
			E O Alabaster Major OC. 200th Fd Coy R.E. 3.11.18.	

D. D. & L., London, E.C. (A10266) Wt W5300/P713 750,000 2/18 Sch. 52 Forms/C2118/16.

SECRET

WAR DIARY

OF THE

200th Field Company, Royal Engineers.

FOR THE MONTH

OF

November 1918

(Volume. XXV).

200th FLD COY R.E.

WAR DIARY
or
INTELLIGENCE SUMMARY.

(Erase heading not required.)

Army Form C. 2118.

November 1918.

Instructions regarding War Diaries and Intelligence Summaries are contained in F. S. Regs., Part II. and the Staff Manual respectively. Title pages will be prepared in manuscript.

VOL. XXV

Place	Date	Hour	Summary of Events and Information	Remarks and references to Appendices
	1.11.18			
29/U.26.95.40			Coy H.Q. and dismounted personnel at 29/U.2.6.95.40. Transport at Work, building bridge for lorries across ESCAUT CANAL near MOEN, 29/U.6.a.3.1. span 75 feet, bottom of canal to roadway ft. Materials carted from GERMAN Dump at KNOKKE 29/O.15.d.9.8. A few H.V. shells near H.Q. at 10.00 p.m. Weather fine, warm and hazy.	
	2.11.18		Work as for 1.11.18.; site of bridge shelled for about 3/4 hr. No damage. Weather showery.	
	3.11.18.		Lorry bridge at MOEN completed. Reconnaissance made by Lt LAMMON for a bridge to take 60 pr MK II at KLYTTE 29/O.35.a.1.9. Weather showery.	
	4.11.18.		Clearing site for bridge at KLYTTE. Debris of girders causing trouble. A few H.V. near H.Q. at 16.00 hrs. Weather fine.	
	5.11.18.		As for 4.11.18	

Army Form C. 2118.

Instructions regarding War Diaries and Intelligence Summaries are contained in F. S. Regs., Part II. and the Staff Manual respectively. Title pages will be prepared in manuscript.

WAR DIARY
or
INTELLIGENCE SUMMARY.
(Erase heading not required.)

Place	Date	Hour	Summary of Events and Information	Remarks and references to Appendices
KNOKKE	6.11.18.		Whole company and transport marched to KNOKKE Dump, where billets were made.	
			Nos 1, 2, 4 Sections under Lt EVANS finished clearing site of bridge at KLYSTTE and prepared some of the framing.	
			Heavy rain all day.	
	7.11.18		Nos 3 & 4 Sections continued work at KLYSTTE.	
			Nos 1 & 2 made cork footbridge and gave demonstration to C.E. II. Army at KNOKKE.	
			Capt HILL took over temporary command of 201st Fld Coy.	
			C.R.E.'s conference giving details of work for each Fld Coy in event of operations.	
			Weather cold and damp.	
	8.11.18		Lt BUMTSTEAD reconnoitred for erection of tide gauge at BOSSUYT.	
			Company employed on making footbridge material; 1-100ft of German floats, 1-40ft of German floats, 2-40ft cork, 3 rafts of petrol tins.	
	9.11.18.		Company started making floating bridging and materials for rafting gone.	
			at 10.00 hrs C.R.E. directed reconnaissance to be made by Lt LANNON for pontoon bridge across SCHELDT; decision to bridge at ESCANAFFLES.	
			Company employed all day loading materials for other companies and preparing pontoon equipment. Moved off at ~~2.3~~ 20.30 hrs; first wagon able to approach site 03.30 hrs 10.11.18. a party under Lt PEARSON threw a footbridge across SCHELDT at 21.30 hrs.	
ESCANAFFLES	10.11.18		Pontoon bridge at ESCANAFFLES (6 pontoons) and road approaches completed and transport crossing 08.25 hrs; maintenance of bridge with continuous traffic all day. Company billeted in ESCANAFFLES.	

D.D. & L., London, E.C.
(A10266) Wt W5300/P713 750,000 2/18 Sch. 52 Forms/C2118/15.

Instructions regarding War Diaries and Intelligence Summaries are contained in F. S. Regs., Part II. and the Staff Manual respectively. Title pages will be prepared in manuscript.

WAR DIARY
or
INTELLIGENCE SUMMARY.
(*Erase heading not required.*)

Army Form C. 2118.

Place	Date	Hour	Summary of Events and Information	Remarks and references to Appendices
BEAUREGARD	11.11.18		Company moved from ESCANAFFLES with a view to bridging at WATTREPONT. News regarding cessation of hostilities received while on the march, and company diverted to near BEAUREGARD between ANSEROEUL and CELLES.	
			Bridge at CELLES reconnoitred by Lt PEARSON.	
	12.11.18.		General clean up and rest. Bridge at CELLES being built by 171 Tun Coy	
	13.11.18		Baths and work on roads.	
	14.11.18.		As for 13.11.18. Reconnaissance of traffic routes in area ESCANAFFLES, CELLES, WATRIPONT.	
	15.11.18.		as for 14.11.18.	
	16.11.18.		Work on bridges started by 29th Div at AINIERES	
HEESTERT	17.11.18.		Moved to HEESTERT.	
LUINGNE	18.11.18.		Moved to LUINGNE.	
	19.11.18.		General clean up.	
	20.11.18.		Thanksgiving Service in morning.	
	21.11.18.		Education and Resettlement Schemes explained.	
	22.11.18.		Physical Training and Baths	
	23.11.18.		Each Section paraded complete with transport for inspection.	
	24.11.18.		Church Parade.	

D. D. & L., London, E.C.
(A10266) Wt W5300/P713 750,000 2/18 Sch. 52 Forms/C2118/15.

Instructions regarding War Diaries and Intelligence Summaries are contained in F. S. Regs., Part II. and the Staff Manual respectively. Title pages will be prepared in manuscript.

WAR DIARY
or
INTELLIGENCE SUMMARY.
(Erase heading not required.)

Army Form C. 2118.

Place	Date	Hour	Summary of Events and Information	Remarks and references to Appendices
LUINGNE	25.11.18.		Sections under own officers, refitting and cleaning	
	26.11.18.		as for 25th. All Fld Coys placed under command of O.C. 200 in 21st Inf Bde Group for purpose of move to BLARINGHEM Area.	
	27.11.18.		Route march	
	28.11.18.		Rifle exercises and overhauling bridging equipment which had been lifted from R. SCHELDT by 202 Fld Coy	
LINSELLES	29.11.18.		Marched to LINSELLES. Joined 21. Inf Bde Group.	
CROIX AU BOIS	30.11.18.		Marched to CROIX AU BOIS in ARMENTIERES Staging Area.	
			G. O. [illegible] Major O.C. 200 Fd Coy R.E.	

D. D. & L., London, E.C.
(A10266) Wt W5300/P713 750,000 2/18 Sch. 52 Forms/C2118/16.

AB
SECRET

V836

WAR DIARY

OF THE

200th FIELD COMPANY, ROYAL ENGINEERS.

FOR THE MONTH OF.

December 1918.

(Volume XXVI)

Instructions regarding War Diaries and Intelligence Summaries are contained in F. S. Regs., Part II. and the Staff Manual respectively. Title pages will be prepared in manuscript.

200th Fld Coy R.E. WAR DIARY or INTELLIGENCE SUMMARY. December 1918

(Erase heading not required.)

VOL XXVI

Army Form C. 2118.

Place	Date	Hour	Summary of Events and Information (Reference HAZEBROUCK 1/100,000)	Remarks and references to Appendices
BAC ST MAUR	1.12.18.		Marched from CROIX AU BOIS to BAC ST MAUR in 21st Inf Bde Group.	
ST VENANT	2.12.18.		Marched to LA HAYE, near ST VENANT. 22 Km on a muggy day.	
AIRE	3.12.18.		Marched to AIRE	
	4.12.18.		Making home comforts and cleaning up.	
	5.12.18.		Building cookhouses and Regtl Institute.	
	6.12.18.		as for 5.12.18. and bunking.	
	7.12.18.		As for 6.12.18. Visit by C.R.E. in the morning to discuss general matters of interior economy with a view to grouping 3 Fld Coys as a battalion.	
	8.12.18.		Parade in marching order in morning. Church Parade in afternoon.	
	9.12.18.		Lt BUMPSTEAD and 4 NCO's joined 89th Inf Bde to supervise hutting etc.	
	10.12.18.		Conference of Coy Comdrs under CRE ref accomodation of Bdes. Coy bathed at LA LACQUE.	
	11.12.18. 12.12.18. 13.12.18.		} Fitting up barracks, and Regtl Institute. Also rooms for Instructional work.	

D. D. & L., London, E.C.
(A10265) Wt W5300/P713 750,000 2/18 Sch. 52 Forms/C2118/16.

Instructions regarding War Diaries and Intelligence Summaries are contained in F. S. Regs., Part II. and the Staff Manual respectively. Title pages will be prepared in manuscript.

WAR DIARY
or
INTELLIGENCE SUMMARY.
(Erase heading not required.)

Army Form C. 2118.

Place	Date	Hour	Summary of Events and Information	Remarks and references to Appendices
AIRE	14.12.18.		Dress rehearsal for ceremonial parade.	
			Inspection of barracks by C.E. XIX. Corps.	
	15.12.18.		Church Parade.	
	16.12.18		Medal ribbon presentation by a/G.O.C. 30th Divn.	
			Regimental system adopted as regards duties in the 3 Fld Coys.	
	17.12.18.		Work on improvement to billets etc.	
	18.12.18.		As for 17.12.18.	
	19.12.18.		As for 17.12.18. Visit by XIX. Corps Commander.	
	20.12.18.		As for 17.12.18. Details for Bde hutting arranged.	
	21.12.18.		Work as for 17.12.18 in morning; football in afternoon.	
	22.12.18.		Church Parade.	
	23.12.18.		Work on improvement to billets.	
	24.12.18.		As for 23rd. Section with 89th Inf Bde rejoined.	
	25.12.18.		Xmas celebrations. Church Parade, dinners, and smoking concert.	
	26.12.18.		Necessary fatigues only carried out.	
	27.12.18		General Fatigues	
	28.12.18		Half holiday.	
	29.12.18		Sunday. Church. Tug of War inter Company. Won by 200.	
	30.12.18		Preparing for move.	
	31.12.18		Company moves	

X Hill Capt RE
OC 200 Field Coy RE

D. D. & L., London, E.C.
(A10266) W1 W5300/P713 750,000 2/18 Sch. 52 Forms/C2118/16

SECRET

WAR DIARY

OF THE

200th. Field Company, R.E.

FOR THE

MONTH OF

January 1919

(Volume XXVII)

200th FLD COY R.E.

WAR DIARY
or
INTELLIGENCE ~~SUMMARY~~.
(Erase heading not required.)

Army Form C. 2118.

JANUARY 1919

Instructions regarding War Diaries and Intelligence Summaries are contained in F. S. Regs., Part II. and the Staff Manual respectively. Title pages will be prepared in manuscript.

VOL. XXVII

Place	Date	Hour	Summary of Events and Information	Remarks and references to Appendices
	1		The Company moved to HUCQUELIERS	
	2		" " " ETAPLES	
	3		" " engaged on billet construction.	
	4		Delousing Station taken over + company employed on it	
	5		Work on delousing station	
	6		" " " " #2	
	7		" " " " + baths.	
	8		" " " "	
	9		" " " "	
	10		" " " "	
	11		" " " " for half day. Have the afternoon off work.	
	12		The Coy have the day off work.	
	13		Work on delousing station	
	14		ditto.	
	15		ditto. + baths.	
	16		ditto.	
	17		ditto.	
	18		ditto for half day. Have the afternoon off work	
	19		The Coy. have the day off work.	
	20		Work on Delousing Station.	

D. D. & L., London, E.C.
(A10266) Wt W5300/P713 750,000 2/18 Sch. 52 Forms/C2118/16.

Instructions regarding War Diaries and Intelligence Summaries are contained in F. S. Regs., Part II. and the Staff Manual respectively. Title pages will be prepared in manuscript.

WAR DIARY
or
INTELLIGENCE SUMMARY.
(Erase heading not required.)

Army Form C. 2118.

Place	Date	Hour	Summary of Events and Information	Remarks and references to Appendices
	21		Work in Debussing Station. Hand over to the Canadian RE's this day.	
	22		Coy are employed on cleaning & painting waggons.	
	23		Coy are employed loading transport and loading on to train.	
	24		Coy entrained at ETAPLES for DUNKIRK and diverted to BERGUES.	
BERGUES	25		Detrained at BERGUES, 37 hrs after commencement of entrainment; L/Cpl RIMMER injured at 01.00 hrs by an engine running into the truck in which he was travelling.	
	26.		Settling into HOYMILLE CAMP with RASC; 15 men demobilised.	
	27.		Commenced work on R.A.O.C. Depot, our own new camp, and stables.	
	28.		Continued work commenced 27th. CRE 30 Div visited company and promised to take up the question of working hours.	
	29.		as for 28th. 2 men demobilised.	
	30.		as for 28th Two lorries attached for duty. 4 men demobilised	
	31.		as for 28th 3 men demobilised. O.C. Coy pointed out to DORE BERGUES that latter was a junior officer and therefore not entitled to a daily state showing numbers sick, on leave, on guard or other employ except work.	

G. O. Calcutt
Major
O.C. 200th Fd Coy R.E.

D. D. & L., London, E.C. (A10266) Wt W5300/P713 750,000 2/18 Sch. 52 Forms/C2118/18.

SECRET

WAR DIARY

OF THE

200th Field Company, Royal Engineers.

FOR THE MONTH OF

February, 1919.

(Volume. XXVIII).

VR 3

200th FLD COY R.E.

WAR DIARY
or
INTELLIGENCE SUMMARY.
(*Erase heading not required.*)

(VOL. XXVIII)

FEBRUARY 1919.

Army Form C. 2118.

Instructions regarding War Diaries and Intelligence Summaries are contained in F. S. Regs., Part II. and the Staff Manual respectively. Title pages will be prepared in manuscript.

Place	Date	Hour	Summary of Events and Information	Remarks and references to Appendices
BERGUES	1.2.19.		Work on repairing & improving stables for our own animals, also building our own camp and depot for D.R.O.S.	
	2.2.19.		Sunday. Hot spray baths in camp for whole company	
	3.2.19.		as for 1.2.19.	
	4.2.19		do	
	5.2.19		do	
	6.2.19		2Lt PEARSON rejoined from hospital, sappers employed on works BERGUES.CAMP 2Lt FITT arrived from Base Depot	
	7.2.19		2Lt. BUMPSTEAD on 14 days leave to U.K do	
	8.2.19		2Lt PEARSON to U.K for demobilization do	
	9.2.19		CAPT F.M. NEWTON arrived to take over command from MAJOR E.O. ALABASTER ordered to U.K for duty	~~do~~
	10.2.19		~~do~~ Sappers employed on works BERGUES CAMP	
	11.2.19		do	
	12.2.19		CAPT: H de C. TOOGOOD rejoined from leave do	

D. D. & L., London, E.C.
(A10265) Wt W3300/P713 750,000 2/18 Sch. 52 Forms/C2118/16.

Army Form C. 2118.

Instructions regarding War Diaries and Intelligence Summaries are contained in F. S. Regs., Part II. and the Staff Manual respectively. Title pages will be prepared in manuscript.

WAR DIARY
or
INTELLIGENCE SUMMARY.
(Erase heading not required.)

Place	Date	Hour	Summary of Events and Information	Remarks and references to Appendices
BERGUES	13.2.19.		Work continued on R.A.O.C. Depot & Camp.	
	14.2.19		do do	
	15.2.19		Company moved to camp at Sheet 19. O.15c.2.5.	
	16.2.19		The following acting promotions were made.	
			813444 Cpl. Walker H. to be A/CQMS.	
			81835 Cpl. Collis F.J. to be A/Sergt.	
			81620 L.Cpl. Hooton J to be A/Corporal	
			155327 L.Cpl. West G.W. to be A/II Corporal.	
			145427 L.Cpl. Medlycott C.H. to be A/II Corporal.	
			541757 L.Cpl. Tullet H. to be A/II Corporal.	
			564218 Sapr. Wilson E.A. to be L/c Corporal.	
			83536 Fr.Cpl. Palfrey G. to be A/Fr. Sergeant.	
	17.2.19		Work continued on R.A.O.C. Depot & Camp. Weather - wet	
	18.2.19		do do do	
	19.2.19		do do do	
			Lieut. E. Evans RE. rejoined from leave.	
	20.2.19		Work continued on R.A.O.C. Depot & Camp Weather wet	
	21.2.19		do do do do	
	22.2.19		do do do do	
	23.2.19		Weather fine - cold do	
	24.2.19		Work on R.A.O.C. Depot & Camp continued Weather fine - cold	
			II Lieut. A.D. Bumpstead RE rejoined from leave.	

P. D. & L., London, E.C.
(A10266) Wt W5300/P713 750,000 2/18 Sch. 52 Forms/C2118/16.

200th Field Coy R.E.

Instructions regarding War Diaries and Intelligence Summaries are contained in F. S. Regs., Part II. and the Staff Manual respectively. Title pages will be prepared in manuscript.

WAR DIARY

~~or~~

~~INTELLIGENCE~~ SUMMARY.

(Erase heading not required.)

Army Form C. 2118.

111

Place	Date	Hour	Summary of Events and Information	Remarks and references to Appendices
Bergues	25.2.19		Work continued on R.A.O.C. Depot and Camp. Weather cold - fine	
	26.2.19		do do " wet.	
	27.2.19		do do " dull.	
	28.2.19		do do " dull.	
			Capt. H. de C. TOOGOOD left the Company to proceed to H.Q. DES VERTON (Authy. L of C wire DA 14939 of 23/2/19)	

E. Evans Lieut ~~Capt~~ R.E.
f. O.C. 200th Field Company R.E.

D. D. & L., London, E.C.
(A10265) Wt W5300/P713 750,000 2/18 Sch. 52 Forms/C2118/16.

WAR DIARY

VR 39

OF THE

200th. Field Company, Royal Engineers.

FOR THE MONTH OF

MARCH. 1919.

(VOLUME XXXIX).

200th Field Coy R.E.

Instructions regarding War Diaries and Intelligence Summaries are contained in F. S. Regs., Part II. and the Staff Manual respectively. Title pages will be prepared in manuscript.

(VOLUME XXXIX)

WAR DIARY
or
~~INTELLIGENCE SUMMARY.~~
(Erase heading not required.)

MARCH 1919.

Army Form C. 2118.

Place	Date	Hour	Summary of Events and Information	Remarks and references to Appendices
BERGUES	1.3.19		Work stopped on R.A.O.C. Camp, and all personnel employed thereon transferred to the R.A.O.C. Depot. Weather fine.	
	2.3.19		Summer Time adopted. -do-	
	3.3.19		Work continued on R.A.O.C. Depot. 2 Platoons 25 Battn. K.R.R.C. attached for work. Weather wet.	
	4.3.19		Work continued on R.A.O.C. Depot. Weather wet.	
	5.3.19		do do Weather unsettled.	
	6.3.19		do do do wet - windy.	
	7.3.19		do do do dull & windy.	
	8.3.19		do do do fine - cold. The 2 platoons of 25th Battn. K.R.R.C. were relieved by the 6th South Wales Borderers (Pioneers) for work.	
	9.3.19		Weather fine - cold.	
	10.3.19		Work continued on R.A.O.C. Depot. Weather dull - cold.	
	11.3.19		do do do do.	
	12.3.19		do do. Work commenced on R.A.O.C. Camp. 2/Lieut. R.C.P. JAMES R.E. rejoined from R.E. Survey Battn. Weather fine.	

D. D. & L., London, E.C.
(A10286) Wt W5300/P713 750,000 2/18 Sch. 52 Forms/C2118/16.

Instructions regarding War Diaries and Intelligence Summaries are contained in F. S. Regs., Part II. and the Staff Manual respectively. Title pages will be prepared in manuscript.

Sheet II

Army Form C. 2118.

WAR DIARY
or
~~INTELLIGENCE SUMMARY.~~

(Erase heading not required.)

Place	Date	Hour	Summary of Events and Information	Remarks and references to Appendices
BERGUES	13.3.19		Work continued on R.A.O.C. Depot and R.A.O.C. Camp. Weather fine - cold.	
	14.3.19		do do do Weather wet.	
	15.3.19		do do do Weather fine Capt W.A. EVANS R.E. joined the Company, to be 2nd in Command.	
	16.3.19		Weather fine - very cold.	
	17.3.19		Work continued on R.A.O.C. Depot + Camp. Weather fine - cold.	
	18.3.19		do do do do do	
	19.3.19		do do do do do	
	20.3.19		do do do Weather cold - snow.	
	21.3.19		do do do do - damp.	
	22.3.19		do do do do - wet	
	23.3.19		Weather fine - Cold. Capt W.A. Evans R.E. left to join the 201st Field Company R.E. for duty.	
	24.3.19		Work continued on R.A.O.C. Depot and Camp. Weather fine - cold.	
	25.3.19		do do do - do -	
	26.3.19		do do do - do - Major F.M. Newton R.E. left unit to proceed on leave, crossing on 27.3.19.	

D. D. & L., London, E.C.
(A10266) Wt W5300/P713 750,000 2/18 Sch. 52 Forms/C2118/16.

Instructions regarding War Diaries and Intelligence Summaries are contained in F. S. Regs., Part II. and the Staff Manual respectively. Title pages will be prepared in manuscript.

WAR DIARY
or
INTELLIGENCE SUMMARY.
(Erase heading not required.)

Sheet III

Army Form C. 2118.

Place	Date	Hour	Summary of Events and Information	Remarks and references to Appendices
BERGUES	26.3.19		Lieut. J.C.B. WAKEFORD R.E. joined the Company from R.E. Bridging Battn.	
	27.3.19		Work continued on R.A.O.C. Depot and Camp. Weather squally.	
	28.3.19		do do do Weather fine - cold.	
	29.3.19		do do do Weather cold - snow.	
	30.3.19		Weather fine - cold.	
	31.3.19		Work continued on R.A.O.C. Depot and Camp. Weather fine - cold.	

E. Evans Lieut R.E.
O/C 200th Field Company R.E.

D. D. & L., London, E.C.
(A10256) Wt W5300/P713 750,000 2/18 Sch. 52 Forms/C2118/16.

200th FIELD COMPANY
No. A/B/16
Date ......
(COUNTY PALATINE) R.E.

HEAD QUARTERS ... 30 ...

Vol 40

War Diary

of the

200th Field Company, Royal Engineers

for the month of

April 1919.

(Volume XL.)

200th Field Company RE

WAR DIARY
or
INTELLIGENCE SUMMARY.
(Erase heading not required.)

Army Form C. 2118.

Instructions regarding War Diaries and Intelligence Summaries are contained in F. S. Regs., Part II. and the Staff Manual respectively. Title pages will be prepared in manuscript.

(VOLUME XL)

APRIL 1919.

Place	Date	Hour	Summary of Events and Information	Remarks and references to Appendices
BERGUES	1.4.19		Work continued on R.A.O.C. Depot and Camp. Weather fine - later snow	
	2.4.19		do do do Weather fine.	
	3.4.19		do do do Weather fine.	
			Lieut I.C.B. WAKEFORD R.E. left the unit to proceed to England. Authority (A.G. 55/7271(O). dated 21.3.19).	
	4.4.19		Work continued on R.A.O.C. Depot and Camp. Weather fine.	
			II Lieut R.C.P. JAMES R.E. left the unit to proceed to 76th Field Company R.E (Western Division) Authority (W.A. 15649. 30 Division A.2968)	
			45 Other Ranks (Retainable men) left the unit to report to C.R.E. 62nd Highland Division.	
			5 Other Ranks (retainable men) who are on leave in the UK were wired to report direct to 62nd Highland Division.	
	5.4.19		Work continued on R.A.O.C. Depot and Camp. Weather fine.	
	6.4.19		Weather fine - dull.	
	7.4.19		Work continued on R.A.O.C. Depot and Camp. Weather fine - warm	
			1 Officer and 24 O.R. from 942 A.E (ARTIZAN) Coy attached to unit for rations.	
	8.4.19		Work continued on RAOC DEPOT and CAMP. Weather fine - warm	
			II Lieut F.H. FITT R.E. left the unit to proceed to 138th (A.T.) Company R.E for duty in the Clearing up Army. (30th Division letter No A/2290 d/ 1/4/19)	

D. D. & L., London, E.C.
(A10266) Wt W5300/P713 750,000 2/18 Sch. 52 Forms/C2118/16.

Instructions regarding War Diaries and Intelligence Summaries are contained in F. S. Regs., Part II. and the Staff Manual respectively. Title pages will be prepared in manuscript.

WAR DIARY
or
~~INTELLIGENCE SUMMARY.~~
(Erase heading not required.)

Sheet II

Army Form C. 2118.

Place	Date	Hour	Summary of Events and Information	Remarks and references to Appendices
BERGUES	9.4.19		Work continued on the R.A.O.C. Depot and Camp. Weather fine.	
	10.4.19		- do - - do - - do - Weather fine - dull - some rain.	
	11.4.19		- do - - do - - do - Weather dull - chilly.	
			Major F.M. NEWTON R.E. Returned from leave in U.K.	
	12.4.19		Work continued on the RAOC Depot and Camp. Weather wet and dull.	
	13.4.19		Weather fine - windy	
	14.4.19		Work continued on the RAOC Depot and Camp. Weather very windy & wet.	
	15.4.19		do do do do Weather wet - windy	
	16.4.19		do do do do Weather dull - wet.	
			Capt. F.M. NEWTON R.E. left the unit to proceed to join the 63rd Field Company R.E. (Lowland Division) on 16.4.19. Authy. H.Q. L. of C. Area No. W.A. 15649 d/24/3/19.	
	17.4.19		Work continued on RAOC Depot & CAMP. Weather fine - dull.	
	18.4.19		Weather dull - rainy.	
	19.4.19		Work continued on RAOC Depot & Camp. Weather fine - warm.	
	20.4.19		Weather dull - windy	
	21.4.19		- do - - do -	
	22.4.19		Work continued on R.A.O.C. Depot & Camp. Weather fine.	
	23.4.19		do do do dull.	

D. D. & L., London, E.C.
(A10266) Wt W5300/P713 750,000 2/18 Sch. 52 Forms/C2118/16.

Instructions regarding War Diaries and Intelligence Summaries are contained in F. S. Regs., Part II. and the Staff Manual respectively. Title pages will be prepared in manuscript.

WAR DIARY
or
~~INTELLIGENCE SUMMARY.~~
(Erase heading not required.)

Army Form C. 2118.

Sheet III

Place	Date	Hour	Summary of Events and Information	Remarks and references to Appendices
BERGUES	24.4.19		Work continued on R.A.O.C Depot — Weather dull - later rain The detachment of 6th South Wales Borderers (Pioneers) left the unit to report back to their Battalion at WIMEREUX. Lieut E. MALLINSON R.E. joined the unit as O/c Cadre.	
	25.4.19		Work continued on R.A.O.C. Depot — Weather dull - cold	
	26.4.19		do do — Weather wet.	
	27.4.19		Weather dull - cold. - later wet	
	28.4.19		Work continued on R.A.O.C Depot — Weather dull - cold	
	29.4.19		do do — Weather cold - wet.	
	30.4.19		do do — Weather cold - windy	

Eric Mallinson Lieut R.E.
O/C 200th Field Coy R.E.

D. D. & L., London, E.C.
(A10266) Wt W5300/P713 750,000 2/18 Sch. 52 Forms/C2118/15.

War Diary

of

200th Field Coy R.E.

for

May 1919

200th Field Company R.E. WAR DIARY or ~~INTELLIGENCE SUMMARY.~~ Army Form C. 2118.

(Erase heading not required.)

Instructions regarding War Diaries and Intelligence Summaries are contained in F. S. Regs., Part II. and the Staff Manual respectively. Title pages will be prepared in manuscript.

(VOL. XLI) MAY 1919 41

Place	Date	Hour	Summary of Events and Information	Remarks and references to Appendices
BERGUES	1.5.19		Work continued on R.A.O.C. Depot. Weather wet.	Ceased 2/5/19
	2.5.19		do do Weather windy-wet.	
	3.5.19		do do Weather fine.	
	4.5.19		Weather dull - fine.	
	5.5.19		Work continued on R.A.O.C. Depot. Weather fine.	
	6.5.19		do do Weather fine - warm	
	7.5.19		do do Weather fine - warm.	
	8.5.19		do do Weather fine - warm.	
	9.5.19		do do Weather fine - warm	
	10.5.19		do do Weather fine - warm.	
	11.5.19		Weather fine - very warm	
	12.5.19		Work continued on R.A.O.C. Depot Weather fine - dull.	
	13.5.19		do do do - warm.	
	14.5.19		do do do - warm	
	15.5.19		do do do - warm	
	16.5.19		Weather fine - warm.	
	17.5.19		— do — Received orders to proceed to 178 Brigade Dunkirk at 1100 hours 18-5-19 for embarkation to England	

D. D. & L., London, E.C.
(A10266) Wt W5300/P713 750,000 2/18 Sch. 52 Forms/C2118/16

APPENDIX A.

Account of operations on 3rd - 4th June 1917

On the night of the 3rd - 4th June a new trench in advance of the front line was dug by the 11th S. Lancs Regt. (Pioneers), from I 18 a 5.6 through I 18 a 85.00, I 18 d 45.50. to I 18 a 45.20. The 200th Field Co. RE were ordered to erect 400 yards of wire entanglement from I 18 a 9.0. to I 18 c 5.5.

The entanglement consisted of a line of French wire secured by long screw pickets with a double apron fence. The diagonals were of barbed wire and there was a top horizontal and two side horizontal wires also barbed.

Each of the four sections of the company was given 100 yards of entanglement to erect. Five infantry were allotted to each section for carrying purposes.

Owing to shelling of back areas only five out of 20 infantry arrived at the rendezvous. It was found possible however to carry out all the stores without them. All sections were clear of the front line trench by 10.55 pm. and the entanglement was all completed by 1.15 am. Enemy interference nil.

Orders attached.

[illegible]
Major RE.

O.C. 200th Fld Co RE.

ORDERS

1. On the night of the 3rd–4th June the company will erect wire in front of a new trench which is to be dug. The line will run from I 18 a 9.0 to I 18 c 5.5.
2. Each section will erect 100 yds of French wire entanglement with a double apron. No 1 section will work on the right of the line.
3. The company will leave YPRES in small groups from 6.0 pm onwards and will rendezvous at the CHINA WALL in I 16 a by 8 45 p.m.
4. The sections will proceed to advanced rendezvous at I 18 c 3.7 arriving there by 10.15 p.m. There 5 infantry will be attached to each section for carrying stores.
5. Stores will be taken up at the rendezvous and carried out to the site of the work by a route along the northern edge of ZOUAVE WOOD.
6. Lt HILL RE will proceed in advance to mark out the line of the entanglement. Sections will dump their stores at the rear end of their part of the line and carry on with the work, details of which have been already arranged.
7. On completion of work report will be made to me before moving off.

[signature]
Maj RE

3 June 1917

O.C. 200th Fd Co RE

www.ingramcontent.com/pod-product-compliance
Lightning Source LLC
Chambersburg PA
CBHW080851010526
44117CB00014B/2234